THE EFFECTIVE USE OF MARKET RESEARCH

The Effective Use of Market Research

Edited by
JOHAN AUCAMP

Staples Press   London

Granada Publishing Limited
First published in Great Britain 1971 by
Staples Press Ltd
3 Upper James Street, London W1R 4BP

ISBN 0 286 62741 8

Printed in Great Britain by
Cox & Wyman Ltd
London, Fakenham and Reading

Contents

CONTENTS

PART THREE

CASE HISTORIES

Editor's Foreword

The Effective Use of Market Research is aimed at the Marketing Executive who wants to find out more about the main types of research and how these can help him in his day-to-day problems. It is also aimed at marketing students, enabling them to get a clear view of how different types of research can be useful. There are no chapters on more technical subjects such as sampling, questionnaire design, editing and tabulating. These are in the realm of the research expert and should not concern the marketing man.

The first section consists of two chapters. In the first, Arthur Ward, Deputy Managing Director of Quelrayn, outlines the information needs of management and touches on one of the problems raised from time to time by management, i.e. the difficulties of communication which sometimes arise between managers and market researchers.

In the second chapter, Reg Clay, Market Research Manager of Colgate-Palmolive, discusses the concept of marketing research as an information system, closely integrated with the daily operational practice of a marketing division within a Company. In the second part of the chapter, he briefly reviews some of the individual market research techniques most frequently used.

In the second section, individual chapters are devoted to a number of market research techniques. Though not a comprehensive list, the techniques described here probably account for 80–90 per cent of consumer market research carried out in the U.K. The subjects covered are:

Qualitative Research
General Usage and Attitude Studies
Market Segmentation
Product Testing
Advertising Research
Test Market Research
Research at Retail Level
Research into Consumer Durables
Research into the Textile Industry

There is still considerable disagreement among market researchers in two of these areas—market segmentation and advertising research. I have, therefore, asked two different authors to write articles on each of these subjects. In both cases the first chapter is a general summary of the technique and its development. In the second chapter, the author expands on specific useful techniques.

The third and final section of the book consists of a number of case histories showing how research results were used to measure the effect of marketing action.

I would first of all like to thank the authors, without whose help this work would not have been possible. I would also like to thank Professor Gordon Wills of the Management Centre at Bradford University, who encouraged me to edit this volume after a two-day seminar entitled 'The Effective Use of Market Research' held at the Management Centre. Three of the articles in this book—Chapters 1, 2 and 14—are based on papers read at the seminar. Chapters 5 and 15 are based on papers read at the E.S.O.M.A.R. Conferences. The other chapters were all specially written for the book.

PART ONE
Information Needs and Information Systems

I Information Needs in Management

A. W. WARD

Assistant to the Chief Executive, Carrington and Dewhurst Ltd.

Marketing information needs vary from one Company to another but the problems associated with identifying the needs, setting priorities and making the most effective use of information are common to most Companies.

This chapter deals with these problems in some detail and, whilst all information sources are not covered comprehensively, a selection of sources with potential significance to the majority of Companies are examined.

Finally, the difficulties of communication which sometimes arise between managers and market researchers are viewed as a problem with a deeper cause.

Making the Best Use of Marketing Information

An effective marketing operation is concerned with a broad field of activity both inside and outside the Company. The definition of marketing information, therefore, should be equally broadly based. It should cover, both in quantitative and qualitative terms, the product, the Company's immediate market (including competitors' activities), the final consumer, the methods and channels of distribution, the social and economic environment in which the product is sold.

This information may be available inside the Company, from outside published sources, from outside sources available to the whole industry for a fee, or from market research commissioned by a Company for its own use.

Being concerned, as it is, with the total marketing process it covers a fairly diverse field of information, which can be classified into three categories according to the needs of the situation:

1 Information required for strategic, long-term decisions.

2 Information required for tactical, short-term decisions.

3 Information required to build up a decision-maker's background of the marketing situation (to act as a direction finder for him to initiate action which may change the course of the Company in the long run, or merely give him a better feel of the situation in taking short-run decisions).

The basic information required for the first two categories is relatively easy to define because it can be related to specific objectives, problems or decision points. The information required in the third category tends to be personal to the decision-maker, and as such it is very difficult to measure its value in helping him to make more effective short-term decisions or, even more important, in triggering off new thinking which results in a decision to chart a new course for the Company's future expansion.

As a general rule the less formal the management structure and planning and control system in the Company, the more the information collected is likely to fall into the third category. Whilst this does not necessarily reflect on a Company's efficient collection and effective use of marketing information in its decision-making processes, the chances are that the information that is available and would be valuable at the strategic and tactical decision levels, is being under-utilized. Similarly, additional information which is being collected for other purposes is collected on a haphazard basis without much thought being given to the use that can be made of it. Such information is likely to be little more than a rag-bag of bits and pieces which, when looked at analytically against the types of decisions made currently, or likely to be made in the future, will be of limited value in building up the background information against which to take these decisions or chart the future course of the Company.

This is a hard line to take but it probably applies to many small- and medium-sized Companies (and possibly to a few big ones as well), some of which may have very adequate collection, storage and distribution facilities for their internal information. Looked at from another angle, what is being said is that marketing information has no intrinsic value, its only value being in the use that is made of it. Making information available represents a cost; benefits only accrue when it is used to make more effective decisions.

There is far too much concentration on how to obtain information and make it available for use and far too little on how to make effective use of it. It is all too easy to neglect the discipline of effective use as a measurement of success and assume that something valuable has been done merely by arranging for a lot of 'interesting' information to be available. A Company can load its costs and management time and reduce the effectiveness and profitability of the business just as easily by producing too much information, without any clear idea as to how it is going to be used, as by ignoring the value of information and working simply on hunch, backed by experience.

What are the characteristics of a Company which makes effective use of marketing information in its decision-making processes?

It does not depend on size, nor does it depend on the number of expert market researchers it has in its employ, nor on the knowledge of information sources or the methods of market research, nor on the information that one has of the specialized services from various market research companies which are now on offer. The essential characteristic of such a company is its attitude towards decision-making in general. Is there a desire in the business to take fact-based decisions?

If there is, then the essential questioning of the traditional ways of doing things and of information that is taken for granted as being factual, and the analytical approach to problem solving and business opportunities required in seeking out and selecting information for decision-making, follows logically on this desire to base decisions on fact.

To make maximum use of information in its decision-making processes, a Company needs to have a systematic approach to planning, appraisal and control of its operations. But this is a secondary requirement and, although important, is not as crucial to success as the desire to base decisions on the best information available.

What has been said refers to the business as a whole and not specifically to the marketing function. This is because the essential atmosphere required to make use of marketing information effectively is a company-wide atmosphere and this cannot survive for long in any one department or function unless it is truly company wide. If fact-based decisions are taken in one functional area only, then there is a lopsided approach to business problems and conflict arises which, in the end, will result in one side or the other winning or a situation of stagnation in the Company.

Defining Information Needs and Setting Priorities

Assuming that favourable conditions for making effective use of marketing information are present in a Company, how should the task of defining information needs and deciding on priorities be tackled?

In order to illustrate one approach to this problem, let us look at a Marketing Director taking up a newly created post in a Company which had always been able to sell what it produced and has not had to think too deeply about marketing in a wider context than keeping its customers happy.

Although the Company is making an adequate return on the capital employed in the business, its profits are now on a plateau after a rising trend for a number of years. The Managing Director knows that his manufacturing and buying are efficient, believes that he has an above-average sales team but realizes that he knows very little about the market to which his Company is selling, apart from his invoiced sales and sales to customers by product group. He appreciates that if he is going to return to a rising profit trend he must tackle the problem from the marketing end of the business. As it happens, his Sales Director (a first-class salesman who got the job on this score) is about to retire and he decides to use the opportunity to appoint a Marketing Director from outside the Company and a Sales Manager from inside the Company to support him.

The new Marketing Director, in addition to being in charge of the total marketing operation, is specifically charged with responsibility for seeking ways of increasing profitability on existing product lines (by increased sales or increased margins or both) and seeking out new products and markets with growth potential which can be exploited with the Company's existing know-how.

The Managing Director does not expect results tomorrow, but he wants to see the way ahead in the current financial year and increased profits in the following years. The Marketing Director knows he is on a tight schedule and a tight budget and that he has to show results fairly quickly in order to gain the confidence of his colleagues and subordinates. He has no previous knowledge of the products and markets served by the Company and has only the minimum of internal information, derived from salesmen's performance and customer offtake.

So here we have ideal conditions for the effective use of marketing information, with the right amount of support and the right amount of pressure from above to keep his feet on the ground in terms of cost and in terms of early results from efforts and expenditure. He had an above-average sales operation, a keenly costed and acceptable product and the minimum of marketing information. Where does he go from there?

His immediate concern is to gain as much background information on the business as possible, to show results from his information build-up quickly and to minimize the cost of obtaining the information, so as not to affect the cost structure of his department before he feels some benefit from the pay-off. His problem, therefore, is one of priorities. What information is likely to be of most value to him and how should he set about finding it?

He must start by looking at what the Company is doing now because this is likely to get the quickest pay-off. Investigations into new markets and products take more time, normally cost more money, and nearly always take longer to reach the pay-off point than is originally anticipated. He must start, therefore, by taking a close look at the Company's present marketing operating from product planning to the time when the product reaches the final consumer. He must examine the cost structure of his marketing operation and the contribution to profit he is getting from his various product groups and his various categories of customers.

This initial stage of his investigation will have given him a good opportunity to build up his background information of the marketing operation and he will now be in a position to decide what aspects of his operation are controllable in the short run and in the long run. It is on these two aspects that he should concentrate his attention. The next stage in his investigation will be to take a closer look at what he can control and try to evaluate, roughly, how changes in these areas are likely to affect the level of Company profits and how quickly results are likely to be forthcoming.

When he has completed this investigation he is in a position to decide on his priorities, pinpoint the gaps in his information, decide what level of accuracy he requires in order to take his decisions, get some idea of the likely cost (in money terms if he has to use outside sources, and in money terms and in terms of the organizational problems which may be encountered in obtaining internal information) and then evaluate this against what he can afford and what benefits are likely to accrue in a specified period of time.

In short, he should concentrate on the information he needs to take those decisions which are likely to have the greatest influence on the Company's profits in the required time span.

There is a great temptation, in this type of situation, to gather as much information as possible without too much concern for its immediate use. This is partly due to the fact that all information is interesting to a new man and is of some use to him since it is supplying him with background. Often the best trained marketing men are the worst offenders. Their experience has probably been obtained in one of the large packaged consumer businesses where marketing information is available in depth on every aspect of the Company's marketing operation. He has thus become used to basing most of his decisions on detailed marketing information, which he takes for granted. When he moves to a medium-sized company in a senior marketing position he often takes with him his preconceived ideas on information requirements and is so horrified when he learns how little information is available that he sets up a programme to obtain more information, based on his previous experience, without considering the particular problems of the Company, the limited resources at its disposal and the likely pay-off period. In his defence, one can say that at least he intends to use the information for decision-making purposes and that as he gets to know the limitations of the business he will probably trim his sails accordingly. The real danger man is the one who has not had his rigorous training in fact-based decision-making, and who sets up a programme to obtain a full range of information without any clear idea as to how he is going to use it when he gets it.

This is a trap into which a person can easily fall unless he is continuously on his guard and asks himself, in respect of every significant piece of information which he thinks he needs and which is not readily obtainable, 'What use am I going to make of this information?' If he finds this difficult to answer he can try a simple exercise to simulate the situation. He can ask himself what he will do if the answer to his information request comes out at each of three different levels or as a number of different alternatives, whichever suits the situation best. He can then test his reaction as to how the different answers will influence the decision he has to make, or how significant the various answers would be in influencing his view of a situation. This should help to clear his mind as to whether he needs the information at all, or, at least, it should give him some idea of the level of accuracy he requires. And he should always keep firmly in his mind that the higher the level of accuracy he asks for, the more it is going to cost and, almost certainly, the longer he is going to have to wait for his information.

The problems facing the Marketing Director in the Company used in this example were special one-off problems, but they have served to illustrate an approach to getting to grips with an unknown situation. In the absence of a plan of action similar to the one described, it would be possible to obtain a considerable background knowledge without actually building up a coherent body of information to assist in coming to grips with the situation.

His next task would be to build up his information requirements for planning and control for the business under normal conditions at the strategic and tactical levels and to consider what background information he required (the three categories of information requirement outlined earlier). Some of this information would be on a regular basis from internal and external sources and other aspects would be periodic or one-off. But all his requirements should go through a rigorous analysis of the use that is going to be made of this information and he should reconsider his requirements at least once a year. He should also analyse his requirements into the three categories and if he finds a large proportion falling into the third category his alarm bell should start ringing.

In the early stages of development of a marketing information system, especially when marketing personnel are learning to use the information effectively, it is anticipated that most of the information would be gleaned from internal records or contact with customers and potential customers. However, as his concentration turned from the present to the future, so his information requirements would broaden and he would be more likely to turn to outside sources and agencies. He would be likely to become more interested in assessing how far his current products had run in their life cycle so that he could anticipate the requirements for new products. This would lead him on to look at gaps in the market with potential for growth which his Company could fill. He would also be concerned about his Company's market standing (and that of his brands if any) and share of market. He would also want to look more closely at trends in the market he served and examine the adequacy of his methods and channels of distribution to serve his market.

Some Significant Sources of Information

Up to this point, information has been dealt with in relation to the problem of identifying needs, setting priorities and creating the right conditions in a Company for its effective use. The efforts which are put into making certain that the information is used correctly can be partly nullified by failure to adopt an equally rigorous, analytical approach to examining the information sources.

Although it is not intended to deal exhaustively with this aspect of information, some potential sources do call for special comment, either because they tend to be under-utilized, or because they are so well recognized that the questions have become stereotyped, or are no longer even posed, because the answers appear to be self-evident.

FINANCIAL INFORMATION

Financial information on the marketing operation is more easily available and more valuable as an aid to effective decision-making than any other single type of information. Unfortunately, it is probably the most under-utilized type of information. This is because most marketing men have only a sketchy idea about the accounting process and, if the truth be known, secretly feel that financial information is more likely to be a weapon to be used by accountants against them than a tool to help them improve their performance.

A marketing man cannot consider himself fully in charge of his area of responsibilities unless he is as familiar with the cost structure, contributions by product group, and the return on investment as he is with his sales volumes and customer turnovers.

MARKET POTENTIAL

This is an area of information which is full of pitfalls. Should you look on total industry sales as equivalent to the market potential for your Company? Is this a useful proposition if a major part of the market is served by a number of Companies equally as strong as your own? Is it more meaningful to think of potential in terms of opportunities in respect of customers and prospects rather than in global figures?

These are questions which have to be answered separately in respect of the individual circumstances of a Company and its industry. For instance, a manufacturer of men's topcoats selling all his output under his own brand name would be led sadly astray if he considered his market share was the percentage his sales made up of the total sales for the market as a whole, and, therefore, the potential for his branded products was related to the total market. The potential for his branded sales is likely to be far more realistically assessed by relating it to the total sales of the retail outlets which are his customers or prospective customers for branded merchandise selling at his price level. Looked at in this way it would probably become clear to him that if he wanted to increase his business beyond a certain point he would have to go for a different type of customer, probably selling unbranded merchandise, at a much earlier date than he would have anticipated had he concerned himself with total industry sales only.

Marketing men should beware of relating Company potential to global figures. In almost every industry a Company's true potential market is much smaller than would appear from this total market approach. Total market figures, and share of total market calculations, are often 'interesting' rather than 'useful' to small- and medium-sized Companies. It is much more valuable to

know the size of the segment of the market your Company is
serving and its growth rate.

THE PRODUCT

There is probably more ignorance about customers' reasons for
buying a Company's products than in any other part of the marketing operation. This is mainly because most Companies think
in terms of the intrinsic value of their products rather than in
terms of supplying a need or a 'bundle of satisfactions' to their
customers.

This is, by now, a marketing cliché with which most marketing
men would agree, yet they do not consider it applies to their own
Company. The truth is that we all become so involved in our own
Company's operation and in the products it sells that we build up
loyalties which erode our critical faculties.

The danger in this area is that more often than not we do not
recognize how ignorant we are about our products. We allow a
folklore to build up around them as to why customers buy, and
these ideas are looked on as fact and used as such.

If these ideas and loyalties are deeply ingrained, it is better to
obtain outside assistance to take a closer look at this critical area
of market information.

PRICING

Ask any salesman of any product what he thinks about the price
of his product and nine times out of ten he tells you his Company
is charging too much. Many Sales Directors will give you the
same answer. On the other hand, if you ask a Managing Director
about the price of his products, he will almost certainly tell you he
is charging too little, but that his Sales Director says that they will
lose a massive amount of business if they put up their prices.

Pricing decisions have more effect on a Company's profits than
most other decision areas in the business and yet they are often
taken with little or no information about the likely effect of a price
change on volume sales. Admittedly, it is very difficult to obtain
information which might be useful in making pricing decisions,
but it is such a vital area in its effect on Company performance
that the preconceived ideas of both the Sales Director and the
Managing Director on price should be questioned.

If pricing is to play its full part in the marketing operation the price sensitivity of the market must be tested in ways which do not commit a Company to changing the prices of its volume sellers before it is fairly sure of its ground. A close examination of ways and means of putting into effect experiments which will yield meaningful information will more than repay the time and effort put into the preparation. Undoubtedly, success in this area will give a Company a tactical advantage *vis-à-vis* its competitors.

TRADING POLICIES OF INTERMEDIATES

Most Companies know very little about the policies, problems, strengths and weaknesses of their outlets, as against the peculiarities of their buyers. This applies particularly to the consumer trade, but it also applies in industrial marketing whenever there is an intermediary between the manufacturer and the final user.

This information is of considerable value to most Companies, but it is absolutely vital to a Company which is selling an almost identical product to that of its competitors and, therefore, has to rely far more on the total sales package (i.e. the satisfactions built around the product).

Since the main contact with the customer is with the buyer, his importance is often overrated and information about the policies and other restraints within which he has to work is almost ignored.

INFORMATION ON COMPETITORS

As in the case of buyers, Companies usually know a lot of gossip about their competitors but have very little information about their trading policies and pricing policies.

Most Companies rely too heavily on their salesmen passing on 'information' about their competitors when they feel like it. It is worth the effort to have a positive check on competitors' activities at regular intervals and not to rely solely on the sales force to obtain the information.

These examples were chosen to illustrate the need for experiment, and for analysis and critical appraisal of the various sources of information which are available to a Company in its day-to-day operations. As indicated earlier this chapter is not intended to be a comprehensive survey of all sources of marketing information.

Communication between Managers and Market Researchers

Most Companies do without an internal market research department and only occasionally employ outside market research Companies or consultants. These same Companies may make very effective use of internally derived marketing information but they often find difficulty in dealing with the professional market researcher who may be called on to do a specific job for them. In fact, much of the benefit of such contact can be nullified by what is generally considered to be poor communication. But is communication the real problem or is it the outward expression of something more fundamental? Is the problem more likely to be concerned with the attitude of mind of the manager and the researcher in their assumptions about their own and their opposite numbers' responsibilities and expertise rather than with an inability to communicate?

The expertise of the market researcher is often misunderstood by management. He is an expert in the techniques of market research. He may also be a very rounded person, with wide knowledge and considerable wisdom in business matters. But, on the other hand, he may be a very narrow specialist whose judgement is no worse and no better than that of the man who has commissioned him to carry out the work. In fact, if he has limited experience of the business world in general, the chances are that his judgement will be worse than that of the manager who has commissioned him. Unfortunately, there is a natural tendency in dealing with experts to judge the whole man on the impression he gives of his technical competence (this is as true of dealings with the medical profession in private life as it is of those with market researchers in business).

In consequence, the manager who knows little about market research often expects too much from his market researcher, and he will take for granted the man's ability to understand his problem and the business environment from which it has been drawn and his ability to come up with a satisfactory answer. Little attempt is made, therefore, to do more than state the problem or pose some questions to which he requires answers. If there are limitations in his techniques, then he looks on it as the researcher's job to explain and not his to probe.

On the other hand, the researcher who has communication difficulties tends to consider that the manager he deals with should know the limitations of his techniques and be able to formulate the problem satisfactorily. If the manager has any doubts, it is up to him to express them and not for the researcher to volunteer information.

Thus, the manager and the researcher, under these circumstances, are committed to their own narrow roles and have a certain fear of trespassing on the other man's area of expertise. The responsibility is neatly split between manager and researcher – the former to pose the problem and the latter to answer it – and the scene is set for a classic case of poor communication.

The only way round this difficulty is for a change in attitude of mind. Instead of considering themselves to be committed solely to their personal roles they must see themselves as being committed to solving a business problem. In this way the search for a solution becomes a joint venture and a joint commitment.

It is sometimes said that if management commissions market research, and at the end of it the results only tell it what it already knows, then the fault lies with management for posing the wrong questions or problem in the first place. This may be realistic if one takes a narrow view of the manager's and the researcher's separate responsibilities but not if one considers that they have a joint commitment to solve the problem.

Information is only an Aid

Great stress has been placed on using marketing information effectively in the decision-making process. But what if there is inadequate information to give a clear guide as to what the decision should be? This situation is much more dangerous in a Company in which management is used to having comprehensive information at its disposal than it is in a Company in which decisions are normally taken on hunch, backed by experience. In the former case, it is easy to fall into an attitude of mind in which decisions are not taken – or are delayed until a decision is forced by a crisis – because the information available is inadequate to point to a clear course of action. Such a situation indicates a delegation of responsibility. A manager is responsible for taking decisions in time for them to be effective, using the best information available, even if this information falls short of what he would like to have for his guidance. True, he risks making a wrong decision, but that is a normal management risk.

Having issued this caution, let it be said that it in no way invalidates the general message which has been developed in this chapter, namely, that Companies should have a firm commitment to base decisions on the best information available, and to create the conditions which will make this commitment effective.

A Company does not need to be large to implement this approach to the decision-making process. In fact, one man, in a strategic position, can create the right conditions and, if he is sufficiently astute, can influence other functional areas of the Company by example. It does not require great intellectual capacity. It is mainly a question of creating an atmosphere in which people are able to question accepted traditions and methods of operation; in which an inquiring spirit and an analytical approach to problems becomes normal; in which people are able to discuss their problem areas openly and are encouraged to apply themselves to the discipline of painstakingly seeking out fact as the basis for the decisions they take. It takes time and patience for the atmosphere to percolate through a Company, but it can be done and it can operate down the Company structure to a much lower level than most people would think possible.

The results are worth the effort and marketing men, who must essentially have a Company-wide view, have a vested interest in seeing that all decisions in the business are based on the most up-to-date and comprehensive set of facts available, and that information requests and output are geared to this end.

2 | Marketing Information Systems and Some Individual Market Research Techniques

R. C. CLAY

Marketing Services Manager, Colgate-Palmolive Ltd.

Introduction

The first part of this chapter deals with the concept of marketing research as an information system closely integrated with the daily operational practice of a marketing division within a company.

This concept is put forward in the belief that this is the most effective way to utilize the range of individual marketing research techniques.

The second part explains in brief some of the basic individual M.R. techniques. This is not intended to be either a complete inventory of techniques or a detailed exposition of each; that would require a separate book in itself. The purpose is simply to bring the attention of the reader to some of the more widely used methods, some of which are dealt with in full detail by other contributors, e.g. General Usage and Attitude Surveys, Product Placement Research, Market Segmentation and Advertising Research.

Marketing Information Systems

INFORMATION — THE RAW MATERIAL OF EXPERIENCE

The *ad hoc* application of particular marketing research techniques does not necessarily limit their individual values. But, as is the case with most business practices, the more marketing research is planned into the total marketing system the more profitable will be its yield, and the easier it will be to assess its worth.

The application of marketing research must be considered within the context of planning for profits. This sphere of planning is a senior management function involving the application of resources based upon the corporate experience. And, in turn, this corporate experience is the collation of all information obtained by a company.

The total corporate experience needs to be organized through a number of information systems. R. & D. have their technical library, their procedures manual and their logbook of experiments. Production are well organized with their formulation and procedures manual. Sales Division have their account cards and files, and their computerized achievements.

In a similar manner, the marketing division of a company needs to organize its own particular experience. Marketing research provides a suitable means of achieving this organization, and should be charged with this specific corporate responsibility. This responsibility takes marketing research out of the area of *ad hoc* application and builds it in as an integral part of marketing with a permanent and continuous function.

CHARACTERISTICS OF A MARKETING INFORMATION SYSTEM

The construction of a system can be likened in many respects to the construction of a house. The raw materials of a house consist of bricks, tiles, cement, wood and metal; but the variety of structures which can be built from these basic materials seems endless.

In a similar manner, the raw materials of a marketing information system are a range of data collection techniques, methods of analysis, and systems of data storage and retrieval; and the manner in which they can be organized is also seemingly endless.

The operation of the M.I.S. will at any point in time be dependent upon the ability of marketing management to correctly recognize its information needs and to know how to utilize the information. These requirements will vary over time with changes in personnel, in skills, and with the competitive market circumstances.

These circumstances require the M.I.S. to be flexible in its organization, and consequently make it difficult to be categoric about the structure of the system. The need for flexibility has resulted in the recognition of maintaining basic disaggregated data files. Aggregated data, such as volume trend analyses, purchasing penetration and average volume per buyer trends, and repeat purchase patterns can then be formed as required, and changed according to needs.

However, within this flexibility of general approach it is possible to identify certain fundamental characteristics which any M.I.S. must develop.

1 The system must have a clear understanding of the general areas of information to be covered. The system has a responsibility for pinpointing these areas, but this responsibility must also be shared by management.

2 The system must have a battery of valid and standardized techniques for data collection. Standardization is essential to maintain comparability of data over time, but the techniques will need to be systematically reviewed for competence.

3 The system must have standardized techniques for aggregation and analysis.

4 The system must have data storage and retrieval procedures which meet maximum flexibility of application combined with minimal time lapse.

5 The system must be operated by staff of sufficient calibre to correctly link marketing management with the information system. This linkage involves guidance on the identification and definition of information needs, as well as the location and analysis of the relevant data.

THE GROWTH OF A MARKETING INFORMATION SYSTEM

Particular care was taken in the previous section to refer to the characteristics of a M.I.S. rather than to specific forms of structure. This was deliberate because it is important to recognize that the system must be bespoke to the company it is to serve, and not some 'ideal' or 'model' structure.

In some respects this makes the development of a system an easy task because it can take shape from the demands made upon it. But if it is to grow into an effective unit it must develop within a disciplined appraisal and re-appraisal of the marketing information objectives.

Every company has its system of marketing. The systems may vary considerably in the extent of sophistication or formality, but there is in every case an agreed sequence of actions. This marketing system is the ground plan for establishing the M.I.S. – is the basis upon which the initial information objectives are defined.

In the beginning the information system should be no more and no less complex than the marketing system. If it is less complex, then information will be inadequate and experience lost, and if it is more complex, then some of its effort will be wasted or it may even confuse by its complexity.

When the information system is set up to match the marketing system, the two will start a process of feed and feed-back and develop into a more effective organization. This is achieved because the information system will, over time, convert the stream of information into appraised and documented corporate experience. This experience will assist the marketing actions to be more effective and develop a need for other kinds of information, thus in turn changing the information system.

In the early stages the more simple techniques will be employed, very often only utilizing basic market measurements. But as the learning process gets under way the demand will grow for solutions to more difficult information problems, resulting in the use of pre-tests and predictive analytic models.

This feed and feed-back process simplifies the initial setting-up of an information system. It need only be as complex as current requirements, and should be established to conform entirely to the actual company marketing system rather than to some 'ideal' system. From this point on it promotes the growth of the marketing system and grows itself accordingly.

Individual M.R. Techniques

As indicated previously, the marketing information system is a series of individual M.R. techniques organized to form a comprehensive information system, which is integrated with the general marketing system.

The following is a brief description of some of the individual M.R. techniques. Each technique has, over time, been the subject of much individual write-up. Consequently, it should be pointed out that the following descriptions constitute only simple introductions to the techniques.

To help clarify the descriptions, five sub-headings have been used: Purpose of Technique; Method; Measurements Taken; Analysis of Measurements; Application of Technique. These sub-headings have been used whenever relevant; not in every case is the description of the technique amenable to such a detailed breakdown.

CATEGORY ANALYSIS

Purpose

To secure, for new product development, all immediately available information to determine that the size, trend, and probable opportunities of the market are consistent with the product development policy of the company. Also to ensure that the technology of the product category is within the achievable scope of the company.

Method

Data is collected from company library, government sources, research agencies and trade publications.

A system needs to be developed for a formal assessment of the data in a way that will satisfy company policy requirements.

The study would also involve a detailed investigation of the nature of the products or services already existing.

EXPLORATORY STUDY

Purpose

The Category Analysis will have provided a good framework of facts about the market. It will also have raised a number of questions. The purpose of the Exploratory Study will be to seek a more precise understanding of the nature of the vital questions that need to be answered. Only questions are important at this stage, *not* answers.

Method

The Exploratory Study involves the first searching contacts with the potential customers for the goods or services to be offered.

The scope of the study is small in scale, but deep in penetration. For consumer goods or services, group discussions and depth interviews are employed. For industrial goods, consultations are held with those responsible for buying decisions and with the user engineers.

BEHAVIOUR STUDY

Purpose

To obtain up-to-date, precise and comprehensive *statistical* appraisal of behaviour in the market, as a basis for deciding on the range of opportunities existing, or to assess the results of attempts to change behaviour.

Method

This is a sample survey technique involving the selection of a large representative cross-section of potential consumers, large being defined as sufficient to provide analysis by all necessary sub-groups to whatever degree of accuracy is required.

In the case of a 'housewife' type of study, there are four major steps:

1 The preparation of a survey plan stating information objectives and method of securing data.
2 Pilot study to test questions and data collection methods.
3 Collection of full data.
4 Analysis of data and report.

An 'industrial' type of study would follow a similar procedure, except that in some cases the potential market involves only a few people. In such cases a near census is inevitable and often necessary.

Measurements

The measurements, or data collected, should embrace the total behaviour cycle involved. In the case of a 'consumer' type product this could involve:

(*a*) Product purchased by type, brand, pack size, price
(*b*) Place of purchase
(*c*) Frequency of purchase
(*d*) Method of use (in full detail)
(*e*) Frequency of use
(*f*) Volume used

(g) History of usage to show significant events leading to change in behaviour

(h) Awareness of product field – of brands, differences in uses, developments

(i) Exposure to influences affecting behaviour (media, women's clubs).

Analysis

The sort of data collected on behaviour studies requires a multiple stage analysis programme. The initial stage would involve a series of straight counts across all data collected, usually analysed by the obvious demographic breaks, such as age, class, family size, geographic region, etc.

The second stage would involve so-called 'cross-analysis' to assess interaction between specific kinds of behaviour, e.g. frequency of use by brands used. The extent of this kind of analysis is indicated by the first stage analysis, and also by the questions which have been formed during the Exploratory Study.

The third, or final, stages of analysis would be special cross-tabulations to seek support for any hypotheses about market behaviour suggested by previous analysis; or simply to clarify previous analyses.

Applications

If the study was conducted to assess the results of attempts to change behaviour in the markets, then the application is in the nature of a progress report.

However, if the study is part of a product development programme then the immediate application is limited without an attendant motivation study which explains the reasons behind the behaviour pattern. The motivation study is dealt with in the next section.

This is not to say that a behaviour study has no application without a motivation study, but rather that the application is limited. Details of volume used and purchasing frequency could guide decisions on pack-size range. But it may be necessary to have an assessment of attitude towards the amount of acceptable expenditure on any one purchase occasion before any unusual pack-size ideas are entertained.

On its own, the behaviour study can be used to stimulate ideas on the way to approach a market, or seek support for any ideas already in hand. It can also go some way to answering the questions formed at the Exploratory Stage.

Together with the Motivation Study it provides a comprehensive long- and short-term marketing planning instrument.

MOTIVATION STUDY

Purpose

To explain the motivations behind the behaviour pattern.

Method

This particular field is still developing fast and many diverse views are held on the best way of handling the study.

A full broad-scale study forming part of a product development programme would include a segmentation analysis, this being designed to split the market into consumer groups each seeking a different range of satisfactions. For example the toilet soap market could be segmented into deodorant soaps, beauty/skin care soaps, and general family usage soaps.

But motivations would also be investigated on aspects such as the aesthetic and functional aspects of packages, user images and brand images (to be related to the segmentation analysis).

The usual general procedure is a two-stage study:

Stage I: A psychological investigation of the market, involving depth interviews and group discussions, to assess the content of the motivational pattern.

Stage II: A large-scale quantitative study to sort out the relative importance of the various aspects of the motivational pattern.

One method of approaching this type of study is to conduct a Stage I psychological investigation from which is drawn a set of hypotheses about the significant motivations in the market, and about the opportunities which exist. The Stage II study then seeks information to confirm or deny these hypotheses.

An alternative approach is to use the Stage I study to establish a range of criteria upon which people discriminate between brands or between alternative patterns of behaviour. The criteria used are reduced to simple elements. For example, a discrimination between brands would be made on the basis of such criteria as:

Expensive	Not expensive
Good value for money .	. Not good value for money
Well packed. . . .	. Poorly packed
Modern	. Traditional
	etc. etc.

At the Stage II study a large sample of people would position their opinion of each brand along these scales, and might also express their 'ideal' brand in a similar manner.

The scales would then be converted into numerical values and subjected to a factor analysis. The purpose of this being to sort out the criteria which significantly discriminate between brand choice or different modes of behaviour.

The fact of the matter is that people hold very many views about things, but there may be only a few of their ideas or beliefs which have any real influence on their behaviour, or brand choice. The purpose of the factor analysis is to sort out the effective discriminating criteria.

The analysis will also 'cluster' the discriminating factors into groups to produce market segments. In this way it is possible to isolate groups of people who hold similar views, these 'views' consisting of the discriminating factors which occur in unison to control a person's particular behaviour.

Applications

The Motivation Study, together with the Behaviour Study, forms a comprehensive marketing planning instrument which is used to:

(*a*) Formulate marketing and product concepts

(*b*) Set marketing objectives in terms of consumer targets and market sizes.

PRODUCT FORMULATION AND CONCEPT TESTS

Purpose

To obtain a consumer assessment of the product and concept relative to competition.

c

Method

No tests of this kind are of any value unless they are conducted within a clearly defined framework of product objectives, these being derived from the company's product policy and from previous behaviour and motivation studies.

In simple terms, consistent with price range, is it the intention to produce a product of superior performance to that of leading competition, or is one to take advantage of the company's superior marketing organization and settle for a parity product? If superior performance is the objective, precisely in which aspects of performance is superiority to be achieved? If parity is the objective, precisely on which criteria is it vital for parity to be achieved?

The traditional procedure in testing is to first test the product 'blind', that is without any means of identifying the origins of manufacture. The purpose of the 'blind' test is to obtain a consumer assessment unbiased by image characteristics resulting from the reputation of the company.

However, for the blind test to be of any value it is necessary that there should be significant performance characteristics of the product which can be objectively appraised apart from image influences. For example, the true appreciation of a perfume is to a significant extent dependent upon its price, packaging characteristics, and house name. Take these away from a perfume and you may just be left with an amber-coloured liquid with a smell. The personal appreciation of a perfume is dependent upon its image and its 'reverence' by the people it is intended to impress — it would be difficult (but not necessarily impossible) to test perfume outside of these influences. On the other hand, a bicycle has to satisfy clear ergonomic objectives and be compatible with certain 'image of self' characteristics, and is considerably more amenable to assessment in a blind situation.

Following the blind test, which should have established whether the product has met the product objectives, the next step is to test identified by brand name together with a statement on the product concept; the statement being presented in the form of an advertisement.

A comparison of the blind and identified tests can be very

revealing of the consumer influences exerted by the brand name and the product concept.

When conducting such tests the results should be used to indicate areas of strength and weakness in a product, rather than as a forecast of the product's sales potential. Nobody has yet proved a way of projecting product test results. Some of the reasons for this are obvious; in the test there is created 100 per cent awareness and availability of the product. This level of penetration is rarely achieved on market and obviously limits the product's potential. There is also the 'gratitude' factor at work which can favour a new product presented free of charge for testing. However, despite these problems the tests can provide much guidance on the nature of consumer reaction.

There are a number of schools of thought on the best testing procedures, and it is advisable to seek reliable advice for specific problems. Some prefer the monadic test involving one group of people testing the competitive product only, and a matched group of people testing the new product only. Adherents of this system claim that a monadic assessment is the natural way that people normally assess a product 'on market'.

Others prefer the paired comparison test in which a single group of people test both products 'side-by-side'. Adherents of this system claim that it is more sensitive to what are often only slight differences between competing products.

In some cases the nature of the product, its price and method of usage and results precludes paired testing: medical remedies being a case in point.

Applications

As already indicated, the major value of the product test is to provide a profile of consumer reaction to indicate relative strengths and weaknesses.

No method has yet been found of projecting product test results in terms of market success. But by testing alternative formulations and concepts it is possible to sort out which of those available will present the toughest attack on competition.

PACK TESTS

Purpose

To check out the functional aspects, to ensure that the aesthetic design supports the intended image of the product, to ensure that the pack establishes a clear identity for the product, and to ensure that the pack has a satisfactory impact relative to competition.

Method

The tests are carried out under three headings:

(*a*) Usage – functional aspects
(*b*) Opinion – image aspects
(*c*) Physical – impact and identity aspects.

Usage and opinion investigation is carried out by observation and free discussion techniques followed by large-scale in-home corroboration tests.

The physical tests are conducted by electronic tachistoscope and eye camera devices which measure the 'stand-out' value of packs when displayed among competition. These tests also establish speed of identification and the extent to which the design 'traps' the eye within the confines of the design or lets it wander off the pack on to outside objects.

NAME SCREENING

Purpose

To ensure that a name is compatible with the intended image of the product, and has no unwanted associations, or confusions with other names.

Method

These are usually quite small-scale investigations to check:

(*a*) *Familiarity:* The extent to which people believe they have seen the name before. This may be unwanted if the introduction is to play heavily on 'newness'.

(*b*) *Memorability:* The extent to which the name can be recalled after a brief exposure. Some words are strangely difficult to register in the mind.

(*c*) *Compatibility:* Linking names with product fields to ensure there is no association which might cause confusion.

(*d*) *Similarity:* The extent to which the name reminds of other names.

(e) Negative Association: The extent to which the name is associated with things or ideas which might cause a negative attitude.

Application

The use of name testing must be conducted with discretion and a clear idea of specifically what it is hoped to get from the test.

In many respects, the name test is a negative test, meaning that it is conducted to ensure that there is nothing wrong with the name rather than trying to find the best name.

Given time and good promotion, words can be built up to have the desired connotations. The name test usually only justifies itself when there is a reason to have cause for concern.

ADVERTISING TESTS

Purpose

To assess the ability of the advertisement to achieve impact and communication of the message, and to create the desired image reaction.

Method

Tests may be carried out 'pre-publication', meaning before actual on-market use, or 'post-publication', meaning after actual on-market use.

In pre-testing, advertisements are exposed to groups of people in the form of press advertisement 'folder tests', or on screens in theatres, caravans, etc. In post-testing, people are contacted shortly after the advertisements have appeared in the press or on TV.

There are numerous 'set techniques' for carrying out these tests which the advertising agencies will be able to describe. However, one thing that is common to all the tests for a satisfactory study to be achieved is the preliminary statement of the communication and image objectives of the advertisement, and the assessment standard by which the advertisement is to be judged.

When setting the communication objectives it is not sufficient simply to refer back to the general statement which was the original brief for the advertisement. It is necessary to go through the advertisement phrase by phrase, and through each individual visual aspect, and to check with the creative team the communication role of each phrase and aspect. And then to get a clear and detailed statement of how the items are intended to meld together to achieve the total communication content.

This exercise is intended to produce a concise, objective, and agreed statement about the advertisement as the basis for the test. The necessity for this is because most advertisement tests have to rely upon a considerable amount of freely worded answers from 'viewers'. This creates many problems of interpretation which are best anticipated before the test rather than after.

If one of the 'set techniques' is used there are usually a number of questions which produce 'scores' and 'score norms'. When norms are available, it is advisable to decide, again before the test, what score levels will constitute a satisfactory advertisement.

In the absence of norms it is only possible to be arbitrary and select some agreed criteria.

The communication objectives and judgement standard ensure the closest possible approach to an objective assessment of subject-matter which is prone to much subjective assault.

RETAIL AUDIT

Purpose

To provide a continuous coverage of the flow of goods through retail outlets.

Method

Representative shop panels are contracted to provide regular information. The information is obtained at fixed intervals of time, usually monthly or bi-monthly. At each call auditors take two measures:

1 A count of all stocks held in the store.

2 A count of all deliveries made to the store since the previous visit. This information is derived from invoices and delivery notes.

Measurements

From the two counts mentioned above six basic measurements are computed:

1 HANDLING DISTRIBUTION. The proportion of stores which have

carried or 'handled' the products at some time since the previous audit call. This is sometimes referred to as 'maximum distribution'. Handling is verified from invoices or other delivery records.

This measure can be computed in two ways: either as 'shop distribution', meaning the proportion of individual stores; or as 'sterling distribution', meaning the proportion of total sterling turnover accounted for by those stores handling the product.

The two measures in combination allow statements such as 'the brand is in 50 per cent of the stores, which between them account for 75 per cent of the total grocery turnover'. This kind of analysis indicates the extent to which the product has got into the larger as opposed to the smaller stores.

2 WITH-STOCK DISTRIBUTION. The proportion of stores which have stock at the time of the audit call. Again this can be expressed either as 'shop' or 'sterling' with-stock distribution.

The difference between the 'handling' and 'with-stock' figure gives a measure of the 'out-of-stock' position.

3 RETAILER PURCHASES. Volume and Sterling measurements of goods purchased direct from the manufacturer, or indirect from wholesalers or other factors. The information is derived from invoices or other delivery records.

4 RETAILER SALES. Volume and Sterling measurements of goods purchased by consumers 'over-the-counter'. Retail Sales information is derived data from the following formula:

$$\frac{\text{Stock at}}{\text{1st Call}} + \frac{\text{Deliveries}}{\text{Between Calls}} - \frac{\text{Stock at}}{\text{2nd Call}} = \text{Sales}$$

5 RETAILER STOCKS. Volume and Sterling measurements of goods held in the retail stores at the time of call.

6 STOCK COVER. The length of time current stocks will last at the current rate of Consumer Purchases.

7 MISCELLANEOUS. The above six measures are traditionally the standard Retail Audit measures. From these measures numerous secondary statistics can be derived: averages, such as average stocks per stockist, average consumer purchases per shop handling, or average selling prices. For new product coverage, cumulative distribution can be computed to show the extent to which the sales effort is penetrating (and losing) stockists. A measure can also be taken of the proportion of stores making a purchase of the

goods – known as purchasing distribution. Finally calculations can be made of stock dispersion to indicate the locations of over- or understocking.

Analysis

Obviously, the extent of the analysis will depend upon the size and composition of the sample, but it should seek to show:

(a) Regional results – sales or TV regions.
(b) Store type results – Multiples, Co-ops, Independents, etc.
(c) Competitive brand shares and volumes.
(d) Product type or size variations.

Application

One of the prime considerations in contracting retail audit information is panel coverage and market representation. The store panel, whether it be grocers, chemists, hardware stores (etc.), should account for the major share of the product field's national turnover. The definition of 'major share' is subjective, but it is advisable to seek a 60–70 per cent minimum coverage. In addition, the pattern of trade through the panel should be as close as possible to the total 'all outlets' national pattern, as far as it is known.

If these conditions can be met satisfactorily the retail audit can be applied in many ways.

1 TOTAL MARKET SIZE AND TREND. A combination of audit share estimate and actual ex-factory shipments can be utilized to project total market size. The accuracy of the projection will depend upon panel coverage and representation.

2 SALES AND PRODUCTION PLANNING. Market trend information can provide the basis for both long- and short-term sales forecasts, and in turn production schedules.

3 EFFECT OF OWN AND COMPETITIVE SALES PROMOTION POLICIES.

4 PROGRESS OF NEW PRODUCTS.

5 MEASUREMENT OF SALES FORCE EFFECTIVENESS.

6 MEASUREMENT OF DISTRIBUTION STRATEGY AND TACTICS. In cases where direct regular calling is limited to economic accounts, the audit can indicate progress made to distribute via wholesalers or other factors.

7 STORE STOCK CONTROL. Stock cover needs to be kept consistent with journey cycles and dispersed adequately to meet demand. Patchiness in under- or overstocking is to be avoided.

CONSUMER PANEL

Purpose

To provide a continuous coverage of consumer purchasing.

Method

A representative panel is contracted to provide regular information either by purchasing diary or by personal interview. The information is collected weekly.

This information covers:

(*a*) Product and brand purchased.
(*b*) Pack size and price.
(*c*) Details of special offer (price cut, banded pack, etc.).
(*d*) Place of purchase.

Measurements

From the basic data listed above it is possible to compute the following measurements:

1 CONSUMER PURCHASES. The volume and value of goods purchased by product category, brand and pack size.

2 PENETRATION. An important feature of the consumer market is the proportion buying a particular product category, and any one brand within the category.

Trends in penetration can be plotted, and in the case of new products cumulative penetration can be plotted to check on the extent of 'trial'.

3 AVERAGE VOLUME PER BUYER. A brand's participation in the market is the result of the number of people who buy it (penetration), and the amount they buy.

By plotting the trend in the average volume per buyer and using this in conjunction with penetration a simple, but useful, understanding is obtained of market movements.

This kind of analysis can be enhanced by plotting the results by type of consumer.

For example, by heavy/light users to see in which group the changes are occurring.

4 BRAND SWITCHING. Consumers switch between brands for a variety of reasons. In some cases their needs vary at different points in time, whilst in other cases they find several brands equally acceptable to their needs. Whatever the reasons, a considerable amount of switching takes place in some product categories, and a switching analysis pinpoints the direct competition.

In some product categories, what appears to be brand switching in the family purchasing records is in fact only coincidental purchasing. This occurs when different brands are being purchased for different family members. However, this is no less important because the 'domestic' brand is still probably vulnerable to the other brands in use in the home.

5 REPEAT PURCHASING. Particularly in the case of new product launches a measure of the level of repeat purchasing is a necessary indicator of the developing success of the launch.

6 SOURCE OF PURCHASE. Because the consumer panel picks up purchasing from all kinds of retail outlets it provides a comprehensive coverage of the total market, and enables an estimate to be made of the relative importance of each kind of sales outlet.

Analysis

Consumer Panel is amenable to all types of demographic and media exposure analysis and experiments have been made to classify people by psychological dispositions such as 'traditional/reserved' or 'experimental/changeable'.

Some of the more recent analysis has included calculations of projected market share on new products, and estimates of eventual trend effect in established product movements.

Such projections are, of course, always made on the basis of a number of assumptions which are difficult to make in any dynamic market situation. But the resulting analysis is a useful device for explaining the underlying sales movements of a brand.

Applications

Consumer Panel data takes over where Retail Audit leaves off, that is, the Consumer Panel explains in consumer terms the Retail Sales Figure of the Retail Audit.

The two techniques are really complementary to each other, but because they have in common one of the most vital of marketing statistics – Sales – they tend to be thought of as being alternatives.

As regards the sales figure, one criticism levelled at Retail Audit is that the panel coverage often leaves out a significant share of the total market. Consumer Panel, on the other hand, by recording what people buy (as opposed to what shops sell) approximates more closely to the total market position.

Other advantages of the Consumer Panel data include the fact that sales can be analysed by demographic or other relevant characteristics, to help assess the effectiveness of media advertising and sales promotion schemes.

The applications may be summarized as follows:

1 Total Market Size and Trend.
2 Sales and Production Planning.
3 Effect of Own and Competitive Sales Promotion Policies.
4 Progress of New Products.

PROMOTIONAL EXPERIMENTS

Purpose

To assess the relative effectiveness between different sales promotion (below-the-line) techniques.

Method

The assessment of below-the-line activity on-market is often impossible because of the effects of all other sales efforts. Consequently, a relative assessment of whether it is, for example, more profitable to sample or coupon can be obtained by small-scale experiments.

The approach used is to set up panels of people, using different but matched samples for each experimental promotion. The promotions are then put into effect and recalls on the samples assess purchasing reaction. This is a difficult research technique as anonymity and rigorous experimental control need to be exercised.

Similar kinds of experiment can be conducted on in-store promotions like price cutting and banded packs, etc.

PART TWO
The Main Types of Market Research

3 | Qualitative Research Studies

JOHN R. GOODYEAR

Managing Director, Market Behaviour Ltd.

To make the most effective use of any type of research, the user needs to have a reasonably clear idea of the techniques and approach involved, what its advantages and limitations are, the occasions and situations when it can be of most value, the sorts of problems to which that type of research is applicable, and how to make the most use of its findings. It is the intention of the writer that this chapter should fulfil that need for future users of qualitative research.

What is Qualitative Research?

The reader may have been introduced to qualitative research by any one of a number of different names – motivational research, exploratory research, psychological research, unstructured research, etc. This proliferation of names reflects, to some extent, the different ways in which the practitioner and the user alike approach qualitative research. It seems relevant, then, to begin by attempting to give an outline of the development of this type of research, the techniques employed in it and the approach which it involves.

THE DEVELOPMENT OF QUALITATIVE RESEARCH

Market research as a business tool is essentially a twentieth-century device, and qualitative techniques in market research really only began to be employed in the 1930s. It was not until the forties and fifties, however, that qualitative research studies made much impact.

The development of qualitative research was the result both of an increasing awareness that questionnaire surveys did little to explain or predict consumer behaviour and of developments in psychology and the social sciences which provided alternative approaches to the study of consumer behaviour.

It is now generally accepted that straightforward, direct questioning of the consumer will often fail to elicit equally direct, honest answers. The consumer may not be aware of the real reasons for his or her behaviour, or may be aware of them but be unwilling to explain them.

Qualitative research employs indirect methods to isolate, understand and evaluate those attitudes, beliefs, pressures, wants and needs which underlie, influence and determine consumer behaviour.

The qualitative researcher, while often starting with an academic qualification in one field of study only, is more often a generalist than a specialist. He (or she) employs a multidisciplinary approach to his studies. He utilizes concepts and principles such as primary and secondary drives, rationalization, projection, unconscious desires, self-image, social pressures, environmental pressures, etc., derived and developed from psychology, psycho-analysis, sociology and anthropology. And the techniques which he employs, again derived and developed in the main from these same sources, set out to probe below the surface response and to expose the underlying determinants of behaviour.

QUALITATIVE RESEARCH TECHNIQUES

Just as there are many names for qualitative research, so there are many techniques which are often associated with it. Projective techniques such as Rorschach tests and Thematic Apperception Tests — in which the individual is, respectively, asked to say what he feels an ink-blot represents, or what he feels is happening, or has happened, in a picture — are often mentioned, but less frequently used. Since it is generally agreed that many years of training and practice are necessary to become adept at the interpretation of Rorschach test results, few qualitative researchers could use such a technique effectively.

The two techniques which are employed most widely by the qualitative researcher are the depth interview and the group discussion. Both approaches have a common link, the interview in each case being relatively free and unstructured, allowing the respondent(s) to develop lines of thought and associations and ideas in a given context and in a sympathetic and relaxed environment.

The depth interview

Many people seem to object to the name 'depth interview' in qualitative research, perhaps because of its closer association with psycho-analysis than with the business world. Other names, such as 'focused interview', 'unstructured interview', 'intensive interview', 'non-directive interview', etc., are therefore often used synonymously. However, the term 'depth interview' seems to remain the most widely used and best known.

Essentially, the depth interview is a development from the psycho-analytic free association technique which encourages the free flow of words, ideas, feelings, thoughts and images in response to stimulus subjects or words. Practically, the depth interview in market research differs in many ways from its clinical counterpart. Whereas the individual undergoing psycho-analysis may have as many as five 'interviews' a week with his analyst for many months and even years, the depth interview in market research is usually a once-only interview with an individual selected to meet certain specified demographic and usership criteria. The analysand visits the analyst at his consulting rooms, but the depth interview in market research is normally carried out in the respondent's own home. The psycho-analyst may end up with hundreds of hours of 'interview' material; the qualitative researcher normally spends one and a half to two hours over a depth interview, etc.

Despite the many differences, however, there are even more similarities, and the skilful interviewer can obtain a wealth of information within the space of two hours. Let us briefly consider what is involved in a depth interview, and what sort of person makes a good depth interviewer.

As we have noted, the interview normally takes place in the respondent's own home – a familiar and secure environment within which the respondent can be relaxed and at ease. The depth

D

interviewer must be a friendly and relaxed individual, sympathetic
to the moods and personalities of others, perceptive and aware
not only of what the respondent says but also of how he says it and
the gestures, expressions, hesitations and mood changes which
accompany the remarks.

Although depth interviews are often called unstructured or
non-directive interviews, it is rare in the context of market research
for the interviewer to carry out such interviews without at least
some outline plan of the broad areas which he or she wishes to be
discussed. Most depth interviews, therefore, begin by introducing
some part of the subject-matter for discussion which is felt to have
only peripheral or background relevance, and the first ten minutes
or so of the interview – while possibly yielding useful data – essentially serves the purpose of a warm-up: allowing the respondent
time to relax and become accustomed to the interview situation
and allowing the interviewer to make an initial appraisal of the
respondent and establish an empathetic relationship.

The interviewer proceeds from there, encouraging the respondent to talk freely and openly about the subject under discussion,
always appearing attentive and interested, probing and following
through all points of interest and relevance raised, re-phrasing
questions to encourage further discussion, guiding discussion
back to the subject-matter when digressions prove to be unfruitful,
always looking for the reasons behind the behaviour and attitudes
described.

The depth interview is a global affair, the interviewer is working
with, and reacting to, many different cues. The facial expressions,
posture changes and muscle tensions of the respondent must all be
taken into account when interviewing.

The good depth interviewer enjoys the work, has a real and
continuing interest in the people interviewed and is normally
capable of establishing a good interview *rapport* with respondents
of widely different socio-economic and educational levels.

Equally, and despite quite frequent initial hesitation, most people
enjoy being interviewed. They are put in a situation where they
have a captive audience, where their views, ideas, feelings and
motivations are obviously seen to be important and worth while.
The interviewer is a stranger whom they are unlikely to meet in
their normal social context, and they can gradually unwind, relax

and even be a little indiscreet in what they say. Their social mask can be allowed to slip a little, they find less need to be guarded in what they say and often the interview situation provides them with the first opportunity in a long time to discuss taboo subjects relatively freely.

It is in such interviews that the qualitative researcher gathers much of his data.

The group discussion

The group discussion as a technique must acknowledge its origins as lying in the areas of social psychology and psychotherapy, but again there have been modifications and again there are differences.

In the view of the writer, the optimum size for a discussion group is six, seven or eight individuals. If one has more than nine people, the group tends to fragment and split up into sub-groups. The interest of the individual members of the group is not sustained and group interaction decreases. If one has fewer than five respondents then not only does one tend to get less group interaction and greater fragmentation, but also the buyer of the research is getting poor value for his research moneys.

The types of venue for group discussions vary, but the writer is firmly of the belief that once again a private house is the most suitable setting. If one recruits one's group discussion respondents from the suburbs to attend a central location one may be biasing the sample somewhat. It may be that only those of a more adventurous, more extraverted personality will accept the invitation to attend, or that those with young children or other domestic ties will decline because of the travelling time and extra effort involved. If the discussion is to be held in a hotel, then other problems may arise: respondents of lower socio-economic status being intimidated by the unfamiliar setting.

We have found that, by using recruiters of similar socio-economic background to the respondents to be recruited for a group discussion, and by holding the discussion in the living-room of that recruiter's house, we can achieve the best results.

The recruiter, working on the basis of agreed quota sample requirements, contacts suitable respondents within a two or three mile radius of her house. Respondents then do not have far to travel, the recruiter will look after their children during the discussion if they wish to bring them, and the discussion group is carried out in a familiar environment.

All discussion groups – as most depth interviews – are tape-recorded. The researcher carrying out the group interview arranges the respondents in an open circle or horseshoe shape in front of him or her.

The task of the group discussion interviewer is similar to that of the individual depth interviewer – but more difficult because of the number of people involved and the need to retain some degree of control. The skills needed are also similar, all the same skills being required plus some extra ones to control and encourage discussion.

The good group discussion interviewer not only has the ability to encourage the respondents to talk, discuss and interact as a group, he (or she) also utilizes his own posture and expressions as cues and stimuli for respondents. If group members are tense and nervous, the group interviewer can help by relaxing and leaning back in his seat; if the group is lethargic and slow, discussion can often be stimulated as a result of the interviewer sitting on the edge of the seat, alert and leaning forward; if any one individual begins to dominate the discussion, the group interviewer can usually introduce someone else into the discussion just by turning away from the dominant respondent and looking with interest and expectancy at someone else. The respondents in a discussion group quickly become adept at reacting to such cues.

Discussion groups have a similar purpose to that of individual depth interviews. They are also looking for the consumer's underlying motivations, wants and needs, but in a different context. The discussion group is encouraging interaction, assessing the attitudes of the individual and the group and of the individual *vis-à-vis* the group. The group interviewer is not only noting and probing the feelings and attitudes put forward by each respondent, but also observing and following up the reactions to those feelings and attitudes from other group members. Patterns of behaviour begin to emerge and can be explored, hypotheses take shape and can be investigated.

Again – as in the individual depth interview – a bond is often formed in the group. The social mask may again slip, and although some respondents in a group interview will quickly adjust it, many allow it to fall aside and forget it. Discussions about such normally taboo subjects as vaginal deodorants, bad breath, and sanitary protection suddenly stop being reticent and fears, anxieties and lack of knowledge are brought out into the open.

Group discussions provide the qualitative researcher with considerable insight into the behaviour of the consumer and have proved to be an extremely valuable research tool.

SUMMARY

In summary, then, qualitative research can be seen to have developed from psychological and psycho-analytical origins, being modified along the way by sociological and anthropological methods and theories, and being influenced ultimately by the needs of the manufacturer and his marketing and advertising teams.

Qualitative studies involve intensive, wide-ranging, in-depth interviews with relatively small samples of target market consumers, normally selected for interview on a quota sample basis.

The qualitative researcher, in his interviewing, attempts to develop a relationship with his respondents which allows free, relaxed and unguarded discussion to take place.

The analysis of qualitative research data is a complex and time-consuming operation, but one which normally results in achieving considerable insight into, and understanding of, the motivations, pressures, wants and needs which underlie consumer behaviour.

Some Applications of Qualitative Research

As we have noted earlier, the two main techniques used in qualitative research studies are the individual depth interview and the group discussion. Perhaps the major advantage of both of these techniques is their flexibility. Not only are they flexible in so far as they allow the interviewer to follow up and probe any interesting points which arise during the interviews, but they are also flexible in their application. Both individual and group interviews are used in advertising development and evaluation, new product development and product testing, and pack-design evaluation, as well as being used to provide a basic motivational breakdown of consumer attitudes and behaviour within a particular market.

In the following pages, some examples will be given of how qualitative research studies can help in various problem areas.

BASIC MOTIVATIONAL RESEARCH STUDIES

There are many reasons for carrying out a basic qualitative examination of consumer attitudes and motivations. A company may be considering entering a new product field and need a basic understanding of the behaviour and attitudes operating within a new and unfamiliar market. Another company – a tobacco manufacturer would be a reasonable example – may already be successfully operating in a particular market, but may – because of constant new product development and frequent price changes – need to institute regular investigations of this type in order to ensure that his marketing, advertising and new product plans remain in tune with the consumer's wants and needs, and take full account of changes that have taken place. And yet another company may use a basic qualitative study of this kind as the first step in a multi-phasic segmentation research programme aimed at identifying and describing target market consumers in other than demographic terms.

Very often, base-line studies such as these not only provide the manufacturer with a clear understanding of consumer dynamics, but also provide bonuses such as the identification of a new product opportunity, a new approach to advertising his brand, or even a tentative blueprint for all aspects of a new brand. A study which we carried out in 1965 and which began as a qualitative appraisal of housewives' attitudes, motivations, behaviour and selection criteria in the lavatory cleanser market may serve to exemplify this point.

We found that most of our respondents effectively split lavatory cleaning into two activities: (i) dealing with perceptible stains and odours, (ii) dealing with hidden factors.

Smells and visible stains presented few problems and could easily and effectively be dealt with by almost all of the housewives. The housewife's greatest concern and anxiety was with what could not be seen: with what was hidden 'round the bend'.

For most of our respondents round the bend was where the majority of germs were to be found. It was also seen as a place where there might well be stains which needed removing. Many of these housewives were prepared to admit the presence of germs, and described the lavatory as a danger zone, a potential breeding ground for germs, and as a possible threat to the family's health.

The housewife, however, is faced with a dilemma here. The germs are believed to exist, but cannot be seen. Products are bought to kill germs, but their efficacy must be taken on trust — dead germs are as invisible as living ones. Similarly, she will buy products to remove the stains which she believes lie just around the bend. Again, she must have faith in product claims; since she cannot see if there is a stain there to begin with, she cannot see whether it has gone after using the product. A frightening situation.

In this context, the housewife needs reassurance that the steps which she has taken have been effective. The majority of our sample dealt with this situation by the simple process of rationalization. They convinced themselves that the absence of stains where they *could* see, and either the absence of offending smells or the presence of a clean, fresh smell were positive indicants of the absence of germs and stains where they could *not* see.

Lavatory cleaning involved the use of products for dealing with hidden problems, and products for dealing with perceptible problems. Ultimately, the housewife might stand back and use the cleanliness/whiteness of the lavatory pan and the absence of offending smells as evidence of the effectiveness of products such as disinfectants, bleaches, and specific lavatory cleansers — any or all of which may have been tipped or sprinkled into the lavatory to deal with invisible stains and germs.

In summary, then, the housewife in cleansing the lavatory was dealing with stains she could see, stains she could not see, germs which were invisible, odours which were present and odours which might arise in the future. She was using various combinations of products such as scouring powders, detergents, disinfectants, bleaches, deodorant blocks, deodorizing aerosols and specific lavatory cleansers in her efforts to deal with these problems.

Many of the products used had to be taken on trust since the housewife had no way of assessing their effectiveness. To reassure herself, the housewife therefore needed to provide rationalized 'evidence' of effective cleaning and germicidal action. The criteria employed were the cleanness and whiteness of the pan and either (or both) the absence of offending smells or the presence of a clean, fresh smell.

We were then able to go one step further and, after considering the products currently used by our respondents for 'round the bend' and their attributes and images, we were able to suggest how our client might approach the development and promotion of a new lavatory-cleaning product. Our evaluation, in outline, was as follows:

Current products

(i) Bleaches for lavatory-cleaning which sell on the platform of a strong germicide, but which have the promise of whiteness as a built-in *cachet*.

(ii) Specific lavatory cleansing products which sell mainly on the platform of removing stains from round the bend. No real *cachets*.

(iii) Disinfectants which also sell on a germicidal platform, but with the *cachet* of a clean, fresh, pleasant smell.

A possible new product

The complete lavatory cleanser.

If possible, a combination of both bleach and disinfectant offering double-strength germicidal action with both *cachets* of whiteness and a clean, fresh smell.

This product should be given a brand name chosen to give maximum reassurance.

The report given to the client on this study contained much more information and detail, but the outline given above indicates the sort of information which can be obtained and the way in which an exploratory qualitative project can often provide additional benefits.

QUALITATIVE RESEARCH AS AN AID TO THE DEVELOPMENT OF EFFECTIVE ADVERTISING

Qualitative research studies can help in maximizing the effectiveness of advertising in various ways. One fairly simple point to make is that whatever approach an advertisement may employ, it is wasted unless it is understood by the consumer.

The archetypal British holidaymaker abroad provides us with a reasonable analogy. His approach to the non-English-speaking native who does not understand his requests is to repeat his request, still in English, but more loudly. He has not taken the trouble to learn the language and often complains bitterly when his attempts to communicate meet with failure.

Some advertising failures may result from similar language problems. To communicate effectively with his target market the advertiser must understand and be able to use the consumer's language and vocabulary. Qualitative research can serve as an invaluable source of reference in this context. The qualitative researcher is in constant touch with the consumer. Depth interviews and group discussions provide a ready source of consumer language and phraseology. Reports on qualitative studies usually provide verbatim quotations from the interviews to support and elaborate the findings reported. Far from devaluing the work of the copy-writer, the intelligent use of qualitative research in this context will tend to maximize the communication effectiveness of his ideas and increase his success.

Another area in which qualitative research can be valuable to the advertiser is in the isolation of concepts, messages and images which are meaningful and attractive to the target market. Thus, while the older man may be attracted to a brand of pipe tobacco which offers mellow, aromatic flavour and relaxed satisfaction, the young man may be much more interested in a brand which seems to confer on its user increased virility and a magnetic effect on attractive girls.

Very often advertising which is based on the consumer's answers to questions posed in conventional questionnaire interviews will be less effective than it might have been. The simple straightforward answer, while often making good sense, is equally often only a small part of the total picture.

The findings of a study which we carried out early in 1967 will show how qualitative research can often probe below the surface and, in so doing, provide information which will lead to more meaningful advertising approaches.

The project in question had two main objectives:
(i) To explore and evaluate housewives' motivations for slimming and weight-watching.

(ii) To evaluate five alternative approaches for future advertising for an existing slimming aid.

Our research findings were as follows:

1 The fat woman, like the nonconformist in most societies or groups, is treated as something of an outsider and is aware that she may be the object of scorn, pity and prejudice.

2 Our respondents seemed aware that slimness is essentially a modern ideal of physical beauty, resulting in part from a greater emphasis on youth. Fashion and public opinion being geared to the young, the youthful, slim figure was felt to have become today's ideal.

3 It seemed that the desire of some of the women to be slim reflected their desire to become more emancipated and enjoy more of the privileges of the man.

4 Many of our respondents complained of being conditioned and imprisoned by the slim person's attitudes towards, and expectations of, the fat person. They feel that they are expected to by happy, jolly, good-natured and able to take a joke at their own expense.

5 It was generally felt to be true that the fat woman has to work harder to get her fair share of love and attention; this refers not only to the love that friends and relations can give, but also to the kind of attention that a stranger can show. The man in the street, passing by, knows nothing of the fat woman's cheerful and friendly personality, he just notes her appearance and her body. Because the fat woman feels that her body is unprepossessing and ugly, the reaction of the stranger to her physical appearance alone is of great importance. The fat woman who feels that she must be unattractive because of her overweight thus craves for admiration from strangers, not necessarily for her as a person, but for her as a cipher – as a symbol of womanhood.

As a result of consideration of our findings, the following conclusions were then put forward about women's reasons for slimming:

Women want to become slim because slimness represents an ideal state. Many women feel that by achieving this state they will become the sort of women they would like to be in other ways as well; those who crave elegance feel they will be elegant when they are slimmer, those who feel insecure consider security to be the slim woman's prerogative, those who want to excite their husband's sexual interest feel that they can do this by becoming slim, and those who feel that they are ageing expect to recapture their youth by returning to the weight they were when they were young. Slimness, therefore, can be all things to all people. It represents each individual woman's idea of her most successful self and is seen as a panacea which will relieve the fat woman of her troubles and anxieties. Thus, when a woman wants to lose weight, she is not just thinking of becoming a specific weight, or having certain proportions, she is also a dissatisfied woman who hopes that, by slimming, she is going to become the woman that she wants to be. Slimness is the secondary goal, the primary goal is success.

Given the basic appreciation of the motivations, pressures and desires underlying the housewife's approach towards slimming, together with the comments and reactions of our respondents resulting from exposure to the five advertising approaches already prepared, the research was able to provide the agency's creative team with a valuable framework for the development of a new promotion for the product in question.

Although qualitative research studies are mainly used early on in the development and evaluation of advertising, they can often be useful at later stages in the evaluation of 'finished' advertising.

OTHER APPLICATIONS OF QUALITATIVE RESEARCH TECHNIQUES

The specific examples of research results given in the past few pages should be sufficient to illustrate the type of findings one can expect from a relatively small-scale qualitative study.

The various additional applications of qualitative research studies will be mentioned more briefly, since space does not permit examples to be given in each case.

Pack design evaluation

A qualitative approach is often employed, both as a diagnostic measure and as a first 'weeding-out' evaluative step, in the development of new pack designs.

It may be decided, for example, by a cigarette manufacturer

that a particular brand needs a new pack design. The manufacturer, having approached two design houses, may have ended up with six or seven alternative new designs. The ultimate intention may be to carry out a large-scale quantitative evaluation of alternative packs – perhaps including a pseudo-product-test – but to do this with six or seven packs would be complex, unwieldy and expensive.

A small-scale qualitative pilot study, however, could provide information which might allow the client to reduce the alternatives to two or three packs only. At the same time, the research would also provide information regarding consumer attitudes towards the designs, the product and user imagery evoked by the designs, the perceived situation-appropriateness of the packs, etc., which would be useful not only for the construction of the questionnaire for the large-scale study to follow, but also for guidance in the future creative development of the brand's advertising.

Qualitative research into packaging and pack designs is not limited to reducing the number of alternatives to be evaluated by larger-scale quantitative research. Many projects commissioned to explore packaging are diagnostic and developmental studies which aim to explore imagery and associations to materials used in the pack, the shape and construction of the pack, the design and the colours used on it, the logo-style and copy, and so on. Indeed, this application of qualitative research would seem to be becoming more and more necessary to the manufacturer. The growth of private label goods and the increased competition generally for shelf space in supermarkets makes it essential that packs should be working ever harder and more effectively at point of sale.

New product development

Qualitative research is extremely valuable, and frequently employed, in new product development work. Very often new product concepts are generated as by-products of qualitative studies commissioned for other purposes. A qualitative examination of housewives' attitudes towards cold desserts, for example, might well provide the client with several suggestions for new products in this market.

Frequently, however, qualitative studies are initiated specifically as part of a new product development programme to identify gaps in a specific product field, to isolate weaknesses in competitive products, to uncover consumer wants and needs and to indicate potential new product opportunities. Often a new product concept can arise simply as a result of looking at a product field and its component brands in a new way. Too often it is forgotten that the consumer's perception, evaluation and structuring of a product field may be completely different from that of the manufacturer or marketing man. Because of its global and wide-ranging approach, qualitative research provides the manufacturer with the opportunity of seeing his market through the consumer's eyes, and the new perspective provided can often be extremely rewarding.

Qualitative research can, and does, also play a valuable part in evaluating new product concepts. With an ever wider choice of products and brands being made available and an increasing sophistication on the part of the housewife, it is becoming increasingly important for the manufacturer to check new products for consumer acceptability/desirability throughout their development. The cost of failure even after test-marketing only can be very high, and yet the data available suggest that in recent years less than 50 per cent of products which have been test-marketed in the U.K. have gone on to a national launch. We are not intending to suggest that carefully planned and executed qualitative research will guarantee success, simply that it may uncover information earlier in the gestation period of a new brand and thus help to guard against expensive failures.

In-home product testing

The use of discussion groups and individual depth interviews as a means of obtaining a detailed evaluation from consumers of new product samples which they have tried out in their own homes has also increased in recent years.

More and more manufacturers seem to have appreciated that the type of detailed information which is obtained from the consumer using such an approach can be of real value in the development and modification of their products.

By combining a product test with an advertising test – for example, having the same product placed with each of forty-eight respondents but exposing three matched sub-groups within that total sample each to a different advertising strategy for the product at placement – one can obtain further useful information. Alternatively, a series of different packs, each containing an identical product, could be used, again providing potentially useful information.

One of the major points in favour of qualitative research is its flexibility: a flexibility which makes it appropriate to most problems and to all product fields.

The development of more effective questionnaires

An application of qualitative research which is often forgotten or glossed over is as an aid to the development of a more effective and complete questionnaire.

The importance, in advertising, of talking the same language as the consumer has been mentioned earlier in this chapter. The same point holds good when one is developing a questionnaire. While the qualitative interviewer is free to ask a question in many different ways in search of information, the interviewer using a structured questionnaire is normally following specific instructions and asking set questions. It seems much more likely that the answers obtained will be meaningful if the questions are too.

A qualitative pilot study of this kind is not only useful as a means of improving the way in which questions are asked, however; it is also valuable as an insurance that the questionnaire will cover all of the appropriate areas. As was noted earlier, the consumer may see things differently from the manufacturer and a failure to take this into account could prove disastrous.

How to Get the Most from Qualitative Research

The two previous sections of this chapter have attempted to show what qualitative research involves and the ways in which it can be usefully employed. In this final section we would like to offer the user a series of guidelines which – if applied – should ensure that he makes the most of the research he commissions.

DON'T RELY ON QUALITATIVE STUDIES WHICH WERE
CARRIED OUT SIX YEARS AGO

It is an undeniable fact that people change. They change as a result of experience, as a result of social and environmental pressures, as a result of fashion, and so on. Because of this, it can be extremely dangerous to rely on old research. This is usually recognized by companies which are working in product fields which change or develop rapidly – such as cigarettes or deodorants – but may well be forgotten in relation to an apparently static market.

For example, the story of how it proved necessary, some years ago, to market an incomplete cake-mix – leaving the housewife to add an egg – has become a cliché, but developments in the convenience foods market generally, and the growth of convenience desserts in particular, could indicate that a cake-mix with egg included may no longer be such a disastrous idea. The housewife may now be ready for such a product.

USE QUALITATIVE RESEARCH EARLY

In many of its applications, qualitative research is used diagnostically. This is especially true of its use in the evaluation of advertising. To be of most value, the research results should be available in time to allow the advertiser and his agency to make use of them. This sounds obvious, yet all too frequently such research loses its value because it is put in hand too late for its findings to be acted on. Sometimes this is unavoidable, but in many cases earlier action could be taken and more use could be made of research findings.

TAKE CARE OVER SAMPLE SELECTION CRITERIA

Qualitative studies almost invariably deal with quota samples. Although sample selection is always important in all types of market research, in qualitative studies where sample sizes are relatively small it is particularly important.

Careful consideration should be given to the question of the target market. If, for example, Imperial Tobacco were considering changing the Gold Leaf pack design and wanted to carry out some qualitative research to get consumers' attitudes to six or seven possible new designs, it would not be sufficient to define one's sample as 'male and female cigarette smokers'.

Although the views of regular smokers of Cadets, Diplomat, No. 6, and No. 10 on this subject could be interesting, they would almost certainly be largely irrelevant since few smokers change up to a more expensive brand. It would, however, be important to talk to a cross-section of Gold Leaf smokers and smokers of competitively priced brands, and – in anticipation of future price increases – to talk to smokers of more expensive brands.

USE THE BEST RESEARCHERS YOU CAN FIND

In qualitative research the abilities of the individual researcher are of paramount importance.

He or she must not only be able to conduct a group discussion effectively, he must be able to understand the consumer. He must have empathy, insight and creativity, and be able to apply these abilities in his interpretation of the information he gathers. Ultimately, also, he must recognize the importance of relating his findings to the client's problems. While he may find psychoanalytic or sociological concepts of real value in his consideration, analysis and understanding of the consumer's motivations, his conclusions and recommendations must be oriented towards the client's marketing and advertising problems.

REMEMBER THAT QUALITATIVE RESEARCH IS USUALLY SMALL-SAMPLE RESEARCH

Most reports on qualitative research have a preface which says something like:

'It should be borne in mind that this report is based on an evaluation of data gathered from a sample of only XX consumers. The findings should therefore be viewed as hypotheses which require validation.'

It may, on occasion, be relevant to carry out qualitative research and use its findings without recourse to quantification. Similarly, a large-scale quantitative study might have relevance on its own. Most often, however, a combination of both will give the most valuable and reliable results.

MAKE THE BEST USE OF THE QUALITATIVE RESEARCHER

As a final point in this chapter we would like to suggest that many users of research are currently not making the best possible use of the qualitative researcher as an individual.

In many ways, the qualitative researcher represents the closest and most sympathetic link with the consumer available. He is in constant and direct contact with the consumer in discussion groups, spending often as many as 250 hours in the year listening and talking to the consumer in direct face-to-face situations, as well as spending even longer listening to the tape-recordings of such discussions before preparing his report.

Round-table discussions of research findings and their implications should take place as a part of all qualitative projects, in addition to any written reports which are prepared. Such discussions allow the manufacturer, and his advertising agency, the opportunity to get the most from the research and from the researcher.

4 Behaviour and Attitude Research

JOHN NOLAN

Senior Research Executive, British Market Research Bureau Ltd.

Introduction

However comprehensive and revealing a survey of the public's use of and attitudes towards a particular product may be, it will never be capable of replacing the need to exercise judgement in deciding appropriate future action in respect of that product. What it *can* do is to limit the alternatives between which this judgement must be made, and to inform it. In this it differs from, say, product testing, or pack research, or advertising pre-testing, where it is often possible to formulate in advance what decision will follow from what range of results: 'With x or better, we'll go ahead; otherwise we'll scrap it.' No such pre-formulation of straight-forward alternatives is possible with the kind of survey we are concerned with here. This is implicit in the name of the research: we cannot normally *control* people's behaviour and attitudes in the way that we can control the nature of a product, its pack, or its advertising. All we can do is attempt to *influence* them.

This means that calculating the results of this sort of survey is likely to mark the beginning rather than the end of its usefulness. It will provide a source from which, hopefully, will stem a plan of action, inspired by the experience, reasoning powers, and creativity of those concerned in this process. This, obviously, has crucial implications for the efficient planning of such a survey: knowledge of the concerns and ambitions of its eventual users is essential. The relative merits of different approaches will vary with the particular ways in which the results are likely to be used.

A second distinguishing feature of this kind of research is that it has a wider application than the other types which have been mentioned. These normally relate to one specific marketing decision, whereas a knowledge of the consumer is likely to be relevant to all such decisions, whatever element in the marketing mix they relate to. A good general survey acquires the status of a 'bible' which is referred to again and again. Paradoxically, comprehensiveness of this kind can only be achieved by the exercise of a great deal of selectivity in the exact coverage given to different topics, since only through this can one avoid placing an intolerable strain upon survey respondents, and upon the survey budget.

The researcher's task is therefore not merely to know the *best* way of doing something. Much more, it is to evaluate the most *cost-effective* way of doing it, and to identify the most economical methods capable of satisfying the various requirements from the survey. Only rarely will he be faced with the need to develop new techniques; most of the time his skill lies in building, from existing techniques, that particular combination which is most appropriate to the context of the market being investigated, and to the particular problems and opportunities facing his client.

The balance of this chapter reflects these preoccupations. In the next section of it a number of the different functions of behaviour and attitude surveys are outlined. The following sections describe respectively the sorts of measures which may be taken in fulfilling these functions, and various methods of obtaining these measures. The emphasis throughout is not on the detailed methodology of various techniques, but on the criteria for choosing between them.

Scope

The precise functions of any survey of behaviour and attitudes will of course vary with the marketing needs of the body for whom it is carried out. It is, however, possible to itemize the main ways in which a thoroughgoing survey of this kind *can* be helpful.

IDENTIFYING MARKETING TARGETS

Marketing activity is becoming increasingly selective in its direction by concentrating on groups which offer greater-than-average prospects of expansion. An inspection of behaviour patterns will often lead to the identification of such groups. For example, if a product is found to have a much larger proportion of its users using it in relatively small quantities than have its competitors, the decision might be taken to concentrate its promotional effort on increasing weight of use among existing users. Here more than anywhere else the survey data has to be interpreted in the light of other knowledge about the product in question.

KNOWING WHAT THESE TARGET GROUPS ARE LIKE

Whether target groups of consumers are defined in this way, or whether they are known beforehand (for example, the situation may be such that all existing users are by definition the object of concern), it can be of great value to know just *who* they are, in terms of such things as age, general opinions, and newspaper and magazine readership.

DESCRIBING THE PROCESSES TO BE INFLUENCED

Given that the ultimate purpose behind a survey is the desire to influence people's behaviour (even if this influence is merely in the direction of preserving the *status quo*) it is clearly useful to know the circumstances of this behaviour.

In what sort of shops is something bought?
At what times?
On impulse?
For a special purpose?
While shopping alone?
After entering a shop to make another purchase?
One or more at a time?
And how is the purchase used up?
Quickly or slowly?
What exactly for?
When?
Who decides this?

The more that is known about the processes involved, the more efficiently can pressure be brought to bear on them.

DETERMINING A PRODUCT'S POSITION IN THE MARKET

With some products it is difficult to know into just which field they fall. With others, it is not at all clear with which other products in that field they are in competition. Consumers' categories often differ from those of producers. Which are the main competitors to a product, and what are its perceived strengths and weaknesses relative to them? It may be decided, in the light of the 'product map' which this sort of question produces, to bolster up a brand's strengths to secure its existing position, or to remedy its weaknesses and thus expand from that position.

SPOTTING OPPORTUNITIES FOR NEW PRODUCTS

This is a function of attitude research which has grown rapidly both in importance and in the sophistication of the techniques used to carry it out. A description of these needs, and merits, a good deal of space in itself, and is provided in subsequent chapters of this book, but it is worth remembering that, while this sort of exercise can be a whole subject in itself, it frequently forms part of the same survey as the other areas described.

IDENTIFYING COMMUNICATION TARGETS

Just as a knowledge of behaviour patterns can form the basis for selecting particular aspects of behaviour on or through which it will be most rewarding to exert influence, so a study of the way *attitudes* are organized can lead to particular beliefs about products, or associations with them, emerging as particularly worth while communicating to the consumer, through either advertising, pack design, any other form of promotional strategy, or the form and content of the product itself.

CHOOSING COMMUNICATION APPROACHES

Once the decision has been made *what* to say about a product, the survey results can provide some leads as to *how* it might best be said, through giving a picture of the broader context of associated ideas in which advertising will be received.

EVALUATING TOTAL MARKETING ACTIVITY

Repeating the survey (or selected parts of it) later in time will show how attitudes and behaviour have been changing in the meantime, and will allow these to be related to objectives previously set. Just as the single survey will set out to explain overall levels of behaviour by identifying those factors which between them determine the consumer's behaviour pattern, so a repeat survey can explain any changes in overall levels, pinpoint the particular changes in people's circumstances and attitudes which have brought this about, and show how marketing activity carried out during the period relates to this.

Measures

The first step in planning a survey must always be a detailed assessment of what will be required from it. What uses are envisaged for it? For what decisions is it going to form the basis? And what are seen as the appropriate criteria on which these decisions should be made? Once this has been done, and only then, the next step is to determine what measurements will be best able to meet these requirements.

It is possible to distinguish five major areas in which measurement may be needed. These are:

A. *Consumption:* How do people behave in respect to the product field or service with which the survey is concerned, and the alternatives within this product field?

B. *Beliefs about products:* What do people think about them? What qualities and associations are they perceived to have?

C. *Requirements from products:* How important are these beliefs? What qualities would people *like* products to have?

D. *More general attitudes:* How does all this relate to more basic motivations?

E. *Classification data:* What sort of people fall into particular patterns with respect to A–D?

This section discusses the principal measuring techniques for each of these areas in turn.

CONSUMPTION

The most obvious and most necessary measurement to be undertaken in any survey is of the behaviour which the survey is designed to help influence, whether this is purchasing, using, eating, drinking, serving, playing, attending or whatever.

While the *need* to measure this may be obvious, however, just what is the appropriate *unit* of measurement is frequently far from clear. To begin with, 'consumption' may be a two-stage process, in which the *purchasing* of a product can be distinguished from its *using up*. Particularly when these occur at different times, and are carried out by different people, it will be desirable, if possible, to try to find out about both. More problematically, it may be necessary to make some sort of choice between them when deciding:

(i) The universe to be sampled;
(ii) The interpretation of the results for action, particularly in choosing between the relative importance of factors believed to influence buying and other factors connected with 'using up'.

This choice often boils down to a judgement as to who makes the real purchasing *decision*. In some cases, this will be the purchaser, but in others it will be the people he or she is buying it for. For example:

'When a request is made, the decision-maker can be the one who made the request: unless the housewife dissents, she acts merely as a purchasing agent to carry the request into action' (Lovell *et al.* 1968).

Secondly, we have to decide in what terms to measure the behaviour we have decided to be appropriate for our purpose. Broadly speaking, there are four (non-exclusive) options:

1 *Questions about recent behaviour*
e.g., 'How often in the last seven days have you eaten X?'
    'How many units of Y have you bought in the last four weeks?'

This approach provides the most *precise* measurement of the overall level of consumption. However, it is by no means so precise as it at first appears, because:

(*a*) Many people are not going to remember too well just what they have done within the stated time span.

In this situation, people typically overestimate the frequency with which they do something: they tend to 'telescope' the frequency in which a given situation occurs. The extent of overestimation is likely to increase with:

(i) Decreasing frequency of purchasing (or use).

(ii) Irregularity of purchasing (or use).

(iii) Diminishing perceived importance of any purchase (or usage).

Thus, a question of this type can provide a fairly accurate estimate of the total market size for, say, fresh milk, or refrigerators, but would seriously overestimate that for breakfast cereals or facial tissues.

(b) Questions about recent behaviour are often answered in terms of perceived average behaviour, when recent behaviour is seen by the respondent as atypical and likely to give, in his opinion, a distorted picture of what he is really like.

(c) People's answers will be affected by the social acceptability of the behaviour being asked about. Consumption of alcohol and tobacco is typically understated, that of toothbrushes and household cleaners typically overstated. This is not necessarily due to deliberate untruths: people tend to believe the best about themselves. This, of course, makes it very hard to 'catch them out'.

(d) If the market is a seasonal one, or conditions at the time of the survey are unusual, the distribution of answers will be unrepresentative.

There *are* many markets where these factors are largely inoperative, and a fairly accurate market estimate can be obtained. In other cases, the information can still be useful as an indication of *relative* levels. Oppenheim's (1966) distinction between validity and reliability is relevant here: A clock which is consistently twenty minutes fast can be just as reliable as one which consistently shows the correct time, i.e. gives a 'valid reading'. Similarly, survey-based estimates can tell us how market size is changing, or how it divides up among different kinds of users, given that they have apparently equal tendencies to over- and under-report their behaviour.

2 *Diary data*

In cases where an accurate estimate of market size *is* required, and interview data does not appear able to provide this, the interview can be combined with a 'consumption diary' to be filled in by the respondent *after* the interview.

3 Questions about average behaviour

e.g., 'How often do you buy X on average?'

'How many Ys do you buy in the average month?'

The tendency to answer questions about recent behaviour in terms of habitual behaviour has already been mentioned. For some purposes, people are right to answer in this way. When, for example, we seek to relate attitudes to behaviour it is more appropriate to do this in terms of what people usually do than in what they happened to do last week, which is likely to have been influenced to some extent by chance or by temporary factors.

Asking people about their habitual behaviour can thus provide a more sensitive analytic instrument, even though individuals' answers may be rather vague and based to a certain extent on guesswork. We can say that it is a less *valid* measure than recent behaviour, but a more *reliable* guide to distinguishing between individuals.

4 Questions about behaviour tendencies

This approach can be taken to its logical extreme by asking about consumption in very general terms indeed, such as 'bought most often', 'bought regularly', 'bought occasionally', avoiding any mention of units. Such measures show how consumers see themselves as standing in relation to a brand, and can be particularly useful in determining the role of specific product beliefs.

To what extent do people differ in their interpretation of such words? A recent experiment carried out by the British Market Research Bureau Ltd stacked up 'subjective' and 'objective' consumption against each other. Respondents were asked which brands of washing powder and tea they considered they used regularly, and which occasionally, and then their actual purchasing frequency for these brands. While *on average* 'regular use' implied much heavier purchasing than 'occasional use', some *individuals* who were regular users of a brand in fact bought it less often than some occasional users:

	Self-assessed use of a brand of washing powder		Self-assessed purchase of a brand of tea	
	Regular	*Occasional*	*Regular*	*Occasional*
Percentage of cases where the brand in question was purchased:				
Once a week or more often	71%	3%	84%	4%
More than once a month; less than once a week	23%	26%	11%	29%
Once a month	5%	20%	3%	22%
Less than once a month; more than once in three months	1%	23%	1%	23%
Less than once in three months	—	28%	1%	22%

It can be argued that in one sense this is desirable, in so far as answers reflect people's differing needs. For example, housewives without children are more likely to describe themselves as regular users of a brand at a lower actual rate of purchasing than are housewives with children. Where answers are relative in this way, the user-groups which result from this sort of question *are* homogeneous in their use of the brand relative to potential use of it, more so than groupings arrived at on 'objective' criteria. Differences in people's definitions which are *not* need-related, on the other hand, will reduce its effectiveness.

A good deal of the variation in actual behaviour can be related to differences in people's basic requirements, for example family size:

	Self-assessed regular use of:			
	Washing Powder		Tea	
	By Housewives:		By Housewives:	
	With Children	*Without Children*	*With Children*	*Without Children*
Percentage of cases where the brand in question was bought:				
Once a week or more often	90%	67%	91%	78%
Less than once a week; more than once a month	10%	28%	7%	15%
Once a month	—	3%	2%	4%
Less than once a month; more than once in three months	—	1%	—	1%
Less than once in three months	—	1%	—	2%

By and large, therefore, such measures can be informative for setting advertising and promotional strategy, in highlighting the differences between individuals who buy more or less of the brand, in proportion to what they might do. They are much less relevant to marketing planning, where the concern is likely to be with the relative value of different sections of the market, in terms of their contribution to total sales.

PRODUCT ATTITUDES

The concepts measured

OVERALL EVALUATION. The extent to which an individual is favourably or unfavourably disposed to the product as a whole. ('Attitude' is sometimes treated as referring *only* to this, following its definition in psychology as 'the amount of affect for or against a given psychological object' (Thurstone, 1931).) The usefulness of this measure varies greatly, depending on its relationship to whatever behavioural data has been collected. In many fields it will mirror behaviour: its only value in these cases is to make sure that there *is* no block between thought and action.

Where it does tell a different story from behaviour, however, overall evaluation can be of crucial importance. This may come about because of a price obstacle (e.g. expensive durables), or because of distribution problems (e.g. Wilkinson Sword razor blades in the early 1960s). Again, there may be no suitable measure of behaviour available to act as a yardstick. In all these cases, it will be important to measure the extent of good- or ill-will, and to be able to relate this to other survey information.

SPECIFIC BELIEFS. These include consumer beliefs about physical and functional properties of the brand, the sort of people and particular uses with which the brand is associated, and the psychological 'added values' promotional activity may have endowed it with. They collectively form what is often referred to as the product or brand image, a useful term since it serves as a reminder that what people *believe* about a brand may not correspond at all to reality, and moreover that people may not *consciously* formulate these beliefs outside the interview situation.

The types of questions used

The *range* of answers to the majority of attitude-questions in a quantified survey is predetermined: the respondent is offered a choice of alternative replies, as opposed to the free-answer approach frequently adopted in exploratory work. Some free-answer questions are frequently included, but these have been aptly described as 'often easy to ask, difficult to answer, and still more difficult to analyse' (Oppenheim, 1966). They do show what thoughts are at the forefronts of people's minds, and how they express them. However, a good deal of this is lost by the need to group answers together in order to assess the frequency with which different kinds of answer occur (an expensive process in itself). Where respondents are expressing themselves in their own language, it becomes much harder to make meaningful comparisons between products, between groups of people, and between different periods in time. Sophisticated analytic techniques can only be used where there has been a good deal of control over the basic data to be analysed. Most surveys nevertheless contain *some* 'open-ended' questions, if only to prevent respondents feeling they are not being given a chance to speak their minds.

There are many different 'closed' techniques of attitude measurement. One basic distinction is between *sorting* techniques, in which the association between a brand and an attribute for an individual is all-or-none, and *scaling* techniques in which degrees of association are established. A number of each type of technique are described in the next two sections.

Some sorting techniques

PRODUCT COMPARISON. The respondent is asked to which particular brand each of a number of different attributes is most applicable:

'I'd like you to look at this list of brands, and tell me which *one* of them you would say had the mildest flavour?... And which *one* would you say had the strongest flavour?...' And so on, through the various dimensions of attitude which preliminary research has suggested are important in the product field. This method is most useful for bringing out any perceived differences between two or more products which are very alike, since it forces respondents to choose between them. It is much less useful in a heterogeneous field, where there may be an 'obvious' answer to each question. In this situation one brand may be nominated by nearly everyone, all others hardly at all. This would mean that although there might well be perceived differences between the latter this would not be brought out.

ATTRIBUTE COMPARISONS. This is the same method 'sideways on'. The respondent is now asked to choose which of a list of *attributes* is most appropriate to a particular *brand*. This makes it possible to compare directly one brand's placing on the different dimensions – but does not permit direct comparison of the placing of different brands on any one dimension.

FORCED CHOICE. The respondent is asked whether or not a specific attribute is applicable to a particular brand:

'I'm going to read out to you the names of a number of brands. I'd like you to tell me for each one I read out whether you would say it had a mild flavour, or whether you would say it had a strong flavour.'

This technique has two main drawbacks. Firstly, it is a lengthy one to administer, since so many questions are involved (the number of products asked about multiplied by the number of attributes).

Secondly, results do not distinguish well between different products, where an attribute is clearly favourable or unfavourable. People forced to answer about a product where they have no information to draw on, or no feeling either way, will normally give the product the benefit of the doubt – and a favourable answer.

Despite these drawbacks, the forced choice method can be the most appropriate one in fields where the different products are particularly heterogeneous. Because each product is asked about separately, the danger of *all* mentions going to one clearly differentiated product is avoided.

FREE CHOICE OF PRODUCTS. The respondent is asked to select which brands he thinks are appropriate for any given attribute. He can select as many or as few as he likes – or none at all if he thinks none are appropriate:

'I'd like you to look at this list of brands. Some of them you may have tried, others you may just have heard about. Either way, we just want your impressions. Which of these brands would you say have a mild flavour?'

And which have a strong flavour?'

And so on. This method is in very common use: for the majority of product fields it is more sensitive between brands, and over time, than any other method (Joyce, 1964). For reasons already mentioned, however, this may not apply to product fields which are either particularly homogeneous or particularly heterogeneous. A further, practical limitation is that there must be at least three competitors in the product field before the method can be applied at all.

FREE CHOICE OF ATTRIBUTES: The free choice method can also be turned 'sideways on' so that the respondent has to choose from a list of attributes which, if any, are appropriate to a given brand. Again, this means that direct comparisons between products are not possible, but that we can compare any one product's placing on different attributes. It can be useful for example, in diagnosing the situation of the 'brand which has everything', where one product dominates the market to such an extent that it would pick up a majority of mentions on all favourable attributes when matched against its competitors.

Some scaling techniques

ORDINAL SCALES. The method described on page 76 can be taken further, with the respondent being asked to place *all* the products in order of appropriateness for a particular attribute:

'I'd like you to look at this list of brands, and tell me which *one* of them you would say had the mildest flavour?

Now which *one* would you say had the next mildest flavour?

And which *one* has the next mildest flavour after that?

And then which *one* after that?...'

Again this can be done 'sideways on' with the attributes being asked about for a particular brand. Again, also, it can be useful in bringing out differences between products. The scale it employs, however, has very uncertain and irregular intervals and respondents may perceive much more (or much less) difference between the first and second products, say, than between the second and third.

VERBAL SCALES. The respondent is asked to select one of a number of statements which best fits a product in respect of a given attribute:

'I'd like you to look at this list of descriptions:
> Very Strong
> Fairly Strong
> Medium
> Fairly Mild
> Very Mild

and tell me which one fits your impression of the flavour of Eden Vale Yoghurt.'

Verbal scales have the advantage that it is easy, when looking at the survey results, to attach some meaning to overall scores. There is, however, a danger that respondents too are likely to attach a meaning to each position on the scale – and that this meaning is likely to be different for different people. Moreover, once again we cannot infer that the different positions on the scale are equally spaced. The difference between 'very strong' and 'fairly strong' may be much smaller, for example, than that between 'fairly strong' and 'medium'.

NUMERICAL SCALES. Here, the variations are many. The scale may run from 0 to 10, or −3 to +3, or may take any other convenient form:

'I'd like you to tell me how many points out of ten you would give Eden Vale Yoghurt for its flavour.'

This method is only really applicable to dimensions on which there is one end obviously favourable. It is a very natural approach to measuring how *good* a flavour is, but clashes with the way in which people normally use numbers as a method of measuring how *mild* or *strong* a flavour is.

SPATIAL SCALES. Here, the positions on the scale have *no* labels. The most frequently used of this type of scale is the semantic differential (Osgood *et al.*, 1957).

'I want you to decide where you think Eden Vale comes on this scale and put a tick in the square which is nearest your opinion.

Mild Flavour [ ] [ ] [ ] [ ] [ ] Strong Flavour

The square at this end would mean that Eden Vale has a very mild flavour, the square at the other end that Eden Vale has a very strong flavour. The other squares represent opinions in between the two extremes.

Now I'd like you to do the same for the next items:

| Looks Attractive | | | | | | Looks Unattractive |

| Expensive | | | | | | Reasonably Priced |

The absence of any labels confers two advantages. It makes it easier to fit different *kinds* of attributes into the same pattern, which can be very important for looking at the interrelationships between them. In addition, because respondents are not faced with given definitions of intermediate positions, there is no obstacle to their regarding the intervals between positions as equal, and it is much more justified to treat the data on the assumption that this is so.

Sorting v. Scaling

These then are the main types of measurement. What are the relative advantages of each? There are these principal criteria for choosing between them:

THE AMOUNT OF INFORMATION REQUIRED. Scaling methods, by their nature, give much more *detailed* information than do sorting methods, but also take rather longer to administer, and are therefore more costly compared to a free choice or comparative sorting approach. The semantic differential has the most to offer, but it is often misapplied in circumstances where the richness of detail it can provide is not required. There is little point in going to the trouble of distinguishing between shades of opinion in data-collection if, at the analysis stage, all that happens is that 'average scores' are calculated to reduce that data to manageable proportions.

THE NATURE OF THE INFORMATION REQUIRED. Less conscious thought is required of the respondent with a sorting technique, and less conscious thought is given. This means that answers are more likely to be associative 'top-of-the-mind' ones in the case of, say, free brand choice, thoughtful considered ones in the case of scale questions. The latter are not always the most appropriate kind of answers, particularly when we are dealing with products for which we have reason to believe that little conscious, considered thought goes into the purchasing-decision, the sort of product which is bought in small quantities often. On the other hand, it *is* likely to be much more appropriate for products where a single purchase is seen as important. In other words, the technique used in the interview should as far as possible make the same sort of demands on the respondent's thinking as does the behaviour with which the interview is concerned.

THE PURPOSE FOR WHICH THIS INFORMATION IS REQUIRED. The free-choice sorting method has been found to be more sensitive over time, and between brands, in grocery product fields (Joyce, 1964), because it does imply a choice between products which a semantic differential approach, for example, does not, and because the more considered replies to a scaling question are likely to produce more stable levels. The latter technique, however, is able to generate much more sensitive cross-analysis, and to provide a much better basis for distinguishing between groups of individuals. Besides these theoretical considerations, there is the practical one that a sorting method may put so large a proportion of respondents into one category that the remainder are too small a number to form a reliable basis for inspection. With a scaling method one can almost always avoid this situation.

PRODUCT REQUIREMENTS

Much of the usefulness of information about people's beliefs about products is dependent on some knowledge of their relative importance. There are two main approaches to this:

1 *Direct questions*

Respondents can be asked to rank attributes according to importance, or to choose between fictional brands possessing alternative groups of qualities or to assess, for each attribute, not only whether it is 'true' or 'false' for each brand, but also the extent to which the possession of it is 'good' or 'bad'.

The trouble with this sort of method is that it favours the 'rational', 'respectable' answer. People are very often unaware

F

of just what they *do* want from a product, and less willing to admit giving a higher priority to some requirements than to others.

On the other hand, it can be extremely useful to know what people believe, or claim to believe to be their requirements: they need *rationalizations* for buying a product just as much as they need *motivations,* and an important consideration in the presentation of a product may be the provision of a ready-made cover story for them. Moreover, since we *know* that 'rational' requirements are going to be distorted, we can allow for this in the interpretation of results.

Once again, the usefulness of this method is dependent on the importance which the informant attaches to the particular decision-making with which the survey is concerned.

The more important they perceive a choice to be, the more likely people are to have some conscious criteria on which to base that choice.

2   *Deduction*

An indirect approach to measuring the relative importance of different attitude-dimensions is to study the relationship between them and the relevant measure of behaviour. This can be done either by correlating individual behaviour and attitude patterns, or by comparing the overall scores for various attributes of different behaviour-groups. Another similar approach is to measure attitudes to an 'ideal brand' and then to calculate how existing brands differ from that ideal.

Implicit in the first of these deductive approaches is the belief that the more an attitude correlates with use, i.e. discriminates between different user-groups, the more likely it is to be causally linked to usership, and hence the more advantageous it is to have consumers (or that section of them with which one is particularly concerned) hold that attitude about the brand.

However, it is not possible to assume automatically that the attitude dimensions on which the major differences occur are necessarily those where favourable beliefs *lead to* use. Rather, use may cause improved attitudes, partly through providing (added) experience of the product, partly because of the drive to eliminate,

BEHAVIOUR AND ATTITUDE RESEARCH 83

or reduce, the inconsistency of committing oneself to the product by buying it, and yet having reservations about it.

Again, then, this approach can produce valuable information, but not a direct statement of the relative importance of different product motivations. What it does provide is a statement of the extent to which attitudes need to be changed in the process of moving from one level of use to another, whether the attitude change temporally precedes or follows the change in behaviour.

GENERAL VALUES

Underlying people's requirements from products, and their resulting brand preferences, are their more general values, needs, and predispositions. Investigating the relevant areas of these basic attitudes can increase the value of a survey in one or more of the following ways:

(i) The information can be valuable in its own right by establishing the climate of opinion in which marketing activities will be operating and by providing for advertisers a picture of the kind of people to whom their advertising is going to be principally addressed.

(ii) It can lead to a more thorough appreciation of data relating directly to the product field, by establishing the framework within which the latter must be interpreted.

(iii) More particularly, by analysing it against patterns of brand behaviour and attitudes, such data provides a line on:

(a) The motivations which increase people's likelihood of using a particular product (or of using it heavily), and hence the most appropriate approach to selling that product.

(b) The ways in which these motivations differ between users of different brands, i.e. the extent to which differences in general attitudes lead to distinctive segments of the market, with some brands meeting one set of requirements and others a rather different set.

(c) The needs which are not currently particularly well catered for, and thus new product opportunities.

Scaling methods have definitive advantages in this area. The questions we are asking are *not* likely to be regarded by respondents as trivial, and are likely to be such as to benefit from a reasonably considered approach. Moreover, since so much of the usefulness of this data comes from its amenability to cross-analysis, it is obviously advantageous to have it in as detailed a form as possible.

Attitude scales are frequently based on more than one question. This is because it is frequently impossible to encapsulate within one statement or question the whole implication of a general attitude trait, and hardly ever possible to be *sure* that this has been done adequately. Moreover, if the matter is approached too directly we are more likely to get a measure of how people see themselves, or how they would like to see themselves, than what they really are. (This of course could still be useful information.) While we can never altogether overcome people's inclination to 'edit' their answers, the temptation to do this is less great if the purpose of the question is less obvious, and if each question appears to be more concerned with attitudes to specific points than with broad attitudinal tendencies.

There is a danger, however, that even with a *set* of questions one or two items may in fact be measuring something rather different. Systematized approaches to item selection have therefore been developed. One such approach is that pioneered by Guttman, and called after him (Stouffer, 1950). This uses the relationship between answers to the different questions to select those questions which by definition form a unidimensional scale.

CLASSIFICATION

Information collected under each of the headings (A) – (D) (page 70) can be, and frequently is, used for the purposes of classifying respondents, or brands, or behaviour or attitude patterns. The term 'classification data' is normally applied in a narrower sense, however, to denote factual information about the respondent which is collected solely or primarily for the purpose of classifying him, in order to see whether or not such variables as age, sex, income, religion, and the possession of relevant durable goods affect the organization of attitudes and behaviour in the field of study, and if so how and to what extent.

Many of these variables are self-explanatory, but for two some explanation seems appropriate:

1 *Social class*

The standard classification technique is not, strictly speaking, one of class at all, since it is based on the *occupation* of the head of the household. This is known as the I.P.A. Social Grade Classification, since it was first developed for the National Readership Survey under the aegis of the Institute of Practitioners in Advertising. It divides the population into six groups, as follows:

Grade	Occupation	Estimated percentage of population
A.	Higher managerial, administrative or professional	3%
B.	Intermediate managerial, administrative or professional	10%
C.1	Supervisory or clerical and junior managerial administrative or professional	21%
C.2	Skilled manual workers	39%
D.	Semi and unskilled manual workers	21%
E.	State Pensioners or widows (with no other earner) and casual workers	5%

The basic advantages of this approach are its

(i) *Objectivity* – interviewers have little control over how a person is classified;

(ii) *Relative simplicity* of application;

(iii) *Comparability* with other survey data, simply because it *is* the standard technique.

At the same time, it should be recognized that it *is* a measurement of occupation, and neither a purely *economic* one (spending power) nor a *cultural* one (the way in which money is likely to be spent).

The normal measure of *spending power* is gross household (or personal) income. This, however, is not the same thing as *disposable* income. Moreover, a proportion of respondents refuse to answer this question, even when all they have to do is to point to the appropriate *range* of money on a card.

A line on likely *spending patterns* can be given by one of the following:

(*a*) *Self-assessed social class.* Where people see themselves on the social scale, or where they would like to see themselves, is obviously related to the way they spend their money. However, the fact that different people evaluate terms such as 'middle class' differently reduces the sensitivity of the term.

(*b*) Magazine and newspaper readership is obviously relevant, particularly from the point of view of *communication* about a product. Its principal drawback as a criterion is its instability over time, as new publications enter and leave the market, or reposition themselves within it.

(*c*) Terminal education age, and type of school attended, can provide relevant criteria in certain circumstances. It has been combined on occasion (Hollingshead, 1949) with occupation, and age (to adjust for changing educational standards), to provide a sensitive and flexible method but one rather complex to apply and thus expensive.

2 *Household structure*

This is likely to be important when researching household goods, and other household products. Breakdowns by size of family and the presence of children of various ages are a very common practice. A more ambitious and more generalized measure of household type is one based on the notion of the 'life cycle' of the family, and which utilizes age, household size, and the presence of children. Many combinations are possible: one example (Hoinville and Jowell, 1969) is given below.

1 Individuals under 60 years.
2 Small adult households (two people aged 16–60).
3 Small 'family' units (one or two adults, one or two children).
4 Large 'family' units (one or two adults, and three or more children *or* three or more adults, and two or more children).
5 Large adult units (three or more adults, none or one child).
6 Older small households (one or two adults, at least one over 60).

Methods

The previous section discussed the sorts of measures that are normally taken in the course of a behaviour and attitude survey;

this one describes the process by which these results are obtained. I have consciously taken the cart before the horse in this way, because in the planning of market research at least that is the appropriate order of things: one must be definite about the precise nature of the cart to be pulled before deciding on the beast to be placed between its shafts.

THE MAIN STAGES OF A SURVEY

Once the appropriate *coverage* of a survey has been agreed and any preliminary research completed the following intermediate stages will have to take place before the final report emerges.

1 *Sampling*

It will be necessary to decide:

(*a*) What sort of people should be sampled.

(*b*) How many.

(*c*) What sampling method should be used and to draw the sample accordingly.

2 *Questionnaire preparation*

This will involve making important decisions about:

(*a*) Question wording.

(*b*) The order of questions.

(*c*) Questionnaire layout.

3 *Pilot survey*

The best planned survey is likely to contain a number of flaws which can only be spotted by actually carrying it out. A small-scale pilot is therefore extremely important; this can also be used where necessary to test two alternative approaches.

4 *Main fieldwork*

Any appropriate modifications to the questionnaire and to the sampling procedure are made. Interviewing for the survey proper is then carried out.

5 *Data transfer*

The data is transferred from completed questionnaires on to either punched cards or computer tape, so that it is capable of being handled by a computer, or some other counting machine.

6 *Data analysis*

The survey information is then analysed by the machine in various ways. A good deal of care will be needed to select from the almost infinite number of possible analyses those ones which will be the most useful for *this* particular survey.

Of these six stages, numbers 4 and 5 are routine in the sense that their basic organization does not differ much between different surveys. There are, however, alternatives at each of the other four stages, which must be chosen between afresh for each survey in the light of its particular aims and context. These are reviewed in turn in each of the next four sections.

SAMPLING

The appropriate sample for a survey will depend on the degree of precision required from the results, and the nature of any sub-groups (e.g. those aged 16–24, those who are light users of a particular brand) which we wish to inspect. This latter consideration may lead us to over-represent particular groups in our sample: to make overall results representative in this situation, interviews from different groups would be weighted to compensate for their over- or under-sampling.

The degree of precision in any set of sample survey results is a function of:

  (i) the *size* of the sample
 (ii) the *methods* by which it is obtained.

The importance of size is self-evident: the larger the sample, the greater the likelihood of obtaining an 'average cross-section' with any chance deviation from this cancelling itself out. But size will not eliminate any *systematic* bias resulting from the way the sample is chosen.

There are two basic methods of drawing a sample: the quota method and the random method. Broadly speaking, the difference between them is that the former specifies how many of various kinds of people are to be interviewed, but leaves the final choice of individuals in the hands of the interviewer. With a random sample she has no such choice: the individuals to be interviewed are predetermined. This makes life much harder for her, since these individuals may live in an inconvenient place, may be out on the first occasion she calls (she is usually required to make at least three attempts to contact each member of her sample), and may finally refuse to grant her an interview. All this is going to considerably increase the cost of the fieldwork, in addition to the costs incurred in selecting the sample in the first place. The cost differential is likely to be particularly great for a survey concerned with a minority group.

On the other hand, a standard quota sample will normally result in a less representative sample, for the following reasons:

1 Controls normally set out the number of particular *types* of individuals to be interviewed, in terms of a selection of age, social grade, sex, housewives v. non-housewives, and use of products: the exact choice will be dictated by the practical requirements of the survey. (Without such controls, we would have a sample of 'good' respondents, remarkably similar in these respects to the interviewers themselves.) An interviewer might, for example, be asked to interview twenty housewives, with the following controls on who these should be:

7 from social grades ABC1
13 from social grades C2DE
9 aged under 45
11 aged 45 or over

This would give a sample which was roughly nationally representative in each of these terms taken separately, but would not necessarily be so when they were taken together. We would *hope* for a pattern like this:

		Social Grade	
		ABC1	C2DE
Age:	16–44	3	6
	45+	4	7

But we *could* get something like this:

		Social Grade	
		ABC1	C2DE
Age:	16–44	7	2
	45+	–	11

There *is* likely to be some sort of bias of this type, because those quotas which are relatively easy to achieve will tend to get filled up first, the more difficult ones achieved together in the last few interviews.

It is, of course, possible to overcome this by specifying inter-locking controls, e.g. age within social grade, but then difficulty and costs quickly rise: if four of five variables were interlocked, the cost of achieving the sample would probably be greater than that of a random sample of the same size.

2 Quotas set in terms of social grade present additional prob-lems. The personal questions necessary to assess social grade are best left to the end of the interview: we must choose between asking them first – and running a high risk of refusal – or relying on the interviewer's snap judgement, which may prove at the end of the interview to have been wrong. There will be obvious temptations in just *how* a borderline case is classified when the interviewer has already filled some sections of her quota. Moreover, the obvious way for her to avoid these dangers is to go to the obvious places, and to fill her quota of ABC1s from stately man-sions, that of C2DEs from slum areas. Conversely, mixed neigh-bourhoods will be under-sampled neighbourhoods.

3 Naturally enough, the more time people spend at home the more likely they are to be interviewed. Thus, a quota sample of housewives will normally over-represent those with small children. (It is worth noticing in passing that even a random method is likely to have deficiencies of the same type, though to a lesser extent, in that people who are out at all three calls, or who refuse to be interviewed, are likely to be atypical of the total sample. A good deal of effort is normally expended in random surveys on keeping the level of non-response from the sample originally selected to maximize not the *size* of the final sample interviewed, but its representativeness.)

Despite its deficiencies of representativeness, the quota method is a frequently used one, since it can often provide information which is precise *enough* for the uses to which it is going to be put. If the main purposes of a survey are comparative, or to do with relationships between different variables, some form of quota sample is probably adequate. The cost of a random sample is normally only justified when it is important to calculate absolute levels, as in the case of the National Readership Survey.

Most samples, of either type, are drawn in two or more stages. The first step in drawing a national survey of housewives, for example, would probably be to select a number of parliamentary constituencies representative of the country as a whole. Then within each of these constituencies a number of polling districts might be chosen. Finally, the individuals to be interviewed would be drawn from these polling districts. The number of *intermediate* units influences the degree of precision in the survey results as well as the number of the final sample of individuals. The greater the 'clustering' of a given sample, the lower its reliability.

Considerable improvements in the quality of quota sampling have recently been made by exploiting to the full the possibilities of multi-stage methods. Constituencies, polling districts with these, and then a number of streets within these polling districts are selected at random. Interviewers are then given quotas of interviews to be obtained within these streets which consist simply of an *overall* figure, or of numbers of men, housewives, and other women where appropriate. No further controls are necessary to arrive at a reasonably representative sample. The reason for this is that the interviewer's freedom of choice is sufficiently constrained by having to obtain her interviews in a few specific streets, and by having to space out her interviews in these streets geographically by leaving four or five doors between them. This method, sometimes called *random location sampling*, avoids or diminishes most of the problems of the older type of quota sampling. One problem *does* remain: that of the 'not at homes'.

THE QUESTIONNAIRE

Once the area to be covered in the questionnaire has been agreed, a number of decisions have to be made as to how this can be best achieved. Both the ordering of the questions and the way the questions are worded can have a great deal of influence on the answers obtained. In addition, a great deal of care has to be given to making the layout of the questionnaire, and the instructions in it, as clear and as straightforward as possible, to avoid possible errors in interviewing or in the transfer of data on to punched cards.

In designing a questionnaire, it is important to:

1 *Avoid asking the impossible*

Seeking out facts which people can't remember, or opinions on topics which they don't know about, is worse than useless, since it is likely to antagonize the respondent and reduce his willingness to answer other questions.

2 *Create a permissive atmosphere*

This will combat respondents' tendency to give what they perceive to be socially acceptable answers. An introductory statement such as 'some people clean their shoes every day, but others don't have the time', suggesting to the respondent that he is not alone in his behaviour, and that there are good reasons for it, can often pay dividends.

A rather different point is that respondents may be reluctant to criticize: this in itself is something which has social pressures operating against it. This can be overcome by depersonalizing criticism, by making it relative criticism ('Things which aren't so good about it'), and above all by making it clear that the voicing of adverse opinions is welcomed.

3 *Be unambiguous*

Ambiguity can creep in in the most unexpected places. The word 'you' for example, may be understood by a respondent to mean himself, his family, or some other reference-group.

4 *Pitch the question at the right level of intelligence*

Technical terms and difficult words must be avoided. So, too, must giving respondents the impression that they are being talked down to. When the sample population covers a wide range of intelligence, this can call for a careful balancing act.

5 *Be careful about loaded questions*

If the respondent is being asked to choose between alternatives, both or all of them should be stated. Otherwise there will be a tendency to opt for an alternative which *is* stated. Each alternative should be given equal emphasis, and, as far as possible, emotive words which would tip the balance one way or the other avoided.

American public opinion surveys in the early 1940s illustrated this danger well when they consistently showed a much higher proportion of the population in favour of war against 'The Nazis' than against 'Germany'.

6 *Be careful about leading questions*

In his excellent book *The Art of Asking Questions,* Payne (1951) describes the case of the snack-bar waiter who brought about a sensational increase in the sale of eggs in milk shakes by asking customers not whether they wanted an egg or not, but whether they wanted one or two. He suggests that this represents an excellent sales technique, but an execrable research one. Much better would be to ask a number of preliminary questions, filtering out after each those respondents to whom the next question is not applicable:

1 Do you yourself ever drink milk shakes?
   If 'Yes'
2 The last one you drank, do you remember if it had eggs added to it or not?
   If 'Yes'
3 And how many eggs were there added to it?

Leading or loaded questions can be deliberately employed in certain special circumstances. Kinsey's study of sexual behaviour (1948) relied heavily on questions of the 'When did you stop beating your wife?' type to counteract the tendency to deny socially disapproved behaviour. In such cases, however, it is difficult to know whether the effect produced is greater or smaller than or equal to what it is designed to counteract.

7 *Guard against contamination*

A great deal of what is said in an ordinary conversation is influenced, one way or another, by what has gone before. The same is true of the interview situation, and it is therefore important to minimize – or at least control – the conditioning of responses to a question by prior questions. To take an obvious example, if we wanted to ask people 'What brands of breakfast cereal can you think of?' we would put this before rather than after a series of questions about specific brands.

Similarly, we would not place questions about a number of competitive products or services, for which we wanted to compare the scores achieved by the different products, after questions asked about one of these products only. This would direct respondents' attention to that brand and make them suspect, probably correctly, that *that* was the products we were really interested in.

Because of the need to avoid conditioning, the shape of a questionnaire can often be likened to a funnel, starting with broad-ranging questions and gradually narrowing down to points of specific interest. For example, a survey of rheumatism remedies might follow the sequence:

> health concerns
> rheumatism
> rheumatism relief
> patent rheumatism remedies.

Certain topics may be *mutually* contaminating, and cannot therefore be properly assessed in the same interview. For example, it is impossible to get an accurate measure of attitudes to a brand and recall of its advertising content from the same questionnaire. If we ask about *attitude*-dimensions first these will act as a prompt to advertising recall. If we ask about *advertising* first, then this will play an unduly prominent part in deciding answers to attitude questions.

8 *Guard against order effects*

The order in which objects or ideas are put to people influences their answers. There is a tendency to choose brands at the top of a list rather than those at the bottom, items which appear in the middle of a list of figures arranged in order of size rather than those at the extremes, and so on. When the survey warrants it, a number of different versions of the questionnaire are produced, with the order of such things rotated so as to cancel out biases.

PILOT WORK

The value of a pilot survey will be obvious from the preceding chapter. The possible blemishes are so many that one or two are bound to escape the most careful abstract contemplation, and therefore the ways in which a pilot can be useful are many.

1 *Assessing interviewing rates*

Given that we wish to achieve a given sample in the main survey, what are the appropriate arrangements, in terms of the number of potential respondents to be selected, and the number of days' interviewing to be arranged? The list from which a random sample is taken may be inaccurate, through being to some degree out-of-date, for other reasons. The pilot will provide an estimate of the extent of this inaccuracy. Similarly, it will show the frequency with which members of a minority group (say, women who use hair colourants) whom we wish to sample on a quota basis occur. Finally, we will be able to see what proportion of those eligible to give an interview will refuse to do so.

On this last point, a more positive approach can be adopted if a high rate of refusal is feared. Two or more alternative approaches can be tried out to discover which one achieves the highest success rate.

2 *Checking respondents' understanding of the questions*

Do respondents *really* understand the questionnaire? And do they understand it in the way we want them to? Scrutinizing the completed pilot questionnaires, particularly when the answers to a number of questions are related to one another, can be extremely informative.

Again, alternative approaches can be tested out.

3 *Checking interviewers' understanding of instructions*

Similarly, a pilot survey will show whether the instructions to interviewers are sufficiently clear, in terms of whom they are to interview, the filters to be applied to particular questions, and how certain answers are to be dealt with. In particular, the pilot will often pinpoint where questionnaire layout needs to be altered to eliminate mistakes.

4 *Maximizing a question's usefulness*

A question to which nearly all respondents give the same answer is not going to be very useful diagnostically. It *may* be an indication of real unanimity, but more often it signifies that the question itself is so extreme that real differences are submerged. It would be particularly important to modify the balance of such a question if one was concerned not with the absolute levels of answers, but with using it to discriminate between different consumers, products, or situations.

5 *Developing code lists*

Verbatim answers to a question at the pilot stage can be used to develop a pre-coded list of answers to be used in the main survey.

6 *Testing the physical factors involved*

Finally, a pilot provides a chance to test out the survey's 'production-line'. This can be important if a number of stimuli and ancillary documents are to be used in the survey. Are we asking too much of interviewers' dexterity, or their muscle-power?

Because the main function of pilot work is to check on previous thinking, it follows that surprises frequently occur. A pilot whose usefulness is conceived mainly in terms of one area can often be extremely revealing in another. It is therefore important to learn as much as possible about all aspects of the pilot, through analysis of the field documents, through interviewers' reports on those parts of the survey which seemed unnecessarily difficult, and through personal observation.

This last approach is often neglected, but it can pay surprising dividends. The person responsible for the research cannot expect his interviewers to have the same grasp of the background to the survey, or of the ways in which the information collected is going to be used, as he has himself. For this very reason, of course, it is important that regular interviewers should *carry out* the pilot, since it will be such interviewers who will have to conduct the main survey. Much can be learned, however, from *observing* two or three of the pilot interviews.

Two or three years ago a large-scale attitude survey I was involved with was based on a questionnaire which began with a number of very general questions and gradually 'funnelled' down to some very specific points. A number of lists were to be shown to respondents in the course of the interview: these were placed on cards, which were then tagged together for convenience. I arranged to observe a couple of the pilot interviews. At the appropriate point in the first interview, the interviewer handed over the cards, the respondent answered her questions on the first card, and then, naturally enough, idly glanced through the remaining cards, and thus hopelessly conditioned the remainder of the interview. I should have anticipated this without a pilot, of course, but it is *always* possible that something like this has been overlooked. The point here is that the interviewer was not aware of this, nor was there any reason why she should have been. As far as she was concerned, the questionnaire had a clean bill of health – particularly because the interview moved so smoothly from one topic to the next!

ANALYSIS

Only a small part of the usefulness of the typical behaviour and attitude survey is realized by an *enumeration* of the various measures which have been taken in the course of the interview. The major part is likely to lie in analysis to establish how the different data we have collected relate to each other.

This is the aspect of market research which has been most expanded in recent years, prompted by the advent of the computer. The possible combinations of cross-analysis for even a medium-sized survey are immeasurable, particularly when we begin to bring a third or fourth variable into the analysis. Still more possibilities are opened up by the idea of multivariate analysis, to determine the relationships between *sets* of dependent variates. If the research budget is not to be exceeded, and the really important results lost in a mound of computer print-out, it is therefore crucial to exercise a high degree of selectivity both in the variables which are to be related to each other and in the techniques used to explore these relationships.

It would be neither feasible nor appropriate to attempt to describe here the mechanics of the main techniques currently employed. What *does* seem worth while is a review of the different *purposes* for which analysis may be carried out. It is possible to distinguish three main types:

   (i) Summative.
   (ii) Descriptive break-downs.
   (iii) Explanatory break-downs.

Properly speaking, of course, the first category is not analysis at all, but its opposite. In the market research terms, however, 'analysis' is normally taken to include all data manipulations, whether these consist of breaking the data down or of building it up.

The more data that is generated by a survey, the more summative techniques are necessary if we are to make sense of the results. Hence, for example, the need for an overall average score from the distribution of answers along a scale. But summarizing may not merely make it easier to grasp the meaning implicit in the original figures, it may also serve to bring out meanings which were not all apparent from those figures. A good example of this is the use of factor analysis to extract from a large number of variables having a common element a smaller number of underlying common factors (Harman, 1960). One common application of this technique is to reduce a large number of specific product attributes to a much smaller number of 'underlying dimensions'.

The difference between *descriptive* and *explanatory* analysis can perhaps best be explained by comparing profile and penetration analyses of product use. A profile analysis of use of a given product is descriptive. It shows what proportion of users belong to various demographic or attitudinal groups, and answers questions of the type:

'How is use of this product distributed among different kinds of people?'
and
'Which groups have the *largest* consumption of this product?'

A penetration analysis of use, by contrast, seeks to *explain* the structure of the market; it shows the proportions of different groups who are users of the product, and answers questions of the type:

'What difference does it make to the user of this product to be in one group of people rather than another?'
and
'Which groups have the *heaviest* consumption of the product?'

Differences here will lead one to infer a causal connection between belonging to a certain group, and likely use of the product.

This is a dichotomy which can be applied to other kinds of analysis and it provides twin tests of relevancy for any projected analysis:

(*a*) 'Will it describe the market in a way which is truly informative?'

(*b*) 'Will it help explain the market in a form which is likely to be actionable?'

Only if the answer to one of these questions is 'Yes' can any analysis be considered worth carrying out. It seems appropriate to conclude by stressing that, at this stage of the survey as at all previous ones, the answer will in each case be determined by the particular uses to which the survey is going to be put.

References

1 HARMAN, H. H., *Modern Factor Analysis*, University of Chicago Press, 1960.

2 HOINVILLE, G., and JOWELL, R., *Classification Manual for Household Interview Surveys in Gt Britain*, Social & Community Planning Research, London, 1969.

3 HOLLINGSHEAD, A. B., *Elmtown's Youth: The Impact of Social Class on Adolescents*, John Wiley and Sons, New York, 1949.

4 JOYCE, T., 'Techniques of brand image measurement', *New Developments in Research*, Market Research Society, London, 1964.

5 KINSEY, A. C., POMEROY, W. B., and MARTIN, C. E., *Sexual Behaviour in the Human Male*, W. B. Saunders, London, 1948.

6 LOVELL, M. R. C., MEADOWS, R., and RAMPLEY, B., *Inter-Household Influence on Housewife Purchases*, Thomson Organisation Ltd, London, 1968.

7 OPPENHEIM, A. N., *Questionnaire Design and Attitude Measurement*, Heinemann, London, 1966.

8 OSGOOD, C. E., SUCI, G. J., and TANNENBAUM, P. H., *The Measurement of Meaning*, University of Illinois Press, Urbana, 1957.

9 PAYNE, S. L., *The Art of Asking Questions*, Princeton University Press, 1951.

10 STOUFFER, S. A. *et al.*, *Measurement and Prediction*, Princeton University Press, 1950.

11 THURSTONE, L. L., 'The Measurement of social attitudes', *Journal of Abnormal and Social Psychology* (1931), pp. 249–69.

5 | Market Segmentation—An Overview[1]

J. A. LUNN
Technical Director, Research Bureau Ltd.

Introduction

Since the publication of Wendell Smith's pioneering article (1955), segmentation has become one of the most influential – and fashionable – concepts in marketing. It '... has permeated the thinking of managers and researchers alike as much as, if not more than, any other single marketing concept since the turn of the century' (Frank, 1968a). It has featured prominently at conferences and seminars and has given rise to a voluminous body of literature. However, simultaneously with this surge of interest, segmentation has become less a single concept than an umbrella topic covering a diversity of issues.

A fundamental distinction is between the perspective of marketing men and of researchers. To the former, segmentation is a *strategy*, whereby products are directed at specific target groups rather than at the total population. Researchers, by contrast, have tended to regard it from a *methodological* standpoint: that is, as a technique; or as a type of survey, geared to the description of fundamental market differences.

Researchers themselves have differed markedly in their emphases. Some, mainly social scientists, have been concerned primarily with developing new criteria for defining target groups: others, mainly statisticians and mathematicians, with the methodological problems surrounding the formulation of these groups.

[1] Based on a paper given at the Annual Conference of ESOMAR/WAPOR, 1969.

Recently, a distinction has developed between consumer-oriented and product-oriented segmentation. The former approach places chief emphasis upon ways in which consumers can be grouped in terms of their requirements; the latter, upon ways in which products can be grouped in terms of the benefits they offer.

This chapter provides an overview of some prominent issues in this area. For reasons of space it deals mainly with research rather than marketing issues, and with consumer rather than product-oriented segmentation. An additional publication (Lunn, 1971) attempts a synthesis of these various standpoints, and gives illustrative case histories. More detailed coverage of the points discussed here can be found in the references listed at the end. Especially noteworthy are the paper by Frank (1968a) and the proceedings of the recent ADETEM Conference (Durand, 1969).

Segmentation and Marketing Problems

A SIMPLIFIED VIEW OF SEGMENTATION

For the marketing man, a simplified view of market segmentation might run as follows:

Markets are not homogeneous. Consumers, that is to say, are not all alike. They have different habits, circumstances, tastes, requirements, and so on, which predispose them to purchase different kinds of products and to use the same products in different ways. At the same time, it is unnecessary to treat each consumer as unique. People can be grouped meaningfully into sub-sets in terms of similar combinations of characteristics. These consumer groupings may well present marketing opportunities. Their potential depends upon a number of factors, not least being that of size.

Products differ also. They differ not only in *real* terms, but more importantly for marketing, in the extent to which consumers *perceive* them as suitable for their requirements.

The essence of market segmentation, then, is to identify exploitable sub-groups of consumers, to design products with optimum benefits, and to promote these products in appropriate ways. In short, to produce goods and services that match consumer requirements — and are seen to do so.

In one sense, segmentation is far from a new concept. Examples can be found long before the 1950s. Take the early days of the motor-car. A Bentley and a Model 'T' Ford might have been regarded as catering for the same market – a novel, motorized form of transport. But equally clearly, they were catering for very different sub-components of this market: that is, for different market segments.

The point is that much early segmentation was accidental, or at best based upon speculation and inspired hunch. The manufacturer would first dream up a product and then look for a market – an approach that led to some striking successes, but to many more dismal failures. Nowadays, segmentation is carried out more systematically. This has come about in part through an increasingly more scientific approach to management, and in part through advances in the understanding and measurement of the determinants of consumer behaviour.

DIFFERENT KINDS OF SEGMENTATION PROBLEM

With its emphasis upon tailoring products to people, market segmentation can provide the cornerstone for a company's total planning. It helps to set the basic objectives for the whole marketing operation, and to indicate directions for implementing these. There are, of course, many different kinds of marketing objectives and strategies which give rise to different types of segmentation problem. Prominent amongst these are:

(a) Obtaining a general background description of the market, perhaps to check upon assumptions underlying present policies and future plans.

(b) Identifying market gaps for new product opportunities, either by the development of completely new products or by the modification of existing ones.

(c) Maintaining the sales of an existing brand.

(d) Expanding the sales of an existing brand – for instance, by increasing the purchasing of current buyers, converting buyers of competing brands, or winning over new buyers to the product field.

(e) Positioning a range of product varieties.

(f) Positioning a range of brands within a given product field.

It is important to bear these differences in mind. For the particular problem posed will determine the kind of data to be collected and, therefore, the analysis techniques required.

MARKET CONSTRUCTION

Despite its current popularity, some marketing men view the concept of segmentation with suspicion. To concentrate upon certain consumer groups implies the deliberate exclusion of others. Is this not to turn one's back upon possible sales? But this is very much a question of facing up to reality. In an increasingly affluent society, purchasing is becoming more discretionary and less concerned simply with basic necessities. Concepts such as the 'global market' and the 'average consumer' are becoming outmoded. A product aimed at everyone may well satisfy no one, and in the days of mass production the price of failure is high.

At the same time, segmentation is not entirely a matter of focusing down. This is partly because certain target groups may well be compatible, in the sense that a product directed at one such group will probably attract at least some consumers from another.

Also relevant here are product life cycles. Take the case of frozen foods. At first, there was only a small and limited market for this product type, a market that could be clearly defined in terms of certain psychological characteristics. Frozen-food buyers were people with a low concern for nourishment, low confidence and involvement in cooking, and with little concern for the traditional ways of preparing food: at the same time, they were highly experimental and therefore interested in trying new and different things. At first, marketing activity concentrated upon people with this combination of characteristics. But, over time, the product group has gained wider acceptance. The psychological characteristics listed above have lost their force. Now the questions for segmentation are less to distinguish frozen-food buyers from non-buyers than to distinguish between buyers of different types of frozen food.

Fig. 1 illustrates this trend in terms of one scale, 'experimentalism', where product 'A' was one of the earliest types of frozen food, product 'B' a type launched two years prior to the survey in question, and product 'C' a very recent launch. It can be seen that types 'C' and, to a lesser extent, 'B', were achieving sales to the more experimental housewives, but that a lack of experimentalism was no longer a barrier to buying type 'A'.

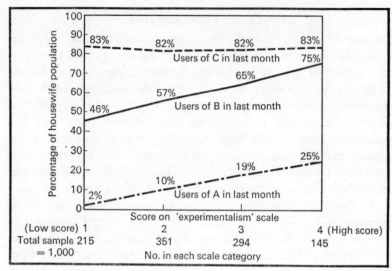

FIG. I. Relationship between 'experimentalism' scale and three product types.

In the light of these considerations, it might be suggested that the term 'market segmentation' should be replaced by the term 'market construction'. The latter has more positive connotations, and does more justice to the range of marketing activity that can follow a typical 'market segmentation' project (Lunn, 1971).

Market Segmentation and the Researcher

GENERAL

To turn from marketing men to researchers. The role of the researcher in this area is to provide a comprehensive description of the market as a background to marketing action. As indicated above, the exact procedures adopted will depend upon the nature of the specific segmentation problem. It is, however, possible to specify three general issues with which researchers have been concerned, namely:

the *criteria used* for defining target groups;
ways of *measuring* these criteria;
ways of *grouping* or clustering consumers in terms of these criteria.

These are discussed below: criteria on pages 105–15; measurement and grouping on pages 115–22, as part of a general review of segmentation methodology.

SEGMENTATION CRITERIA

(a) WHAT DO WE REQUIRE FROM THESE CRITERIA? It has already been pointed out that for the marketing man to produce a 'universal product' for the 'average consumer' is to run the risk of missing important market opportunities. Likewise, for the researcher to represent data in aggregate form, rather than analysed by relevant criteria, is to provide information that may well be misleading. What then are the main requirements from these criteria? Basically there are four: that they should be discriminatory, diagnostic, easy to measure, and possible to exploit through marketing action.

Clearly, we are only interested in criteria that pick out differences in market patterns. However, the distinction between current and potential discrimination should be borne in mind. A particular consumer requirement may well be present in a product field, but remain, as yet, unsatisfied. This might be due to a failure to identify the requirement, or to the failure of past marketing activity to exploit it.

Discrimination alone is not sufficient. Segmentation criteria should increase our *understanding* of the market, and thus help with marketing strategies, whether these are concerned with the formulation of the product or with ways of promoting it.

It is equally important that criteria should be easy to measure under normal market research circumstances. Only then is it possible to provide market descriptions based on sufficiently large sample sizes; or to reach specific target groups through marketing action, and thus to test out the effects of this action. Hence, the importance, as emphasized below, of developing precise measuring instruments for psychological and other 'intangible' characteristics.

Segmentation criteria must also contain full potential for practical exploitation. This cannot be emphasized too strongly. There is little point in following a comprehensive market description study with the proviso — 'but there is no way in which you can use it'. Researchers should, therefore, be on the look out for consumer characteristics which marketing men can influence directly – e.g. through advertising appeals. And preferably for characteristics which help in the communication of these appeals, for instance through relationships with media.

(b) DIFFERENT KINDS OF CRITERIA. Consumers can be described in terms of an almost unlimited number of characteristics. Those most commonly used in segmentation include the following:

> Consumer behaviour
> Demographic variables
> Other situational variables
> Physical variables
> Psychological variables
> Media habits.

Consumer behaviour

The most straightforward way of classifying consumers is in terms of their behaviour: e.g. heaviness of buying in a product field, brand purchasing within product fields, different ways of using the product. These data are fundamental to most market appraisals, and are relatively easy to collect, even though we cannot always take their accuracy for granted – see the controversy over survey versus panel methods of recording purchasing. (Parfitt, 1967; Broadbent & Mooney, 1968.)

The value of behavioural data for segmentation has increased in recent years in the light of a considerable body of research involving a wide range of sophisticated techniques. Such research has increased our knowledge of consumer behaviour in general – e.g. of the nature of brand loyalty – as well as of behaviour in specific markets. It has also provided more precise forms of behavioural classification. Instances of this research are:

(i) the work of Ehrenberg and his colleagues which has led to the development of basic laws of buyer behaviour. (For a summary and references, see Ehrenberg, 1969):

(ii) The clarification of different patterns of brand loyalty and multi-brand purchasing by researchers such as Brown, Kuehn and Cunningham. (For a summary, see Massy et al., 1968):

(iii) A factor analytical study by Massy et al. (1968) of twenty-nine aspects of consumer behaviour in three product categories: coffee, tea and beer. This study revealed four factors common to all three fields, namely a brand loyalty factor, a store loyalty factor, an activity factor (made up of such items as the number of units bought and the number of shopping trips made) and a consistency factor (which indicated regularities amongst purchases of consumers' second and third most popular brands):

(iv) Factor analytical studies by Wells (1967) and Banks *et al.* (1969) of purchasing and usage rates for a large number of consumer expendable fields. The product groupings resulting from these studies were of two kinds – complementary and substitutable. Complementary products were defined as 'those which tend to be consumed jointly in order to satisfy a particular need', and substitute products as 'those which satisfy the same need and tend to be consumed separately'. The factors discovered by Banks *et al.* were given labels based on the products that grouped together in each case – e.g. laundry products, baking products, dairy products, canned goods, frozen products, 'non-smoker'.

Some of these product groupings were as expected, others contained surprises. Wells refers to the approach as 'backward segmentation' and suggests three main applications:

(*a*) To stimulate ideas and guide future research.

(*b*) To simplify marketing strategies, for example by suggesting common policies of couponing and distribution for related products.

(*c*) To increase understanding by stimulating researchers to question why sets of products group together as they do.

All this does not mean that behavioural segmentation is sufficient in itself. For most segmentation problems additional criteria will be required, not least for diagnostic purposes. The understanding of market patterns which lies at the heart of marketing strategies can only be inferred – often very speculatively – from behavioural data taken on its own. There is also the point that behavioural groups are not necessarily homogeneous. That is to say, equally heavy buyers of a product may use it in different ways, and people with the same usage characteristics may have quite different motivations.

There is a further danger in segmentation strategies that are too firmly based upon behavioural criteria. This is exemplified by the 'heavy half' approach (Twedt, 1964), which points out that in many product categories one half of the consumers account for approximately 80 per cent of total sales, and goes on to imply that marketing men should concentrate their efforts on those high volume consumers.

Two telling arguments have been advanced against the 'heavy half' approach. The first, by Haley (1968), points out that

> ...not all heavy consumers are usually available to the same brand—because they are not all seeking the same kinds of benefits from a product. For example, heavy coffee drinkers consist of two types of consumers—those who drink chain-store brands and those who drink premium brands. The chain-store customers feel that all coffees are basically alike and because they drink so much coffee they feel it is sensible to buy a relatively inexpensive brand. The premium brand buyers on the other hand, feel that the few added pennies which coffees like Urban, Martinson's, Chock Full O'Nuts and Savarin cost, are more than justified by their fuller taste. Obviously, these two groups of people, although they are both members of the 'heavy half' segment, are not equally good prospects for any one brand, nor can they be expected to respond to the same advertising claims.

The second, by Frank (1968b), reminds us that the 'heavy half' is already the 'heavy half', and may offer little scope for expansion. Unless our strategies are purely defensive, we should be careful of ignoring the 'lighter half', some of whom may well respond more favourably to changes in our marketing strategies.

Demographic characteristics

Demographic characteristics have long been the most popular criteria for defining market segments. A comprehensive list, covering thirteen countries, is given in a recent paper by Broadbent & Masson (1969). They include sex, age, geographical region, occupation, income, social class, education and household composition. These characteristics have become the basic terms in which marketing men and researchers think about the consumer.

This is reasonable up to a point. Demographic variables describe important aspects of people's circumstances which give rise both to general motives and to particular product requirements. They also act as moderators upon the translation of needs into behaviour: e.g. a low income household may have expensive tastes, but little prospect of indulging them. These characteristics have been treated with increasing flexibility in recent years. For instance, as research has come to indicate the ambiguities of 'social class' (Lunn, 1965), concepts such as terminal age of education have been adopted as replacements or supplements. The concept of life cycle has been an important refinement. This is based upon a composite of variables such as marital status, length of marriage, and of the age of any children in the household (Joyce, 1967). It may often provide a much more sensitive indication of purchasing power and intention than would any of these variables taken singly.

Demographic variables have the advantage of being relatively easy to measure. Moreover, through extended usage, their relationships with other market factors, such as media patterns, have become well known. They do, nevertheless, have limitations. They provide only indirect reflections of product requirements, and are thus of little help on their own in the formulation of marketing strategies. Nor are they entirely free from problems of definition and measurement. The ambiguities of 'social class' have been referred to above. Income too can present severe problems. There is, for instance, the question of definition – should we be interested in gross or net income, in total household income or merely in that of the head of the household? If we opt for net income, what about, say, mortgage or hire-purchase payments, which already incorporate aspects of discretionary spending? Moreover, whatever our definition of income, the respondent does not necessarily know the answer. This can apply particularly to working-class wives. There may also be a reluctance to provide income information which may necessitate the use of elaborate questioning procedures.

Other situational variables

A large number of variables can be specified in addition to those traditionally labelled 'demographic', which describe aspects of the consumer's background situation and environment. These both give rise to product requirements and impose constraints upon the expression of these requirements. They include the ownership of complementary products; for instance, frozen food purchasing is associated with the ownership of a refrigerator. For a comprehensive list, see the recent paper by Agostini (1969).

Use of these variables for market segmentation involves similar advantages and disadvantages to the use of demographic variables.

Physical characteristics

There are many products which either cater for or are affected by the consumer's physical attributes, e.g. skin and hair texture. Such characteristics are obviously important for segmentation. They may sometimes present measurement problems, not least because of the distinction between possessing a particular characteristic and being aware of it or being willing to admit to it.

Psychological characteristics

A growing awareness of the need for more explanatory criteria has led to the greater use of psychological variables, a trend that has been accelerated by advances in psychological measurement. These variables range from general personality traits to specific product field requirements.

It is unfortunate that undue prominence has been given to general personality traits, borrowed for the large part from other fields, such as clinical psychology. This is symptomatic of the *a priori* approach to deriving criteria which has characterized much research in segmentation. There is little reason, on the face of it, why characteristics such as extroversion and neuroticism should show close relationships with people's behaviour as consumers. Yet failure to find such relationships in projects such as the Londoner (1962) led many people to the unwarranted conclusion that no psychological characteristics were likely to be of value for segmentation.

At the same time, personality traits should not be dismissed out of hand. *Firstly,* there are, in fact, product fields where such characteristics are important to consumer behaviour. Obsessionalism is a case in point for household cleaning products. But general personality measures should only be used where there are clear hypotheses about their relevance. *Secondly,* many of the reported studies incorporating personality variables have used rudimentary – and probably inappropriate – techniques for relating these variables to consumer behaviour (see section on Methodology, below). They have, in addition, been guided by over-simplistic views of the buying process. The latter point was emphasized in a paper by Brody & Cunningham (1968). In their study they found more discrimination where personality variables were related to heavy buyers of a product rather than to buyers in general. They also suggested that we should only expect relationships between personality and purchasing amongst consumers who are confident in their ability to judge the performance of the product in question and who perceive the product as a high performance risk.

One of the most promising recent advances has been to classify consumers in terms of attitudinal characteristics. The basic principle has been to derive these empirically through a combination of motivation research and psychometric techniques (Lunn, 1969b). This approach has been found increasingly valuable and has become a regular feature of segmentation projects. For published examples see Durand, ed. 1969; Heller, 1968; and Haley, 1968. Haley has suggested the term 'benefit segmentation', meaning by this the attempt to identify and measure the particular satisfactions that people derive from the usage and purchase of the product in question, and ensure that the appropriate benefits are built into the product.

Attitudinal classification may be conceptualized at several levels of generality. A particularly useful distinction is between:

(i) Relatively specific requirements, which reflect the importance given by the consumer to specific product attributes, whether these are physical (e.g. 'sweet'), functional (e.g. 'easy to use'), or emotional (e.g. 'glamorous');

(ii) More general motives and attitudes which are nevertheless close to the product context, e.g. traditionalism; economy mindedness; experimentalism; health consciousness.

Experience gathered from a large number of studies suggests that the latter can be thought of as broad consumer values, which find expression in a wide variety of product fields. They seem to represent basic psychological mechanisms. For example, the traditional housewife has one set of requirements when buying furniture, another set when buying foodstuffs. In each case, she has different requirements from her non-traditional counterpart. Attitudinal characteristics at various levels have been found by the author to show clear and consistent relationships with consumer behaviour, and have by their very nature been invaluable in suggesting marketing strategies (Lunn, 1971).

Other kinds of psychological variable may well be found valuable for certain kinds of problem. R.B.L. has derived measures of budgeting and shopping styles for use in shop research projects. These have included characteristics such as enjoyment of shopping, shop loyalty and self organization in the shopping task. For long-range planning, measures of general interests and value structures may also be relevant. Moreover, recent work in R.B.L. has indicated the importance of 'quasi-personality' variables such as self-esteem, self-confidence, and willingness to take risks, as well as more specifically product-geared variables, such as involvement in tasks like making clothes, preparing food and so on.

The main advantage of psychological criteria is, of course, their considerable explanatory power. Whether relatively general or specific, they provide direct measures of consumer motivation. They tell us not only *who* buys, but *why* they buy. This does not, of course, mean that we should ignore additional ways of classifying consumers.

In considering psychological variables, we must be careful to select those relevant to the problems in hand, and be ready, where necessary, to develop our own measuring instruments (see below). And in this context, we should be alert to the dangers of focusing too much upon existing specific product field requirements, thereby missing basic consumer mechanisms which could guide new product development.

It has often been alleged that psychological variables are difficult to measure and are highly unstable. Work carried out by the author during recent years leads to the opposite, more optimistic conclusion, which may be summarized by the following points:

(i) RELIABILITY. Given advances in psychological measurement – such as the combined use of factor analysis and coefficient alpha (Lunn, 1969b) – it is possible without too much time and expense to build reliable measuring instruments.

(ii) VALIDITY. By proper attention to construct validity approaches (Cronbach & Meehl, 1955) it is possible to check upon whether the scales measure what we think they do.

(iii) STABILITY. In several R.B.L. studies, respondents have been re-interviewed using the same questionnaire, at time intervals ranging from a fortnight to a year. In all cases bar one, respondents have given closely similar scores on the two occasions. The exception was in a market which had undergone major changes between the two time-periods.

(iv) INTERNATIONAL CONSIDERATIONS. There is increasing evidence of the international applicability of certain psychological dimensions. In some cases, scales originally developed in the U.K. have been found to replicate in research carried out in other countries. In others, similar scales have been developed spontaneously in different countries: see for instance, the work of Wilson (1966), Pessemeir & Tigert (1966), Wells (1968) and Day (1970), whose attitude scales bear a close resemblance to dimensions produced in R.B.L. These findings reinforce the notion that fundamental consumer motivations are being measured.

(v) MOTIVATION AND CHANGE. Reference to fundamental motivations should not be confused with a claim that psychological characteristics will never change. On the contrary, many will, even if over fairly long time-periods. Take the more specific product field requirements: obviously these will change as markets develop and consumers acquire fresh experiences of product possibilities, see (iii) above. Even at the more general level, some dimensions may well change with corresponding changes in the cultural environment: germ consciousness and modernity are cases in point.

MEDIA HABITS

The criteria discussed so far have been of two kinds: consumer behaviour, and characteristics which help to explain and predict this behaviour. Media habits belong to a third category. Their function for market segmentation is to indicate how we may reach the target groups at whom our marketing and advertising strategies are directed. Let us say a target group has been selected and defined as A.B. women under 35 with a high need for glamour. The question arises whether this group has any distinctive patterns of readership or viewing, as a guide to media scheduling.

However, the whole issue of media selection is fraught with controversy, the details of which go beyond the scope of this paper. Belben (1969) in a recent review of the situation concludes:

1 The majority of media plans today are still being produced on the basis of matching the demographic characteristics of the target audience with comparable audience characteristics from the two main industry research surveys.

2 The growth of 'single source' data like A.M.P.S. and T.G.I. is leading to more media plans being directly related to target markets based on actual product usage and purchasing factors. But this method as a basis for media planning in the 70s has still to be fully vindicated.

3 Sophisticated techniques of market segmentation, obtained by grouping the psychological characteristics of people with their product requirements, are playing a significant role in formulating better marketing strategies and, in particular, providing creative people with descriptive as against statistical briefs. In media terms this type of analysis is of limited use owing to the absence of comparable data for the readers and viewers of different media.

As psychological characteristics become more familiar and more widely used, it is likely that corresponding media data will be gathered, perhaps on an industry basis.

There is a case for extending the definition of media to cover travelling and shopping habits. By this means we can take into account exposure to posters and to point of sale activity such as display and promotions. The value of the latter was demonstrated in a recent R.B.L. study, where the target group was strongly characterized by high bargain-seeking tendencies. Research showed that bargain-seekers were much more likely to shop at supermarkets than at counter service stores. This finding had a strong influence on distribution policy for the product in question.

Changes in approach to deriving criteria

It was implied in the preceding discussion that, over the past few years, market researchers have changed their approach to deriving segmentation criteria. To make this more explicit:

Firstly, there has been a move from an *a priori* to an *empirical* approach. In the early days of market segmentation, researchers would try out criteria mainly in the hope that they might prove relevant. A typical example is the use of general personality scales, as in the Londoner (1962), referred to above.

Increasingly, however, researchers have come to adopt the kind of approach discussed later in this chapter, whereby criteria are elicited in 'depth' exploratory stages, rather than imposed *a priori*. The criterion is, as it were, fitted to the consumer, not the consumer to the criterion. The result has been the growth of relatively specific criteria, tailor-made for particular product fields.

Secondly, there has been a search for *explanatory* rather than essentially descriptive criteria. Thus, increasing attention has been paid to psychological and similar characteristics, which increase the understanding of the market and thus, by their nature, suggest appropriate marketing action.

The *third* major tendency is the move towards classification in terms of *multiple* rather than single criteria. There has been a growing recognition that consumer behaviour is determined by a multiplicity of factors—some of these are psychological, some are related to the general social environment, others are connected with the situations in which the product is purchased and used—and that segmentation studies should include all kinds of criteria relevant to the particular problem.

Our awareness and usage of these factors has been increased by recent work on consumer theory (e.g. Howard & Sheth, 1969), and by our ability to make simultaneous assessments of their effects on behaviour as a result of advances in multivariate and taxonomic analysis. (See below.)

SEGMENTATION METHODOLOGY

It was pointed out at the beginning of the chapter that market segmentation studies are of different kinds, and that the nature of the specific problem will determine the methodology to be adopted. It is, nevertheless, possible to map out a broad sequence of stages through which most segmentation projects will pass.

Background clarification

An essential first step is a thorough review of existing knowledge and assumptions about the market. Several sources may contribute—e.g. past research carried out for the company, industry desk research, discussions between researchers on the one hand, and marketing and advertising people on the other. Such discussions are particularly important. The most successful segmentation projects are usually those where, from the outset, there is good communication between researchers and research users; where the researchers have a clear understanding of current marketing problems and possible courses of action; where marketing men feel fully committed to the research, and where they understand its objectives if not necessarily the intricacies of the methodology employed.

One result of such a review should be a clarification of the basic patterns of purchasing and usage in the market, which subsequent research will attempt to describe and explain.

Qualitative exploration

The first step may well have suggested a number of possible segmentation criteria. However, in most cases it will be necessary to carry out qualitative research to ensure that we are aware of all criteria of possible relevance to the problem in hand. This stage is crucial. It provides the foundation for the sophisticated analyses that follow, which are of little value unless based upon salient characteristics. Yet it is the step that has been most neglected in much published research on segmentation, which has too often adopted an *a priori* approach, thereby pre-judging what the important variables might be.

A variety of techniques can be used at this exploratory stage, including the traditional methods of 'motivation' research – e.g. group discussions, depth interviews and projective techniques – and the Kelly Repertory Grid, a recent import from clinical psychology. These techniques have been widely discussed in the literature: see, for instance, the chapter by Goodyear in this book and also Sampson (1971). Suffice it to say here that, as at other research stages, it is important to preserve a flexible approach, selecting those techniques, separately or in combination, which seem most appropriate to the particular study. Where possible, exploratory interviews should be conducted within behavioural or other sub-groups of known importance to the market.

Developing measuring instruments

Just as the more numerically inclined researchers have been apt to neglect qualitative exploration, so the more qualitatively inclined have been apt to neglect measurement. This is unfortunate. For, having identified the relevant variables, it is important to ensure that these are measured adequately. Discussion here will be confined to psychological variables, which are generally considered to present most problems.

Psychological measurement in consumer research has been discussed more fully elsewhere (e.g. Lunn, 1968 and 1969). The basic principle is that of self-report. Statements or phrases are selected from depth interview records and other sources, and presented to respondents in forms such as the following – e.g. 'Everyone should give themselves an occasional treat.' Here respondents would be asked to indicate the strength of their agreement or disagreement. Or in bi-polar form, as in semantic differential type approach – e.g. 'glamorous...not glamorous'. Here respondents would be asked to rate themselves, brands, 'ideal' brands, or other objects of interest, on a seven point scale in terms of attributes elicited at the qualitative exploratory stage.

An important principle is not to rely upon a single item for any particular characteristics, but rather to compose sub-sets of items. Thus, the trait of bargain-seeking might be represented by statements such as:

I hate to buy anything and find it is cheaper elsewhere.

I compare all prices before I decide where to buy.

It's a waste of shoe leather walking round looking for cheap shops.

Having selected sets of items for each of the characteristics in question, it is customary to use techniques such as factor analysis to sort out which items do, in fact, group together in terms of similar response patterns. These procedures both clarify the hypotheses developed at the qualitative exploratory stage about the nature and number of important variables, and also help to reduce each group of items to a small sub-set for use in subsequent research. This last point is especially important where a segmentation inquiry is dealing with a large number of criteria; it is essential to measure each with the maximum efficiency in order to reduce the load on the respondent.

Defining target groups

These first two stages will have led to a list of important segmentation criteria, and, where appropriate, to the development of measuring instruments.

The next task is to determine the main market segments, in terms of these criteria. This can be done in a variety of ways.

(a) The most straightforward is to carry out simple cross-tabulations between aspects of consumer behaviour and the variables that have been identified and measured at previous stages (in statistical terms, the independent variables). Thus, heavy, medium and light buyers of the product or brand, or different loyalty and usership groups, would each be related, separately to criteria such as age, educational level, economy-mindedness, need for fast acceleration and so on. The disadvantage of this approach is that it does not allow for the fact that consumer behaviour is determined by many factors working in conjunction with one another.

One means of allowing for this is to carry out cross-tabulations with the criteria interlaced: e.g. age within economy-mindedness, education level within need for acceleration. This approach ceases to be feasible when there are several criteria, and thus a very large number of possible cross-tabulations.

(b) A more sophisticated approach is to incorporate all the independent variables in a multiple regression or discriminant function analysis (Nunnally, 1967). Briefly, these analysis techniques tell us how much of the variance in the behavioural groups can be accounted for by combinations of the criteria, and also the relative importance of the criteria in accounting for this variance. Thus, 25 per cent of the tendency to be a buyer of chocolate digestive biscuits might be accounted for by a combination of age, household size, economy-mindedness and concern with nourishment.

This has been a popular approach in segmentation and was used, for instance, in the very thorough exploration of personality and purchasing behaviour carried out by Massy et al. (1968).

However, regression-type techniques made certain assumptions, often unwarranted, about the nature of the data; namely that these are additive and can be combined in a linear fashion. In doing so, they fail to take into account *interactions* within the total set of variables. That is to say, where any one variable has a different effect upon behaviour depending upon its combination with other variables, multiple regression will fail to detect this. To take a simple case, two housewives may be equally traditional: but if one is also highly bargain conscious and the other has a low interest in bargains they may buy quite different kinds of products. For a fuller discussion of interaction effects, see Sonquist & Morgan (1964).

(c) A well-known means of dealing with interaction is the sequential dichotomization method, advocated by Belson, Agostini and others. Proceeding in a step-wise fashion, this method searches out those combinations of variables which best discriminate a single dependent variable, e.g. heaviness of buying. An illustration is given in the chapter by Clunies-Ross later in this book. It can be an illuminating way of dealing with cases where the main focus of interest is one particular variable, not necessarily behavioural—e.g. in a recent R.B.L. project it was used to explore the determinants of certain psychological scales, such as traditionalism. In several R.B.L. studies sub-groups have been identified, each representing over 10 per cent of the market, and containing a high proportion of heavy buyers of the product. For instance, in a confectionary project, a group was identified consisting of high sweet-toothedness, D.E. social class, high self-indulgence, and low conservatism. The group consisted of 12 per cent of the sample, and contained 85 per cent heavy buyers of the product, compared with 50 per cent in the total sample. The A.I.D. computer program of Sonquist & Morgan (1964) overcomes, to a certain extent, some of the objections that have been raised against this method: for example, the question of where to dichotomize each variable, and problems of higher order interactions.

(d) There are, however, many occasions where we do not particularly want our target group definition to be determined by a single variable. Here the methods known as cluster or profile analysis are more appropriate. Briefly, these methods group respondents into homogeneous sub-sets with similar patterns of scores. That is, they produce 'natural' groupings, rather than 'predictive' groupings as in the Belson-type approach.

The objective is to maximize the similarity of respondents within each sub-set and minimize their similarities to respondents in other sub-sets. (Green & Frank, 1968a; Nunnally, 1967.)

Cluster analysis is relatively new in market research, but has been extensively—and successfully—used during recent years. For instance, a case was described in a previous publication (Lunn,

1969), where respondents were clustered in terms of their scores on ten general attitude scales, producing six totally distinct groups. Group 1 was highly traditional, home-centred and secure, had little interest in glamour, and was rather unsociable, unexperimental and disinclined to seek bargains. Respondents in Group 2 were in many respects similar – they were traditional, home-centred, uninterested in glamour and not particularly sociable. But, unlike respondents in Group 1, they were insecure, obsessional and very economy minded. A third group – a young-oriented, 'swinging' set of housewives – was opposite to the first two groups in almost all respects. All these groups exhibited clear brand discrimination, as well as indicating certain market opportunities.

The input to cluster analysis need not be confined to one type of data, such as the general attitudes instanced above. Respondents can be clustered in terms of all kinds of segmentation criteria where interactions are expected to occur, although caution should be urged where the data takes different forms – e.g. dichotomous and continuous items.

The whole area of cluster analysis still contains a number of problems. These include the question of whether or not there are, in fact, discrete clusters within the sample in question, whether respondents should be allowed to come into more than one cluster, whether some respondents should be regarded as non-classifiable, and therefore, allocated to a 'dustbin' category, and how many groups should be formed.

On this last point, it is important to balance considerations of preserving the maximum amount of useful information whilst retaining target groups sufficiently large to be realistic for marketing action. A useful procedure is to extract a range of cluster solutions, say from two to twenty, and to examine both the homogeneity and meaningfulness of the groups at each stage. With some data only the groups at one particular stage are sufficiently homogeneous and interpretable to be of value, whereas with other data any one of several cluster solutions would be feasible to take. On the latter occasions, the marketing objectives of the study will determine whether we opt for a relatively large number of specific groupings, or a small number of more general ones. The former option tends to give better brand discrimination, the latter to indicate broad themes running through the data. Amongst the computer programs available in the U.K., the C.R.C. method (1969) offers a useful check on the stability of the groups by splitting the sample in two, and calculating a cluster similarity score at each stage.

Obtaining target group profiles

Having isolated target groups, the next step is to obtain profiles of these groups, based on any data in the questionnaires that might be relevant, e.g. purchase and usage, and brand image ratings.

Further stages

Properly carried out, the stages outlined above will provide a comprehensive background picture of the market. There is a danger in regarding this as the end of the story. In a sense, it is the starting-point. Two particularly important issues here are the following:

(*a*) The target groups that have been identified should form the basis of marketing strategies; for instance, they may in themselves lead to the generation of new product concepts, or help in the checking of existing hunches. In addition, they should now figure at the centre of research for product idea testing, product testing, copy testing, and so on. It is the preferences of the target group that matters, not of the population in general.

(*b*) It is essential to take a dynamic view of market segmentation. Consumer requirements may change, possibly as a result of marketing activity, and we must remain constantly alert to this. It is also important to examine the elasticity of particular segments. It is not enough merely to provide the client with a description of the market, however complete this may be. Researchers should also encourage him to test out the potential of each suggested promotional strategy, by determining the responsiveness to it of the various target groups.

An open-minded approach to methodology

As with segmentation criteria, it is important to preserve an open mind about the techniques used in forming target groups. It is often appropriate to apply several methods in any one study.

Multiple regression may well be used to establish the relative importance to purchasing of the variables amongst the homogeneous groups formed by the sequential dichotomization method. Again, whilst factor analysis may not be the most appropriate technique for clustering respondents (Nunnally, 1967), it helps to clarify the dimensions in terms of which they should be clustered. Moreover, the sequential use of qualitative and statistical techniques can be recommended. For instance, depth interviews amongst respondents in different clusters can provide evidence for construct validity and further ideas for advertising strategy.

Product Segmentation

The history of market segmentation is replete with conflicts between the protagonists of different criteria and techniques. A theme running through this chapter is that many of these controversies are unwarranted: most of the conflicting approaches have a place for at least one kind of segmentation problem. Product segmentation is a characteristic example. This has developed during recent years mainly as an alternative to consumer segmentation (Barnett, 1969). In the author's opinion it is better regarded as complementary.

The chief objective of product segmentation is to identify groups of products which elicit similar responses. There have been two main research approaches towards this end.

The first approach uses the semantic differential and is a logical extension of traditional brand image research. Consumers are asked to rate a selection of brands or products along a series of attitude dimensions, e.g.:

Full of nourishment/Lacking nourishment.
Economical in use/Not economical in use.

Preferably, these dimensions, and the ways in which they are phrased, are determined by prior qualitative research.

The simplest analysis is to compare the various products along each dimension separately. The 'ideal' product (for a particular purpose) may be used as a yardstick, as in Fig. 2.

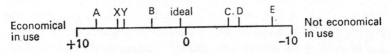

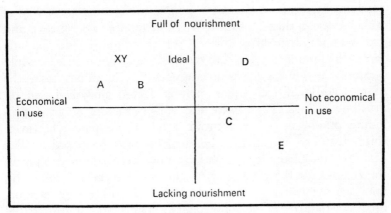

FIG. 2.

The next step is to compare product ratings on all pairs of dimensions, as in Fig. 2.

This provides a series of maps of the product field, which yield two main kinds of information:

(*a*) An indication of which products are competitive in the sense that consumers perceive them as closely substitutable—in this case, products X and Y;

(*b*) An indication of market gaps, in that no products are judged by consumers to provide this particular combination of characteristics—in this case the combination of economical in use and lacking nourishment.

These maps may be extended so that they compare three or more dimensions simultaneously. Computer programs exist which will summarize this information, and also provide supplementary information to indicate the relative importance of particular gaps and groupings, e.g. in terms of market share (see Clemens & Thornton, 1968). Again the 'ideal' brand or product can provide a useful yardstick.

The final step is to use cluster analysis to summarize the total set of ratings for all the products, including the 'ideal'. As mentioned above, these procedures may be concerned either with plotting the positions of existing brands and products or with finding gaps in the total space which indicate new product possibilities. For example, see Thornton (1970) and Lunn (1971).

The second main approach essentially requires consumers to assess products in terms of similarity and/or preference. A variety of techniques can then be used to summarize these assessments, and produce groupings of products. These techniques, which include multi-dimensional scaling, are often termed 'non-metric', mainly because they make fewer measurement assumptions than the more traditional techniques such as factor analysis based on attribute ratings. These have the theoretical advantage of providing purer and more accurate product groupings: however, this advantage remains to be demonstrated in practice. The disadvantage of this approach is one of interpretability. That is, the reasons for the product groupings have to be inferred. This may be overcome to a certain extent by obtaining product attribute data from the same sample. The semantic differential approach provides greater diagnostic power: products are clustered in terms of attributes based on consumer language. For examples of the second approach, see Green *et al.* (1968b) and Stefflre (1968).

An important challenge for researchers is to link consumer and product segmentation. One means of doing this is to work out product groupings separately for different consumer sub-groups. Another is to attempt to represent the consumer and product groupings simultaneously, see Sherak (1969).

Segmentation and Theory

An important recent development in market research has been the increasing attention paid to theory. There has been a greater awareness both of the nature of consumer decision processes, and of the various influences – commercial and non-commercial – bearing upon these processes. A segmentation study provides a snapshot of the market at any one period of time. For a full understanding of the market, and for effective marketing action, we require a consideration of the changes that take place over time. Thus, although this paper has argued for an empirical approach to market segmentation studies, these should fit into a clear conceptual structure of consumer behaviour.

There is no space here for a comparison of different approaches to consumer theory. However, the interested reader might care to contrast three different approaches:

(i) The purely *a priori,* where a theory is adopted from, say, social psychology: see the recent discussions on Fishbein (Tuck & Nelson, 1969);

(ii) The essentially *empirical* approach, where laws are derived solely from the study of consumer behaviour (see Ehrenberg, 1969);

(iii) The more *eclectic* approach, where attempts are made to integrate knowledge about consumer behaviour with a variety of theories from the social sciences (see Nicosia, 1966; Howard & Sheth, 1969; Lunn, 1969a).

In conclusion, this overview of current issues in segmentation has touched upon concepts and techniques of a high degree of complexity and sophistication. These developments are essential for a full description of the market. There is a danger, however, that their very complexity may create a barrier to their usage. Researchers face a challenge in the communication of the results of these studies to marketing men. In the absence of clear communication, research will be wasted and valuable marketing opportunities wasted.

References

1 AGOSTINI, J. M. (1967), 'New criteria for classifying informants in market research and media strategy', *Admap,* Vol. III, No. 9.
2 BASS, F. M., PESSEMEIR, E. A., and TIGART, D. J. (1969), 'Complementary and substitute patterns of purchasing and use', *Journal of Advertising Research,* Vol. IX, No. 2.
3 BELBEN, K. C. (1969), 'Matching media to market segments', *Advertising Management,* October, pp. 27, 28, 30.
4 BARNETT, N. L. (1969), 'Beyond market segmentation', *Harvard Business Review,* January–February.
5 BROADBENT, S. and MOONEY, P. B. (1968), 'Can informant claims on product purchase made at an interview be used for media planning?' ESOMAR-WAPOR Congress, pp. 325–39.
6 BROADBENT, S. and MASSON, P. (1969), 'Informant classification in media and product surveys', *Admap,* January.
7 BRODY, R. P. and CUNNINGHAM, S. M. (1968), 'Personality variables and the consumer decision process', *Journal of Marketing Research,* Vol. V, February, pp. 50–7.

8 COWLING, A. B. and NELSON, E. H., *Predicting Effects of Change*. Paper given at M.R.S. Annual Conference, Brighton, March 1969.

9 CYBERNETICS RESEARCH CONSULTANTS LTD, *The CRC Cluster Analysis Programme*, 1969.

10 CRONBACH, L. J. and MEEHL, P. E. (1955), 'Construct validity in psychological tests', *Psychological Bulletin*, Vol. LII.

11 DURAND, J. (ed.), *Market Segmentation*. Papers from the conference organized by ADETEM, Paris, March 1969.

12 DAY, G., *Buyers' Attitudes and Brand Choice Behaviour*, The Free Press, New York, 1970.

13 EHRENBERG, A. S. C. (1969), 'Towards an integrated theory of consumer behaviour', *Commentary*, The Journal of the Market Research Society, Vol. XI, No. 4.

14 FRANK, R. E., 'Market Segmentation research: findings and implications' in Frank, R. E., Bass, F. H. *et al.* (eds), *Appliances of the Sciences in Marketing Management*, pp. 39–68, John Wiley and Sons, New York, 1968(a).

15 *But the Heavy Half is Already the Heavy Half*. Paper presented to the American Marketing Association's Conference, Philadelphia, 17–19 June 1968(b).

16 GREEN, P. E. and FRANK, R. E. (1968a), 'Numerical taxonomy in marketing analysis', *Journal of Marketing Research*.

17 GREEN, P. E., HALBERT, M. H., and ROBINSON, P. J., 'Perception and preference mapping on the analysis of marketing behaviour' in Allen and Crespi (eds), *Attitude Research on the Rocks*, American Marketing Association, 1968b.

18 HOWARD, J. A. and SHETH, J. N., *The Theory of Buyer Behaviour*, John Wiley and Sons, New York, 1969.

19 HELLER, H. E., 'Defining target markets by their attitude profiles' in Adler and Crepir (eds), *Attitude Research on the Rocks*, American Marketing Association, 1968.

20 HALEY, R. I. (1968), 'Benefit segmentation: a decision-oriented research tool', *Journal of Marketing*, Vol. XXXII, July, pp. 30–5.

21 JOANNIS, H. (1969), 'L'Exploitation des diverses typologies au niveau de la creation' in Durand, J. (ed.), see Ref. 11.

22 JOYCE, T., *The New Housewife. A Comprehensive Study*. Paper of the ESOMAR Congress, 1967.

23 —— and CHANNON, C. (1966), 'Classifying market survey respondents', *Applied Statistics*, Vol. XV, No. 3.

24 LUNN, J. A. (1965), 'Exploratory work on social class', *Commentary*, The Journal of the Market Research Society, Vol. VII, No. 3, July.

25 —— (1966), 'Psychological classification', *Commentary*, The Journal of the Market Research Society, Vol. VIII, No. 3, July, pp. 161–73.

26 ——, 'New techniques in consumer research' in Pym, D. (ed.), *Industrial Society*, Penguin, New York, 1968.

27 ——, *Buyer Behaviour in Practice*. Paper read at the Third Annual Buyer Behaviour Conference, Columbia University, New York, 1969(a).

28 ——, (1969b), 'Perspectives in attitude research', *Commentary*, The Journal of the Market Research Society, Vol. XI, No. 3.

29 ——, 'Segmenting and constructing markets.' In Worcester R. (ed.), *Handbook of Consumer Market Research*, McGraw-Hill, New York, 1971.

30 *The Londoner* (1962), Associated Rediffusion.

31 MASSY, W. F., FRANK, R. J., and LODAHL, T. M., *Purchasing Behaviour and Personal Attributes*, University of Pennsylvania Press, Philadephia, 1968.

32 MORTON-WILLIAMS, J. (1969), 'The marketing man's guide to market segmentation analysis', *Advertising Management*, August, pp. 16–18.

33 NICOSIA, F. M., *Consumer Decision Processes*, Prentice-Hall, New Jersey, 1968.

34 PARFITT, J. (1967), 'How accurately can product purchasing behaviour be measured by recall?' ESOMAR-WAPOR Congress, pp. 507–45.

35 PESSEMEIR, E. A. and TIGERT, D. J., 'Personality activity and attitude predictors of consumer behaviour' in *New Ideas for Successful Marketing*, Proceedings in the 1966 World Congress, American Marketing Association, pp. 332–47.

36 SAMPSON, P. M. J., 'Motivation and qualitative research', in Worcester, R. (ed.), *Handbook of Consumer Market Research*, McGraw-Hill, 1971.

37 SHERAK, B., 'A Beer segmentation and brand mapping study' in Durand, J. (ed.), see Ref. 11.

38 SMITH, WENDELL (1955), 'Imperfect competition and marketing strategy', *Cost and Profit Outlook*, Vol. VIII, No. 10. October.

39 SKELLY, F. R. and NELSON, E. H., *'Market Segmentation and New Product Development.'* Paper given at M.R.S. Conference, Eastbourne, 1966.

40 SONQUIST, J. A. and MORGAN, J. N., *The Detection of Interaction Effects*, Monograph No. 35, Survey Research Centre, University of Michigan, Ann Arbor, 1968.

41 STEFFLRE, V., 'Market Structure studies: new products for old markets', in Frank, R. E., Bass, F. N. *et al.* (eds), see Ref. 14.

42 THORNTON, C., *Researching New Product Openings in Multi-dimensional Space*. Paper read at the Annual Conference of the Market Research Society, Brighton, 1970.

43 TWEDT, D. W. (1964), 'How important to marketing strategy is the "heavy half" theory?', *Journal of Marketing*, Vol. XXVIII, No. 1.

44 TWIGG, J. and WOLFE, A. (1968), 'Problems of communicating the results of market segmentation studies', *Commentary*, The Journal of the Market Research Society, Vol. XX, No. 4., October, pp. 264–78.

45 WELLS, W. D. (1967), *Patterns of Consumer Behaviour*. Unpublished manuscript, University of Chicago.

46 ——, 'Segmentation by attitude types' in King, R. L. (ed.), *Marketing and the New Science of Planning*, American Marketing Association, Fall Conference Proceedings, No. 28, 1968.

47 WILSON, C. L., 'Homemaker living patterns and marketplace behaviour', *New Ideas for Successful Marketing*, Proceedings of the World Congress, American Marketing Association, pp. 305–31, 1966.

48 WINKLER, A., 'Problems in connection with the use of segmentation methods with examples from the field of consumer goods' in Durand, J. (ed.), see Ref. 11.

6 | Different Uses of Market Segmentation

C. CLUNIES-ROSS
Consultant.

General

A general survey on product attitudes and usage has several uses. It describes the general background and will also look at some of the points that may indicate how the market has got there, how relevant a proposed advertising approach appears to be, etc. It will answer certain questions that have been raised recently, e.g. whether purchase frequency is sufficient to support a certain premium scheme.

Segmentation is, currently, a vogue term. It is also a vague one that covers very different approaches. They have in common the idea that different people want different amounts of different products on different occasions – i.e. the market is segmented and not an undifferentiated mass. The marketing application of this approach requires a certain finesse; a policy suitable for one part of the market may be ludicrous for another. Users of segmentation should get close to the research operation to ensure that the research produces results in a form that can be used.

This chapter illustrates three sorts of techniques used in segmentation analysis. The techniques tend to go to extremes: they each start from a certain viewpoint which is formalized and embodied in the analysis. The first thing to settle in using segmentation is this viewpoint. The Table below shows how the content of the research changes to match the situation.

It is seldom that the perspectives remain unchanged. One might start with a broad viewpoint. If the conclusion is that the company should enter the field with another brand then the perspective shifts.

A totally inclusive survey usable for all these purposes has some obvious attractions. It looks a neater, unified approach which

	1	2	3
Perspective	*Global*	*Strategy*	*Tactics*
Examples of Applications	Assessing the long-term development of the market	Setting advertising objectives, ...or...... extending the product field with a new product	Designing a new brand within an existing product field ......or...... designing advertising to modify a brand's position
Data Emphases	Psychological and sociological charac-terization of respondent ......plus...... respondent's 'relationship' with the product field and related ones	Respondent's 'relationship' with the product field and related ones ......plus...... something on brand differentiation	Consumption of the product .....but mainly..... brand differen-tiation

should save both time and money. It does not work out that way unless an awful lot is already known about the product field. The unification imposes a long interview which takes its toll in terms of the quality of the responses. There are prospects for saving time as one does not need to do another survey when one's perspective changes. Enormous discipline is needed; there are so many rela-tionships that can be explored that 'might be interesting'. It is easy to dissipate the savings on such possibilities; complicated computing and executive time are not particularly cheap.

Segmentation is a group of ideas and techniques. It is an expand-ing group. Three general ideas can be picked out as more 'popular' examples:

(*a*) New products are ones that don't already exist. Market segmentation is shown by differences between products or brands already on the market. Gaps between brands indicate possible market segments which are not adequately served by existing brands.

(*b*) One can't plan marketing strategy properly until one knows the structure of the market, in particular who is using the product. This knowledge is the framework on which to build one's plans.

(*c*) The market segments should be allowed to speak for themselves. Market segments are just groups of people who are relatively similar in their needs, their attitudes or their reactions. This structure would guide our assessment of the market's longer-term development.

These ideas will be examined in more detail in the next three sections.

Brand Segmentation

Market segmentation in terms of brands is particularly useful in generating ideas for new products. New brands can, of course, aim at being imitations of successful brands already on the market. There are seldom any great problems in identifying the successful brands. The policy of aiming for a 'gap' in the market poses a different question: 'What sort of brand would be distinctive to the potential consumer?'

The answer to this question is not a number, or a relationship; the answer cannot be properly expressed numerically. The answer is a 'brand' or at least the nucleus of a marketing idea for a new product.

The general area for the new product will have been picked before the segmentation study. It may be an area where the company already has a product, 'so we can capitalize on our goodwill in the trade'; it may be an area related to existing products but not actually covered yet, 'so we won't be competing with ourselves', or it may be in a completely new area, 'a genuine diversification'. This choice will have been made before the brand segmentation study.

The type of technique described here will work best where there is a moderate number of brands, e.g. boxes of chocolates, alcoholic drinks.

It can also be applied where the product field has fuzzy edges: peanuts, crisps, count-lines and other nibblers.

It cannot be applied where there are only two or three brands.

You start by listing all the brands within the scope of the field, that is, all the brands that are of any marketing significance, i.e. over, say, a third of the initial volume you hope your new product will achieve.

The next stage of preparation is a comprehensive but short list of characteristics relevant to the product field. The list covers the way that people think and talk about the products. It is collected by getting people to talk in suitably controlled group discussions, or in individual interviews. The list can be supplemented by your own or your advertising agency's hunches (it will normally be too long already).

The list has to be screened down to a workable number. This is carried out on a pilot survey where the interview consists primarily of the respondent describing one brand on all of the terms using rating scales. The terms are analysed to see which are similar in meaning (correlation and factor analysis) and which distinguish most effectively between brands (analysis of variance, discriminative analysis).

A shorter list of terms is selected with the objectives of covering the full range, being sensitive and being as short as possible.

This abbreviated list is used in the main survey. The respondents will describe more than one brand on the list of terms. The exact number depends on the number of brands known, the length of the list and the level of interest the respondent can be expected to have in the field. It is as well to include some products that are a bit beyond the product area considered. This gives a broader perspective on the consumer usage of terms.

The ratings are assigned numerical values (the results are not particularly sensitive even to quite large changes in the values assigned). The numbers should be set on some notion of 'psychological distance' between the opinions of people giving different responses. A frequent practice is to assign numerical values of 1, 2, 3...to the different responses from one extreme to the other (the scales are sometimes set up to make this 'equal distance' assignment reasonable).

The average rating is calculated for each of the brands on each of the descriptive terms. These ratings, and particularly the relative values of the ratings, show the way in which the brands are seen by the people who know them. The ratings are the raw material for the brand segmentation.

The first stage in using the results is to consider the descriptive terms individually. The average ratings for each of the brands are arranged in order and presented (preferably graphically) and considered, bearing in mind the question: 'Do I believe it?'

The question of belief is basic. If you don't believe the results at this stage you won't be able to carry out the important stage of getting ideas from them.

The brands themselves are the landmarks for translating from the abstract consumer views (average ratings). Belief means being able to accept the ratings and modify any of one's pre-conceptions into place. The end result of this is an understanding of what the various terms *dark, strong,* etc., mean to the respondents.

One thing to check is the contrast between users' and non-users' opinions of the products. Users will normally have a better opinion than the non-users. Thus, if the users' opinions show a higher rating on *dark* than non-users' *for each brand,* it is likely that *darkness* is associated with overall evaluation.

Not too much time should be spent on this secondary aspect of individual aspects. A brief look does help in the appreciation of the meaning of the terms but too long a look leads to an uncomfortably analytic viewpoint which is at odds with the free flow of ideas. It should suffice to make a note of the 'good' end of the scale if there is one.

The first attack on idea stimulation is a natural extension of understanding the scales. It consists of envisaging what the next brand would look like. The existing brands have been arranged, say, in order of increasing ratings for *safety.* This has produced an entirely reasonable order with the simpler, more innocuous, older brands as the safest ones. Is there any way of getting something that would look safer? The things that might occur to you are:

'PLACEBO' – the brand that does you all the good you think it does.

'HERBAL' – the natural remedy.

These examples are brought out to demonstrate:

1 Not all the results are necessarily to be taken seriously. (To be fair it should be pointed out that distilled water has been packaged

and sold expensively as a car battery restorer in the U.S.[1]) Ideas are being generated, not evaluated.

2 Envisaged really means envisaged. The ideas must be made real in some way. A new brand will (almost certainly) be introduced to the public by advertising and so slogans or claims are often a convenient method of pinning down ideas for later examination. The danger is that one tries to polish the slogans; a distraction as bad as analytical thinking.

3 The stimulus of seeing brands arranged in sequence of 'SAFETY' and being asked 'What would the next brand in the sequence look like?' is a much more effective one than the question: 'How can we make a brand that will be seen to be very safe indeed?'

This one-at-a-time approach can be carried out on the aspects that do not have a particularly strong evaluative element. One can explore both ends and any gaps in the middle.

The next stage of investigation is to look at pairs of terms. Pairs can also be plotted out to give an easily appreciated picture of the market. One can then inspect for gaps or combinations of properties not possessed by any brands. These need to be screened in advance because there are so many possible combinations to examine. The screening selects the empty, or relatively empty, quadrants which are not at the bad end of two distinctly evaluative scales, e.g. there is little point in looking for a *weak, not long lasting* analgesic even if the market is wide open. The material is presented as visually as possible and the question posed: 'What sort of brand would occur here?'

The approach starts to break down when one tries to consider three terms simultaneously; there are so many groups of three terms (over a thousand with a list of twenty terms), that results are difficult to present graphically, computerized screening becomes more complex. The task to the imagination is more detailed and, more importantly, less convincing: it is rather like having an advertising platform with three 'main messages'.

Some of the main variations to the above recipe are worth noticing. Firstly there is the 'poor man's' brand segmentation.

---

[1] The defence in court centred on the point that regular topping up with distilled water *IS* good for the battery.

One uses one's own, or other expert, appraisal of the relative position of the brands on the characteristics. This approach can be combined with the former. It may be especially relevant when distribution channels are unusual or complex enough to be taken into account.

Another variation is a more technical one. The original description was in terms of the individual questions asked of the respondents. One can use indexes or factor scores built up from several of these questions. This is going further from the original data but the products themselves still provide the landmarks. The burden of the work is reduced with indexes because the number of characteristics is reduced. The benefit is particularly worth while when some of the questions cover similar characteristics because it avoids suggesting contradictions – e.g. *weak* and *powerful*. (Recognition of contradictions is a distraction into analytic thinking.)

Descriptive terms are often partly evaluative. Indexes can be set up to remove the 'evaluative' side so that the indexes are purely descriptive.

A further variation is to look for 'gaps' more generally, i.e. to look for gaps in the middle of the brands. This is a much more complex operation and can only be carried out on a computer. There are also difficulties in presenting the information about the gap in a simple enough way to stimulate the imagination accurately. As computing costs start to rise at this stage one is not so likely to be inundated as when one looks at more than two characteristics in the original way.

Segmentation by Product Usage

This is the opposite extreme of segmentation from the brand-oriented one described above. It is concerned with the product group as a whole and the objective is to understand it sufficiently to be able to predict, for any individual, whether or not they use the product group, and if so, to what extent. Work along these lines is undertaken to inform marketing and advertising thinking as a whole. It need not be directly related to any particular marketing or advertising 'problem'. Clearly, if we do know about the role of the product group sufficiently to be able to predict the consumption of individuals we are in a much better position to formulate and appraise marketing policy.

This question of telling the buyers from the non-buyers is one of the standard considerations in market research. It underlies the tabulations of buyers by demographic characteristics and buyer profiles. This approach has been extended to take attitude as well as demographic data. These tabulations are very informative. Their main faults are that they tend to be repetitive and long.

The range of points that 'could be covered' can be stretched indefinitely. It is usually difficult to say in advance that, for example, *extraversion* has no relevance to a particular product field...but if it could be relevant should it be omitted? There are limits to the amount of information that one can collect. Generally speaking the way the analysis is to be applied should be used to guide the selection of the data, e.g. product attitudes are most important when advertising strategy is to be planned, but psychological characteristics may rise in importance when one is trying to anticipate the effect of a price cut.

All too often in practice, a survey has been commissioned for some other purpose and it is then decided to see what can be found out about product usage. The question of what should be included then becomes operationally meaningless – all that one can do is omit questions. One should look at the questions and come to some conclusion about how accurately it is reasonable to expect them to predict purchasing. It is better to scrap the analysis than to carry it out on unsatisfactory data.

The segmentation idea is that different sorts of people have different buying rates – or likelihood of buying. One therefore wants to look for the groups with the high buying rates. The complication is that with, say, only twelve characteristics describing a respondent, each of them in two possibilities (e.g. young – old; ABC1–C2DE; with children – without children) there are over 4,000 combinations. Most of these will be unrepresented in surveys of less than 2,000 respondents. The others will have one or two representatives within the sample.

One could consider going to these extremes but the fragmentation is no use because one can't grasp it nor believe it literally. The fragmentation can be lessened by recombining some of the groups. This, of course, leads to combining groups containing buyers and similarly groups containing non-buyers. We then need to describe the composite groups and, lo and behold, we come up with buyer profiles.

One needs, therefore, some form of control to stop the fragmentation from getting out of control. The method given here is subject to all sorts of modifications. We shall take the simplest type of data where each of the questions – explanators – has only two possible 'answers', e.g. young/old; agree/disagree with statements.

The first thing to look at is the relationship between each of the characteristics and buying/not buying. This is brought out by a series of tables showing buying versus the characteristic. Some of these show more relationship than others. The one that shows the greatest relationship is a natural starting-point. Put another way, you select the piece of information about a respondent that you would want if you were restricted to only one. Let us say the product is ice-cream. Then it is very reasonable that the most important bit of information is the WITH/WITHOUT CHILDREN composition of the households. Households without children may well buy ice-cream for different reasons or in different patterns from those that apply to households with children. When differences are expected, or even just reasonable, it is bad practice to suppress them. In such an example it would be natural to analyse the two sub-samples separately. This generalizes to the idea that whenever there is a strong 'influence' on purchasing, the pattern at the high end may well be different from the pattern at the other. Applying the idea across the board leads us to treat the two sub-samples separately whatever the nature of the influence or explanators.

The process then can be repeated on these separate sub-samples. Each can be inspected to find the next questions which show the strongest relationship to purchasing *within that sub-sample*. This need not be the same in both sub-samples. For example, households with children might then be split on whether or not the housewife thought that 'convenience' in desserts was 'very important indeed' for that particular product, whilst those without children were then divided by class.

This sort of result can be conveniently illustrated in chart form. The two numbers in each box give the number of respon-

dents in the sample and the percentage purchasing the product
(the data is hypothetical).

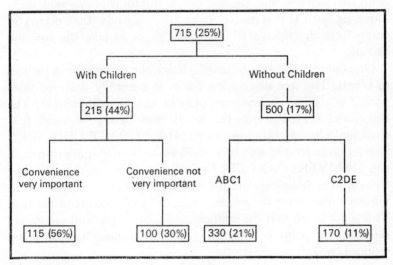

FIG. I.

The resulting sub-samples can also be regarded as samples in
their own right. The procedure is repeated, until a whole 'tree'
is developed.

A halt has to be called somewhere. The main considerations are
the number of respondents and the strength of the relationships.

There is no point in subdividing the sample when there is not a
strong enough relationship to justify it. 'Strong enough' has two
aspects: the chance that the observed relationships are due to the
quirks of random sampling, and the amount of prediction improvements or explanations given by the split. It turns out that neither
of these points can be given an exact statistical definition.

The sample size (the sub-sub-sample that is) is a more workable
idea. It has the great advantage of being familiar – the point that
a sub-group 'contains only 2·3 per cent of the total sample and so
is not worth examining in any further detail' is easily communicated. Technically, it is just as impossible to create an absolute
borderline but, because the point is so readily understood, there
is no real problem of misunderstanding.

The technique could be regarded just as a method of describing or condensing the data. As such it is very effective, being systematic and easy to appreciate. An analytic interpretation is a consequence of an effective description – one should not think of any such technique as 'purely descriptive'. The main mistake that occurs in going from description to interpretation is to take the tree too literally.

One tends to think in terms of 'chains of causality' or sequences of events. The tree description fits in so naturally that one finds oneself accepting its structure without further examination. The first question used to split the sample may be a good, solid, fundamental characteristic, as in WITH/WITHOUT CHILDREN in relation to ice-cream. Or it could be something quite transient, e.g. DELIVERY/NON-DELIVERY OF FREE SAMPLE. The tree could be building from the fundamentals or it could be working back from the purchase occasion, or some mixture of the two. This is not to say that the method sometimes works and sometimes doesn't: the point is brought out as a warning against being seduced by the pretty pattern.

The other drawback is that the analysis can turn out to be circular: people who *like* the product actually buy it. The fault lies in the selection of the questions to be studied and not in the technique itself. Crude cases are easily recognized; other cases are more ambiguous. For example, *convenience* could be circular – especially if this has been the main promotional platform for the leading brands – but it need not be, as when the study is investigating the influences of the different product benefits.

Once you have absorbed the meaning of the tree you have got part of the way. You need also to know why all the other characteristics *did not* appear in the tree: whether they are 'represented' by terms that appear or just had no relationship. Finally you want to review the groups against other characteristics – brand, media usage, psychological, etc. – to provide the current marketing background.

Let us consider some of the variants. We started off by only considering two possibilities for each of the questions asked. Often the questions lead to several possible answers, e.g. strongly agree/agree/disagree/strongly disagree with some statement.

There are several ways of taking all the different answers into account. One is to modify the procedure to allow splits into any number of sub-samples at each stage. The other is to decide in advance on a primary grouping of the responses, e.g. 'strongly agree' and 'agree' versus 'strongly disagree' and 'disagree'. Once this question has been used to split a sample the subsidiary categories are brought into play. Another way is to let the data dictate groupings into the two categories at each stage in terms of the strongest relationship with buying.

Each of these methods has some drawbacks. Selection between them is a matter of choosing between

— too rapid fragmentation of the sample (by splitting into too many sub-samples at each stage)

— building in unwarranted assumptions or overlooking relevant possibilities (by building in some emphasis on the order of the different categories)

— paying too much attention to random sampling effects and losing understandability (by making too comprehensive a search for maximum descriptive power).

No hard and fast rules can be laid down as to the right balance. The larger the sample size the less important is the third consideration — at least in the opening splits. My own inclination is for the third method as it has the maximum descriptive power. Afterwards, when one has seen the results, 'peculiarities' can be eliminated by a preliminary grouping of the answers to eliminate any artificial looking splits (e.g. 'strongly agree', 'agree' and 'strongly disagree' versus 'disagree').

Once this point has been sorted out one can use indexes based on several of the questions rather than the individual questions. This leads yet further from the two-category case. Some form of categorization can be applied, e.g. equal intervals or equal percentages. Alternatively one can look for the two best 'simple' groups, i.e. one end of the scale versus the other or the middle versus both extremes.

One might have data in more detail than buying/not buying, e.g. the number of units bought in the last six months. The technique can be modified to use this data. It will involve the 'least squares', which is the standard statistical way of assessing relationships. This treats equal numerical differences as equal which may not be reasonable in the particular context, e.g. the difference between none and one unit may be considered much larger behaviourally than the difference between one and two units. It is easier to adjust the numerical values assigned than the computer program itself.

The number of variations to the technique, and the warnings on circularity, should have demonstrated that the technique is not to be taken as absolute. The results do sharpen one's understanding of the data; a point that is helped by the graphic simplicity with which the results can be presented.

This sharpened understanding often suggested that the analysis should be conducted differently, e.g. that some of the questions should be combined into an index, that a particular 'split' should be forced, that certain questions should be removed from the analysis. Such a reaction should be regarded as natural and praiseworthy, and be acted on. The statistical analysis was carried out in a vacuum. It did not build in any knowledge about the meanings of the questions whose answers were analysed so assiduously. The best analysis is always a meaningful description of the situation which leads to an effective statistical description of the data.

Grouping the Consumers

The third method of segmentation mentioned was to group the consumers. The idea is that the groups will contain relatively similar people who may therefore be expected to react in a similar manner to marketing tactics. This type of analysis may be carried out at various levels.

It may be applied to basic psychological and sociological data in an attempt to anticipate the long-term trends. Or, at the other extreme, it may be applied to the respondents' perceptions and impressions of the brands currently on the market, to plan brand strategy.

Markets tend to defy predictions about them. Cluster analysis is not the magic key to prediction; it does, however, provide the possibility of integrating psychological insight with other more quantitative data. The need for clustering arises from the nature of survey data. A sample of respondents may be thought of as a set of individuals or, on the other hand, as a composite. There are normally too many of them to be studied at length as individuals and so they are treated as a composite and tabulated in various ways. Clustering respondents provides an intermediate approach.

The relatively small number of clusters permits them to be studied individually and they are homogeneous enough to make this worth while.

Analysis of the general characteristics of the market rarely solves immediate marketing problems. Still, more comprehensive understanding of the market should lead to better marketing plans. Cluster analysis provides a link between quantitative and qualitative market research.

The most practical method of clustering is sometimes called 'centroid clustering'. This has the property that any member of a

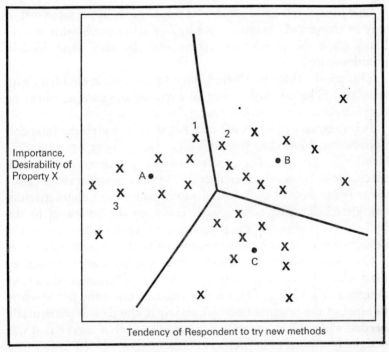

FIG. 2. Three clusters in two dimensions. '1' is much closer to '2', who is in a different cluster, than to '3' who is in the same cluster or to 'A', the cluster centre.

cluster is closer to that cluster average than it is to any other cluster average. Centroid clustering can produce anomalies. Members of the same cluster can still be quite different from each other, and members of different clusters can be very similar (see Fig. 2). These things can happen with all clustering methods. Sometimes the clusters do have definite gaps between them but these occasions arise when clustering brands or words rather than people.

Clusters should not be thought of as definitely distinct groups; they shade into one another. Centroid clustering could be applied to purchasing rate data in which case it would come up with 'Light', 'Medium' and 'Heavy' buyers. The distinction is useful even through Medium shades into Light and Heavy. To make an analogy, clusters are best regarded as having the same sort of precision as social class. The clusters give a good set of stereotypes (cluster centroids) for representing the population over the topics included in the analysis.

One cannot recognize clusters of respondents in the same sort of way as clusters of brands or words. The latter are known beforehand while the people are known only through their filled-in questionnaires.

This means that the clusters have to have their characteristics tabulated. The tabulations should cover all the data, not just the characteristics involved in forming the clusters.

It is necessary to select the range of data to match the intended application. More than that, it is important to have a good understanding of the data. The process for forming clusters is completely mechanical. It uses the idea that the distance between two respondents is the sum of their distances on each of the characteristics considered. These characteristics could be the responses to the individual questions on the questionnaire. This would result in the definition of distance having the same balance as the questionnaire.

One has a better understanding of the data after the survey than when it was being planned. The idea of 'distance' should be designed accordingly. (This is often carried out using factor scores in place of the original data.) A review of the data is particularly needed when the segmentation is carried out on a survey that was designed for some other purpose.

Suppose, for example, that a survey has been largely concerned with attitudes to the 'relaxing effect of the product and the need for relaxation' in connexion with the advertising plans. Other aspects have been covered but in less detail. The clusters formed will relate primarily to relaxation unless the data is 'balanced' beforehand. This is appropriate when the effects of the planned advertising are considered – it is self-defeating within the purpose to reconsider the advertising plans. The clusters, being in terms of relaxation, will 'show that the dominant market structure is relaxation' and so confirm the advertising plans. However, relaxation dominates the questionnaire and not necessarily the market.

Segmentation can be based on data that shows what the respondent thinks of the available brands, what she likes about them and how they could be improved for her. The general aim is to find clusters of people with the same 'needs'. This uses the same sort of data as to consumer-oriented marketing models of brand competition and is subject to the same reservations.

The reservations centre on the validity of the data collected. This raises such questions as:

Can the needs be elicited by straightforward questioning, or are projective techniques required?

Should product descriptions be standardized by incorporating a product test?

But this goes beyond the scope of this chapter.

Review

The first thing to do in considering the use of market segmentation is to decide what you want to use it for and in what sort of form you are expecting the results. You should then compare this with what the research people are expecting to provide and how they expect you to use it.

The next thing to do is to make a pest of yourself by demanding to be informed and consulted at every stage. There is no need to dig into the technicalities much deeper than the level to which they have been discussed here; you must satisfy yourself about why the particular data was selected, why it was collected in the way it was and why it was processed in that particular way.

All this probing will be resented a little bit, but not to worry. This will be balanced out if you use the results, at least if you are seen to use them.

7 | Product Testing

M. COLLINS
Director, Aske Research Ltd.

The Role of Product Testing

When, in consumer research, we talk about product testing, we are referring to methods of assessing the consumer's perception and acceptance of a product. This process must not be confused with technical development research: whilst the latter is concerned with whether or not a product works, the consumer researcher is asking whether the user will *think* a product works. Thus, the scientist may tell us that lather is an inessential ingredient to a liquid detergent and yet the housewife may still need to see the suds before she is able to believe that her washing-up liquid is doing its job.

Consumer research cannot be considered as an alternative to or a replacement for technical development research. In point of fact, the closer the liaison between the two functions, the greater will be the yield from both. A housewife may tell the interviewer that she dislikes one of two samples of ginger cake because it is 'too dry'. Reference to those who formulated the two recipes may be necessary before we realize that this is a criticism of an excessively coarse texture rather than a lack of liquid in the mixture. Similarly, we must rely upon the laboratory to tell us whether or not they can improve the acceptability of the texture of the cake without, for example, losing its flavour.

Product testing amongst the public can be a relevant tool at many stages of a product's life. A new product may be submitted to test in this way prior to marketing on even a limited scale. Marketing policy may be aided by any information as to the groups of the population to whom it has greater appeal. With an existing brand, we may wish to assess a new production technique or measure the possible threat from a new competitor. If our market share begins to decline, we may use product tests as part of a programme designed to investigate the sources of the decline; if then we decide to revise our formulation, we will re-test.

Thus, a product test may be used for any one of a variety of purposes; to answer various questions. This is reflected in the wide range of options open to us when it comes to designing a test for a particular purpose.

Designing a Product Test

Whilst product testing tends to be regarded by many researchers as one of the simpler forms of consumer research, it has, nevertheless, given rise to a good deal of dissension amongst its exponents. This dissension arises from the number of options open at each stage of the research design:

> The type of people to form the sample
> The size of the sample
> The way in which the product is introduced
> The testing method to be used
> The measurement criteria to be employed
> The interpretation of the results.

THE SAMPLE

Clearly, if the results of a product test are to be of marketing value, the answers must be based upon relevant opinions. Whilst this may appear banal, inadequate consideration of the type of people to be represented in the sample must have led to dissatisfaction with the results of many product tests.

The rules are not difficult to formulate or to apply:

(i) The test must be conducted amongst those people likely to be affected by the marketing action resulting from it, e.g. a new product should be tested amongst its target market. A revised formulation should be tested by users of a brand.

(ii) If it is suspected that different groups of the population will react differently to the test, each such group must be adequately represented. Moreover, the sample should, if possible, be divided equally between the groups in the interests of statistical efficiency, e.g. in a diagnostic test of a declining brand, regular users and lapsed users should be equally represented.

SAMPLE SIZE

Because the product test tends to be viewed as a simpler form of research than, say, an attitude survey, it all too often employs a sample which is too small to yield usable results. An idea of the size of sample which could be needed can be obtained from the simple chart below. In this chart, sample sizes are shown against two variables:

(a) The risk of error (R).

(b) The critical preference: the preference level above which marketing significance would be read into the results (C).

This chart is applicable to only simple paired tests, where two products are compared by a single sample of informants.

C R	55:45	60:40	65:35	70:30
1%	2,700	675	300	170
5%	1,600	400	180	100
10%	1,100	275	125	70

Thus, if a preference result for either product in a paired test of 60:40 is considered to be of marketing importance and we are only prepared to take a risk of 5 per cent of making an error by saying either that such a preference exists when in fact it doesn't, or that it does not exist when in fact it does, we will need a sample of 400 informants. Alternatively, if the preference division which is considered to be of marketing importance is a 70:30 split and we are only prepared to accept a 1 per cent risk of error in our conclusion, we will require a sample of at least 170 informants.

If, furthermore, we wish to obtain the same level of accuracy in different sub-groups of the sample, then we will require at least the number of interviews indicated in each of the sub-groups.

INTRODUCING THE PRODUCT

Most product tests are conducted 'blind': the products under test are identifiable only by code numbers, letters or combinations. In some cases, however, it may be desirable to identify the products to informants by using branded packs. This would be done in order to embody in the consumer's reactions the elements of brand image and expectation. Thus, the product tested 'blind' will be judged on the basis of its performance related to the informant's memory of experience in the product field. Judgement of a branded product will be influenced by attitudes and will be based upon comparisons with the expectations established by the brand name.

In most product tests, the objective is to assess only the physical properties of the product and a blind test is more appropriate. Where, however, we are testing a new formulation of a brand with a pronounced image and reputation it is important to judge not only whether the product is, *per se*, acceptable, but also whether it can 'live with' the brand image. In such a case, it is wise to identify the product to the informant.

TESTING SITUATION

The precise method of testing employed will have profound effects, not only upon the results of a product test, but also upon its economics. At the cheapest extreme, we have the on-the-spot test, using informants invited to a hall or to a caravan. This type of approach has two disadvantages: the sample recruited for the test is unlikely to be representative of the population being measured, and the testing situation is bound to be relatively unreal and superficial.

The first of these two problems can be avoided by interviewing informants at home, using some reliable sampling procedure. The second is avoided by allowing the informant more time to test the product and to comment upon it. This is done by leaving the product in the home: a placement test.

The advantage of the 'Town Hall' test, or similar operations, lies in its lower cost. Also, there are instances where any other type of test is not practical, e.g. in assessing the design of a bulky item — a washing-machine or a gas fire. Alternatively, a test of this type may be recommended as a preliminary to more detailed testing, for example, in 'sifting out' absolute 'non-runners'.

Despite these advantages and uses, the wisdom of 'Town Hall' testing should be questioned thoroughly for any project for which it is considered. If there is any risk that a snap judgement could be misleading, the method should be avoided.

It is also important to allow the informant to perform all of the operations necessary to form a judgement of a product. For example, in a test of a food product, the housewife should be given the opportunity to assess all relevant considerations, e.g. ease of storage, ease of opening, preparation, keeping qualities and, perhaps most important, the reactions of those people to whom she is expected to serve the product. Only those elements which we can absolutely guarantee to hold constant can be omitted from the judgement process and, again, only when they can be shown not to have any differential effects upon reactions to other elements of the product.

TESTING METHODS

Probably the most widespread form of test is the paired comparison, where an informant is asked to test and compare two products. Two variations exist:

(i) Simultaneous trial: where both products are in the possession of the informant, allowing of direct comparisons. This approach is the most common and should certainly be used if it is important to force a choice between two products.

(ii) Sequential trial: where, although the informant is asked to test both products, only one is in her possession at any one time. This approach can be said to be more realistic in that the consumer is unlikely to compare competitive brands simultaneously in life. However, it must be recognized that the process of product testing is inherently unrealistic and marginal realism is probably not a satisfactory basis upon which to judge a method. A more important virtue of this method is that it reduces the risk of a single, very obvious difference between two products clouding the whole judgement process.

One advantage of the sequential trial method is that it allows for a greater degree of control of the informant's exposure to the products. This can be particularly important in relation to the order in which two products are to be tested. The 'order effect' is a notorious problem in this type of research: the way in which the order of testing two products may well influence their relative assessments. If it is expected that order effects may influence the results of a project, but paired comparisons are still required, the following rules should be adopted:

(i) Sequential trial methods should be used.

(ii) A time gap sufficient to subdue the effects of the first trial should be allowed before the second trial.

(iii) The order in which the products are tested should be carefully controlled and balanced across the sample.

(iv) If the worst comes to the worst, the sample size should be large enough for the results of the second trial of each informant to be rejected and for the remainder to be treated as a monadic test, i.e. as if each person tested one product only.

A monadic test is one where a sample of informants is asked to test only one product. Their reactions are then compared with those of a second sample of informants asked to test the other product. Statistically and economically, the method is inferior to the Paired Comparison Test, but these disadvantages are fully outweighed in the appropriate situation, such as when exposure to one product may have a strong influence upon reactions to the second or where products differ radically in respect of something which is obvious but not necessarily related to their performance.

Frequently, of course, a testing programme involves more than two products to be compared. Again, the most economical approach is to ask a single sample of informants to test all of the products. This, however, has its dangers. If, for example, in a comparison of three products one is very different from the other two which, in turn, only differ marginally, the large difference will tend to cloud the informant's ability to discriminate between the two relatively similar products. In this situation, three alternative approaches are available:

(i) A series of monadic tests.

(ii) A series of paired comparison tests, facing each of the products with a control product.

(iii) A series of paired comparison tests, facing each product with every other product – a 'Round Robin' design.

The more alike are any two products within the total range, the greater is the desirability of the last of these three options.

MEASUREMENT CRITERIA

The basis of any product test must be comparison, either with another product in the same test or with past experience. No method of absolute measurement of reactions exists or can be developed in isolation, since every predictor relies for its recognition upon past events.

In any individual test, the comparison to be used will depend upon the problem under consideration and upon the availability of relevant data from previous tests. Thus:

1 A new product's performance could be compared with an existing brand in the same field (in which case the brand selected will be that from which our product is expected to gain sales) or with the results of earlier tests of products with known subsequent performance.

2 A revised formulation will be compared with the existing product.

3 A declining brand, tested for diagnostic reasons, will be compared with the brand(s) to which it is thought to be losing ground.

4 A revised formulation designed to check losses to a competitive brand will be compared with that brand and with the existing product.

5 Two or more alternative formulations will be compared with each other.

More than one comparison may clearly be needed in a single test. Thus, a number of variations of a new product designed to compete with an existing brand will be compared with each other and with the existing brand.

Simple preference between two or more products is the most common basis for judgement but is not always appropriate. Thus, it is important in some tests to consider conditional preferences: the product thought to be more suitable for given purposes or situations of some special import. The final selection of criteria will be based upon the action which is proposed at the end of the test.

Suppose, for example, that we are the manufacturers of a leading brand of toilet soap which, we know, succeeds on the basis of an image of simple, unsophisticated efficiency. If we now decide to add to our range by producing a luxury soap intended to sell on a platform of skin treatment, a test of simple preference between the new soap and our existing brand would not be wholly appropriate. It would form one of the relevant comparisons, in checking upon likely losses from our own brand, if these are feared (i.e. if we suspect that some of our customers may be won over by the planned creative platform). Otherwise, we must compare with other brands which are currently fulfilling the selected need in the market. If, then, we have developed more than one version of our new soap, simple preference should not be the criterion for comparing the different formulations. Rather, we must relate our criterion to our platform by choosing the formulation which is preferred for 'kindness to the skin' or some other appropriate verbalization of the requirement. In this way, we will select the product which stands the best chance of surviving with our concept: the product least likely to lead to fatal disappointment of the buyer who has allowed herself to be convinced by our advertising.

Clearly, then, there are a number of points at which basic choices must be made in designing a product test. Very rarely is there one correct method: the choice must depend upon precise and detailed consideration of the objectives of the research. Because the situation is so open-ended, the discussion is best continued in the form of a series of examples based upon actual problems.

Examples of Product Tests

EXAMPLE I — ECONOMICAL TESTING

The product in this case was a supermarket own-branded range of food products for immediate consumption. Within quite narrow limits the range was pre-ordained, the launch was imminent and funds were not plentiful.

On the grounds of speed and economy, 'Town Hall' testing was selected. This selection implied a recognition of certain short-comings in the research, but was accepted on the basis that, in the time available, the only possible use of the research was to weed out absolute non-runners. Since the criterion was not strict, the sample size employed could be small – 100 informants per product. These informants were a selection of people who ever consumed each of the product lines.

The testing method was an on-the-spot trial of the new products in comparison with products drawn from one of two similar ranges of known success. The measurement adopted was simple preference, qualified by spontaneous comments regarding the two products. The latter could, in turn, be compared with known formulation differences between the products.

As a result of the testing, two lines were returned for reformulation and another was re-tested. The latter provides an example of a problem which can frequently be encountered in product testing – inconsistencies in production. The two tests of the same product produced quite different results, a difference which could be traced back to batch production differences. This can occur particularly often with trial manufacture and points to the need for repeat testing or testing over several batches.

EXAMPLE 2 – BLIND TESTING

Here we have a culinary product – a major brand losing ground to a competitor. As part of a programme of diagnostic research, a product test was used to investigate the existence of any physical shortcoming in the declining brand.

This problem permits an almost classical consideration of the points raised in earlier paragraphs. In terms of the sample, three groups were of interest:

(a) Customers remaining loyal to our brand.
(b) Customers converted from our brand to the competitor.
(c) Customers converted to the competitor from brands other than ours.

Clearly, the test should be blind, since the sole interest was in physical properties. It must involve home placement, since differences would be reflected in conditions of use, and it should be a paired comparison test of our product and the competitor, since product differences were only marginal.

The criteria of measurement adopted were extended beyond simple preference to conditional preference for certain aspects of the appearance and performance of the products, including factors which featured in the advertising for the two brands.

This test allowed us to say that both brands were being advertised wisely in that each was preferred for those aspects related to its own promotional platform. Further, these two platforms appeared to be related to a real division of the market, since the users of each brand remained loyal to it in their preferences, even in the blind test. Thus, the results can be set out as:

	Users of A	Users of B
Overall preference	A	B
Preference for items promoted by A	A	A
Preference for items promoted by B	B	B

The conclusion to be drawn is that our brand has in the past held the support of a number of incompletely satisfied customers. The advent of the new brand, providing the qualities they sought, inevitably led to a certain loss of trade. Any attempt to modify our product to match the competitor in this respect must be accompanied by caution to ensure that our existing advantages amongst our loyal buyers are not lost. Further, even if we can achieve this, could we afford to promote our brand on the new platform in direct competition or will this, too, endanger our existing franchise? The final solution was to employ the spare capacity resulting from the decline in sales to produce a second brand, directly competitive with the new brand but capable of living alongside our own existing brand.

EXAMPLE 3 — BRAND NAMES

This case allows us to consider the effects which brand names can have upon reactions to a product. Indeed, it was designed in part to illustrate these effects.

Informants were asked to taste four beers: two light ales and two extra-strength pale ales; and, amongst other things, to rank them in terms of alcoholic strength. Our first sample tested the beers

blind, relying only upon taste and sensation to reach their decision. The resulting overall ranking was:

Strongest —	Light Ale A
	Extra-Strength Ale I
	Extra-Strength Ale II
Weakest —	Light Ale B

A similar sample of informants was asked to perform the same
test, but with branded beers, the branding adding image and
reputation to the bases of judgement, with the following result:

Strongest —	Extra-Strength Ale II
	Extra-Strength Ale I
	Light Ale A
Weakest —	Light Ale B

Not only does this switch illustrate the effects of branding, but
also it points to the danger of accepting responses at face value.
In the blind test, one of the weaker beers was said by informants to
be stronger, on the basis of its tasting 'stronger'. Thus, it is important to relate claimed differences to known physical properties.

EXAMPLE 4 – CONSUMER EXPECTATIONS

As a further example of the way in which reactions can be influenced by expectations, we can take the case of a household cleaning
product. In this case, three different samples of informants were
recruited. At a first interview, each sample was exposed to a
different promotional platform for the product. Informants were
then all given identical samples of the product for test.

At the concept stage, the ratings given for appeal showed a
higher interest in Concept 'D', and a lower interest in Concept
'S', than in Concept 'C' – a ranking D > C > S. When the product
was rated after trial, there were differences between the three
samples, the ranking being C > D > S.

It would seem that Concept 'D' is exciting but dangerous, in
that it builds up expectations which the product, in use, is unable
to fulfil. At the same time, Concept 'S' is so unattractive that it
leads to an underrating of the product in use. Here, then, is what

the product test should be measuring and the reason for its existence alongside laboratory testing systems: it should measure not whether a product works but whether the consumer feels that it works as well as expected.

EXAMPLE 5 — EXTENDED USE TEST

The radically new product always faces the product tester with an extreme problem, due to the lack of a relevant comparison. If the product is in a new field, designed to satisfy a newly recognizable consumer need, there is no existing brand for comparison. It would be unwise to take a product from a different product field for comparison, since reactions will be based upon a different set of circumstances.

In one particular case, this problem was diminished but not solved by comparing the product with two things: the concept and itself. Firstly, a sample of informants was exposed to the concept and questioned. The results appeared to be favourable, although this could only be a subjective assessment. Informants were then given a sample of the product for a trial and were later questioned. Where comparisons were possible, the product in use was better received than had been the concept.

As a third stage, however, a second sample of the product was issued to the informants and, later, a third trial was conducted. At each of these tests, the ratings given to the product deteriorated, quite drastically at the last stage. As a result, the product was shelved for a time.

The establishment of a basis for comparison and, hence, for decision, is only one specialized use of the extended test. The test form is used most frequently either where it is suspected that initial exposure to the product may build up artificially high ratings due to novelty value, or where repeated use is thought likely to exhaust interest in the product or, conversely, where it is expected that repeated experience will be required in order to establish a 'taste' for the product.

EXAMPLE 6 — FACTORIAL DESIGN

In the development of a new product, there are generally a number of ways in which the formulation can be varied. Thus, a new hair-dressing for men might be varied in terms of colour, perfume and consistency. The separation of these three elements for the purposes of product testing is both uneconomical and dangerous. The danger lies in the possibility of two or more of the elements interacting with each other to influence consumers' reactions. Thus, we may find the 'best' colour and the 'best' perfume, but, for some reason of manufacture or perception, the combination of the two may be inferior to another combination of two variations which have mutually beneficial effects.

The type of test suited to a problem of this nature is one employing factorial design. Suppose, for example, that there are two variations of each of the three elements mentioned above – two colours, two perfumes and two levels of consistency: thus, it is possible to combine these three elements into eight different products, i.e.

Colour	Perfume	Consistency
a	a	a
a	a	b
a	b	a
a	b	b
b	a	a
b	a	b
b	b	a
b	b	b

The test can then be designed so that each of a sample of informants compares two of the products, all possible pairings being used. (In our example, there would be twenty-eight pairings.) The results of the test can then be subjected to an analysis technique known as Analysis of Variance in order to show which, if any, of the three variables has a significant effect upon consumer reactions to the product and whether any two or all three of the variables reveal an interaction effect such as that mentioned above.

Separation of the elements for testing could not take full account of these possible interactions. Further, the process would be more expensive. Thus, if we demanded that each factor must be judged by 100 informants, and we conducted the three tests separately, we would need to interview a total of 300 people. In the factorial design, sixteen of the twenty-eight possible pairings of test products would involve comparisons of the two variations of each of the three elements. Thus to obtain 100 reactions to each of these direct comparisons we would require a total sample of less than 200 informants.

EXAMPLE 7 – DISCRIMINATION

In all of our discussion up to this point, we have been dealing only with preferences or conditional preferences. One of the major problems associated with product testing is that of interpreting the results. Suppose, for example, that a paired test produced a preference for product X of 60 per cent and a preference for product Y of 40 per cent: at one extreme, this could mean that the population under study divided into two parts, 60 per cent having a preference for one type of product, 40 per cent for a different type. At the other extreme, it could mean that 20 per cent had a preference for a product like X, the remaining 80 per cent not being able to discriminate between X and Y, but refusing to admit their inability, thus stating a preference at random and dividing equally between X and Y. Alternatively, of course, the true situation could be anywhere between the two extremes. Without definite evidence in addition to the preference result, the only conclusion which could safely be drawn would be that there was a marginal preference for X over Y.

One partial solution to this problem is to repeat the test on the same group of informants, re-coding the test products so that the subject is not aware of the duplication. Thus, in a test to compare two dessert-mixes, we might obtain the following result:

	%
Prefer mix A	55
Prefer mix B	42
No preference	3
	100

On repeating the test, the result might emerge again in favour of mix A:

	%
Prefer mix A	52
Prefer mix B	43
No preference	5
	100

We can now consider the two tests together:

		Prefer A	Test 1 Prefer B	No Preference	
	Prefer A	32	19	1	= 52%
Test 11	Prefer B	22	20	1	= 43%
	No preference	1	3	1	= 5%
		55%	42%	3%	

Thus, 32 per cent of our sample preferred mix A in both tests and 20 per cent preferred mix B in both tests. The remaining 48 per cent of the sample had no preference or gave answers which were inconsistent between the two tests. In interpreting the results, we assume that the 47 per cent who gave inconsistent preferences were, in fact, unable to distinguish between the two mixes. Even then, however, we would expect some of these 'guessers' to be consistent purely by chance. Thus, 41 per cent of our sample stated a preference in both tests but were inconsistent. We would expect a similar proportion to be consistent in their preferences (i.e. to fall in the two marked cells of the table) despite a similar inability to discriminate. Further, assuming that this proportion would be divided equally between the two cells, we can reasonably say that all of the 20 per cent who consistently chose mix B were, in fact, 'guessers' and that only about one in ten informants had real preference, all of them for mix A.

EXAMPLE 9 — TRIANGULAR TESTING

An alternative approach to this problem is the triangular test. Here an informant is presented with three samples, two of which are identical, and is asked to pick the 'odd man out'. Only those informants who make a correct choice are then asked to state a preference. Thus, the test is setting out to answer a dual question: 'Can people tell the difference between these two products and, if so, which do they prefer?'

A test of this type is particularly suited to the situation where a manufacturer wishes to revise his product for technical reasons. Thus, a drink manufacturer, through amalgamation, acquired an alternative method of producing his product and, wishing to rationalize his operation, considered the possibility of rejecting one or other of the alternative production methods open to him. Having a well-established brand, he was not prepared to risk his consumer franchise in order to carry through the rationalization.

The test consisted of inviting consumers of the product to carry out a triangular discrimination test upon the products of the two methods, with the following result:

	Result of test	Random expectation
	%	%
Correct discrimination	52	33
Prefer old	21	16½
Prefer new	31	16½
Incorrect discrimination	48	67
	100	100

This result can be compared with that which might be expected from a sample of informants responding at random (the second column above). Thus, we would expect one-third of our sample to guess the correct answer to the discrimination test and then to divide equally in their preferences. The two columns appear to differ and, on the sample size involved, can be shown to differ statistically.

In our interpretation of the results, we reason that the 48 per cent who gave an incorrect answer to the discrimination test represent only two-thirds of the people who could not perceive a difference between the two drinks, the other one-third having guessed the correct answer.

Thus, amongst the 52 per cent of our sample giving the correct answer, we expect to find 24 per cent who are, in fact, unable to discriminate and only 28 per cent true discrimination. Further, we can reason that the 24 per cent of non-discriminators will state a random preference, dividing equally between the two drinks. Our conclusion, then, to be qualified by statements of statistical accuracy, is that the situation is as follows:

	%	
Able to discriminate	28	(i.e. 52 − 24)
Prefer old method	9	(i.e. 21 − 12)
Prefer new method	19	(i.e. 31 − 12)
Unable to discriminate	72	(i.e. 48 + 24)

The problem then becomes a subjective one: is a minority of 9 per cent who would notice the change and would be displeased by it of marketing import?

8 | Advertising Research

MISS A. BURDUS
Director of Research, Garland-Compton Ltd.

Advertising agencies in this country were amongst the pioneers in the use of market data for marketing planning. Their constant demand for data with which they could establish brand shares and target markets was followed up by demands for further information about the people whom they were trying to reach, inform and persuade. Their insistence on having this data and having it soundly based is reflected in the number of established research companies who owe their foundation if not their present support to specific agencies.

In parallel with this development of basic market measurement techniques which would permit the setting of targets and measurement of results came a demand for pre-testing and post-testing advertising and also for research which would establish basic principles of advertising and give any agency who used these an edge over his competitors.

Basic Principles

Today the emphasis on establishing basic principles is less. This is largely because of a growing awareness of the complexity of the marketing and advertising process. There are very few general rules deduced from research which are not so blatantly obvious that everyone adopts them anyhow, which will stand up in any particular marketing and advertising situation and which will prove to be always sound. The fashion is now for fitting horses to

L

courses and for regarding with deep suspicion any man who tries to sell a touchstone or formula which will serve in all circumstances.

The decline in the race for the alchemist's stone has also partly been the result of people getting their fingers burnt and the realization that we are dealing with a dynamic process. Market research as it exists is largely historical. It is based on information collected about the past and is peculiarly inept at predicting the future except on the broadest of canvasses.

If we try to analyse which elements of an advertisement lead to its success then we find ourselves collecting data over time. Two sorts of data are necessary, an analysis of the advertisement and a measurement of the response of the consumer. There are dangers in both of these. If we analyse too closely what has gone into an advertisement in the past we may neglect completely new elements which might go into the advertisements of the future. If we are concerned about the comparative effectiveness of jingles and orchestral music we may neglect the use of electronic music or the use of silence.

On the other hand measuring response is equally hazardous if we try to carry it out across a lot of different advertising. This is particularly so in respect of advertisements from other advertisers whose intentions we can only guess and whose marketing situation we know only in outline.

Were it possible to use sales alone as a measurement of advertising effectiveness then part of this problem would not exist, but sales cannot be used in isolation for two reasons. Not all advertising is intended to maximize or increase sales, and experimentation has demonstrated what common sense should have suggested, that in many markets other elements in the marketing mix than advertising have the major effect on sales.

Because sales taken in isolation cannot be used as a measure of advertising effectiveness advertisers wishing to assess their campaigns have had to develop special techniques. In doing so they have had to think in terms of measuring the intermediate objectives of their advertising which has meant adopting an implicit or explicit model of how they believe the advertising process works. They have had also to think in terms of specific objectives for particular campaigns such as establishing the brand name, communicating a new message, attracting the attention of a new group of potential consumers and so on.

As people have become clearer about the model of the advertising process which they use and as they have become more specific in their advertising objectives, the feasibility of collecting data across campaigns, across product groups has receded. It can still be done but it has to be done with greater sensitivity and a greater understanding of its limitations than in the recent past.

This does not mean that the search for general principles has been completely abandoned but that people have become more realistic in their objective. In the field of media planning, for example, it is more common to carry out studies which will help determine appropriate expenditure levels, media and media weights for individual brands or product groups than to look for a general solution.

The trend, therefore, has been away from the collecting of general principles and towards research designed to help create better advertising. This implies also a swing away from the pre-testing of advertising, the assigning of pass and fail marks to complete or almost complete advertisements, and towards more constructive research at every stage of the advertising process.

Determining the Strategy

There are four stages of the advertising process at which research can be and is usefully applied. The most important of these is strategic planning, when the marketing man works with his agency in order to assimilate all the data available on his brand and market and to determine from it what his advertising policy should be.

At this stage, therefore, it could be said that the advertiser is using all the data discussed in other sections of this book. He is using government or industry statistics on his market's total size, he is using retail audit or consumer panel information to determine his brand share and the trends within his market, he is using attitude research to determine how people feel about buying and using his product and image research to determine how they see it.

There is a temptation when describing the application of

research in this way to write as if we started each time with a new product and a clean sheet of paper, but in reality our marketing man is also including, in his assessment of his position at this strategic stage, the effects of his previous advertising policy. His specific objectives and his beliefs about how advertising works will affect what measurements he needs on his previous advertising. If, for example, his previous policy has been to try to make people feel guilty if they do not use his product, then he needs at this stage of determining his new strategy a measurement of how successful he has been.

This must not be taken to imply an *ad hoc* approach to research. On the contrary it is crucial to the marketing man that he should be able to make an assessment of his previous strategy in a comparative way and this means that as far as possible his research should be long-term, consistent and comparative.

It is worth stressing that at the strategic stage the researcher can supply the relevant information to the marketing man and to the account group, he can help in the interpretation and he can give his advice, but the strategy will rarely emerge self-evident from the data. In nearly every case at least two alternatives emerge, to capitalize on the things which make you different, or to compensate for them. The decision of which road to take lies with the marketing man.

This type of research, used to determine the advertising strategy for a brand, is important and most researchers would submit that given a limited research budget this is where it should be spent, because getting the target audience, the objectives, the message and the media right are fundamental to the success of the campaign.

Research on Advertisements

This type of research is different from research into advertisements and the effectiveness of advertising campaigns. People have been trying for many years to test advertising and to demonstrate how it could be improved and this is an area of great dispute within market research. The waters have become a little clearer since people began to distinguish more firmly between two forms of research on advertisements: research which is designed to help us make a better advertisement while we are making it, and research designed to demonstrate the potential effectiveness of that advertisement against some outside criterion.

In a paper given at ESOMAR in 1969, Gregory of Gallup demonstrated that there was a difference between what the research managers of advertising agencies and the research managers of manufacturing companies were looking for from research on advertisements; in general the latter were more likely to be looking for tests which would demonstrate likely efficacy, the former were more likely to be looking for ways of building a better advertisement.

Developing the Advertisement

Both these sorts of advertisement research have a part to play in the advertising process but it is important to distinguish between them because they demand completely different research methods and facilities. The major distinction is that creative or development research, designed to make better advertisements, tends to take place while creative work is in process and to help a remoulding, reshaping of advertisements; it must therefore be quick, cheap, flexible and adaptable to the specific problem. Research designed to evaluate the potential effectiveness of an advertisement must be consistent, comparative and outward-looking, comparing the advertisements with some outside criterion, whilst the creative research can look inwards for the best of several possible alternatives.

Looking more closely at the use of research to build better advertisements, it would appear that research has three main functions at this stage and the first of these is interpretation. The information available on the product, the brand and the consumer must be made available to the creative man and this means that the researcher must digest and regurgitate it because it is useless and unimaginative to hand a technically well written but indigestible research report to a creative man and expect him to read it. The researcher must also bring the consumer back to life. By the time the number of people in the market has been boiled down into groups and described as points of a percentage the real housewife, motor mechanic or doctor to whom the creative man hopes to talk has got buried under a welter of statistics.

Qualitative research designed to bring the consumer back to life, to let the creative man hear her talking in her own language about her problems and her views of the product he is trying to advertise, is a very real part of creative research. The researcher is acting as the link between the creative man and the consumer and at this stage he is opening the ears of the creative man to the consumer.

He also must expose the ideas of the creative man to the consumer and this is his other function in creative research, to give the creative man the opportunity of seeing how the consumer is likely to react to his ideas.

With this need in view several agencies have been encouraged to develop and run creative workshops. These vary in their form and facilities but usually the principle is that they are a facility and not a testing procedure. They are a facility whereby the creative man can try out his ideas on the consumer and see which of several concepts is most likely to succeed, whether the pack he is designing is creating the impression he intends, whether housewives are familiar with the phrase he wants to use and whether it communicates what he intends.

The main feature of this type of creative research is that it tends to be inward-looking. It determines which of several ideas is the best, not whether any of these are any good; whether the housewife understands the idea but not whether she is likely to act upon it when faced by both it and the competitive claims. Some researchers concentrate on qualitative research at this stage, believing that the free-flowing ideas of a group discussion or depth interview are more productive creatively than a structured interview. Others prefer quantitative measurements in an experimental design as they like to work from numbers and strict comparisons.

This type of research tends to be carried out in workshops, and workshops imply the bringing of the consumer to the research rather than the research to the consumer. This is principally for two reasons. If creative research is to be useful it must allow rough material to be used. This means that when someone has spent two days making a single mock-up pack we cannot ask him to make twelve more so that interviewers can take them round door to door. We must bring the informants to the pack. The second consideration is cost. Usually people wish to use creative research in a constructive and developing way. If they take three ideas and try them out they don't necessarily want to go ahead with 'the best'; they may want to modify two of them in the light of this experience and try again. This implies a series of small projects and a research bill kept strictly under control. This can be achieved if an informant is subjected to several different tests at the same time in a workshop rather than being asked about one problem only in a survey.

This concentration on small-scale research where comparisons are made between alternatives calls for the use of different statistical techniques from those used in survey work, because at this stage we are concerned primarily with the statistics appropriate to experiments with small numbers of people.

Testing the Advertisement

The same could be said to be to some extent true of evaluative research, research designed to demonstrate the potential effectiveness of an advertisement. At present no one has a technique which can give a simple score which will relate directly to the sales effectiveness from advertisements. Or if such techniques exist they have yet to be proved. In some senses the demands made upon those working in advertising research to demonstrate the soundness of their techniques are greater than those placed upon other sections of market research. Any test of an advertisement should be shown to be sensitive, reliable and valid before it is used. That is, it should discriminate between the advertisements it is designed to test, should do so consistently, and should measure what it is designed to measure. It is relatively easy to demonstrate the first two characteristics for widely accepted tests but the third is more difficult. If the validity of a test of potential effectiveness were to be demonstrated, someone somewhere would have to run both the 'good' and the 'bad' advertisements and watch their effect. As most tests have a certain face validity few people are willing to experiment in this way, although occasionally accidental experiments have occurred. Tests do not usually classify advertisements as harmful or beneficial but rather indicate that if you use one commercial you are more likely to achieve the effect you intend or to achieve it to a greater extent than if you use the other.

Faith in an advertising manager's judgement has meant that sometimes the commercial with the lower score has appeared, but such experiments are not common.

Where a manufacturing company, the only people with adequate access to data, has demonstrated a positive relationship between sales and pre-test results it tends to keep the details of such research to itself. This is understandable, as the data is expensively won.

The constant application of an evaluative technique of some kind has become much more common with the advent of television. This was due partly to the timing of the arrival of a new untried medium, partly to the encouragement of some of the television contractors and partly to the high investment in production and media costs which each television commercial entailed. It was not surprising that the advent of commercial television brought with it new testing techniques which were asked to demonstrate their efficacy with a greater stringency than had been applied in relation to the tests of advertising for any other medium.

Within this category of testing are techniques which in some terminology would be called both pre- and post-testing. The concept of evaluative research embraces both testing a finished or almost finished advertisement when it has appeared on the air or in its intended medium once and possibly in a test area. It is distinguished from other forms of research in that the emphasis is on testing rather than developing and that it involves usually a single exposure of the advertisement.

The concept of testing in this sense implies that the advertisement is being compared with some standard or alternative. Logically the question must be, 'Is this advertisement better than the advertisement the competitor is currently using?' but equally it can be whether the advertisement is up to the standard known to be necessary in this product field, or whether it is better than some readily available alternative. (Should we in fact continue to run the commercial which is currently on the air?)

Such questions imply a direct or indirect comparison and both are used although the former tends to be more expensive than the latter. It also tends, however, to be technically more satisfactory, because when the comparison is indirect it involves either the collection of data over time or the collection of data across brand or product groups or both; neither is entirely satisfactory.

The companies who consistently measure the response to their commercials when they have appeared once on the air tend to make indirect comparisons. Not all companies do this and there is no reason why two new commercials should not be tried in two regions at the same time, or why the response to a competitor's commercial should not be measured when it appears on the screen. In practice it is more common for people who engage in this sort of testing to have a standard test procedure and to evaluate each new score they obtain against scores they have achieved in the past.

Exposing the Advertisement

This type of research, carried out after the commercial has appeared on the network once, tends to be carried out by those who believe it is important that the commercial should be seen in its intended setting. This is a severe constraint because it means that all measures which are applied must relate to what is remembered of the commercial and this type of measurement is therefore used primarily by those who think that the memorability of the commercial is an essential feature of its effectiveness.

Some practitioners compromise here and, while believing that it is important that the commercial should be seen in the home, do not use normal on-air testing but try to simulate the normal viewing situation as closely as possible by bringing small screen portable projectors into the home. Others believe that this type of intrusion destroys the naturalness they are trying to achieve and that once the artificiality of the situation has been accepted there is no advantage in using the informant's own home. The fact that this type of research tends to be expensive and cumbersome and usually necessitating the making of special prints of the advertisements, has no doubt encouraged the acceptance of this view, although a certain amount of this type of research is done and it may well have certain advantages in terms of security and sampling.

If a natural setting is considered important then the ideal situation would be one where the commercial was transmitted through the respondent's own set but at a time convenient to the researcher.

This can be achieved in several ways. The respondent can be asked to watch TV at a certain time, for example, but not told why (and a control sample asked to watch the alternative channel if necessary). In theory a commercial could be piped into her set from a van outside. Unfortunately this device does not appear to be strictly legal in this country.

In the United States there are two other possibilities. There are apartment blocks and other units which have their own system into which special shows and commercials can be fed. These blocks can then be used for trial purposes. The main difficulty with such units is that they tend to contain a homogeneous population not necessarily relevant to the advertiser. The other alternative is a city which has a complete split cable system. This means that the television contractors can feed one set of material into one lot of houses without the consumers being aware of this. The whole town is equipped with both retail audit facilities and diary panels. Sensibly, however, in order to prevent the residents from becoming over sophisticated as respondents the facilities are mainly used for experiments in media weight, strategies and alternative media rather than for testing individual commercials. This facility is unlikely to be developed in this country unless the laws relating to broadcasting and the transmission of television are changed.

There is a considerable body of opinion which holds that attempts at realism are unnecessary. This argument is based on the belief that it does not matter how artificial the test appears to be provided its validity is established. The snag in this is that validity is difficult to demonstrate.

The most common type of testing outside the home is in cinemas used specifically for the purpose. Schwerin (who no longer operates in this country) was perhaps the first practitioner here to test commercials by exposing them to people in the context of a feature film in a small theatre. A.S.L. (A.S.I. in the States) and Clucas similarly use large audiences and large screens. The main arguments against exposure of commercials in this way come from those who believe that the photography on a large screen looks quite different from that on a small screen; and also from those who believe that people react differently in kind as well as extent when in a large group.

The third alternative which is becoming increasingly popular is to show the advertisements to people outside their homes and family circle but in relatively small groups such as are found in the Telpex system, the A.S.L., M.A.P.S. and M.I.L. buses and the new Gallup facility in Regent Street.

Types of Measurement

Of more significance than the location of the testing must be the nature of the measurement, but the two are to some extent interdependent. Thus interviewing the day after a commercial has appeared implies relying on recall of the commercial as a basic measure; use of large audiences restricts the applicability of open-ended questions or autonomic responses. Both these examples are generalizations and open to qualification; other measurements can be used the day after a single showing but in general this would require larger samples and more expensive research and so on.

The choice of measurement used at one time to be dependent primarily on what could be measured and on common sense. Thus it seemed obvious to some people that if an advertisement had been effective people would remember it. The more recent involvement of psychologists in advertisement research, and their insistence that remembering the source of the message is irrelevant to remembering or accepting the message itself, has been accepted by some but has had little effect on those who have found measures of recall of advertising sensible and useful in the past. In circumstances where this experience is backed up by a demonstrated correlation between scores and sales, such persistence is understandable.

While criticizing what has been measured in the past, new practitioners have been encouraged to postulate what should be measured and have had to point out that this is dependent upon how you believe advertising works and what you were trying to achieve (Joyce, 1967). In place of common-sense measurements there have been attempts to create models of the advertising process and to develop measurements which relate to them. In some cases the models have been *post hoc* and in some the measurements no more standardized or valid than those developed without the theoretical framework. Some, but not all, of the measurements that are used have been tested for sensitivity and reliability; few, if any, have been shown to be valid.

The most prolonged debate in this area was probably stimulated by Schwerin's insistence in the mid-1960s that their competitive preference measure, which was the cornerstone of their technique, could be shown to be related to sales. The debate between the theoreticians and statisticians was prolonged and Schwerin no longer operate in this country. It is improbable that any company would put up such strong claims for any one of their measuring instruments today.

The measurement consisted in outline of asking people to choose which brand from a product group they would prefer to have if they were to win a competition. The same question was repeated later in the testing session after the commercial had been shown and the shift in response was believed to be related to the effectiveness of the commercial in persuading people towards the brand.

This measurement has several variations, some more practical than others. A.S.L. include a similar question but do not imply a series of competitions, believing that some gamblers think their chances improve when they switch choices. A similar but more sophisticated and very stringent technique is used by some companies in the United States when they show three commercials together, the test commercial and the current commercials from the two leading competitive brands. The informant is asked her product choice before the test and again having seen the three commercials, and the score is calculated on the basis of the number who move towards and away from each brand.

This pattern has many variations. Sometimes people are not asked questions at both stages but are given vouchers to spend, points to allot and so on. All the measurements are designed to determine whether the consumer is more likely to choose your brand after exposure to the advertisement than before.

The striving for reality in connexion with the vehicle of exposure (in the home, in a bus, in a cinema) is also seen in the measurements which are made. The most common, when low-priced packaged goods are involved, is to ask the informant to select a brand as a gift at the end of the test session, but the problem of the person who chooses atypically because of the test situation rather than because of the advertisement is inherent. Yankelovitch in the United States has experimented with releasing people in a supermarket immediately after a test session, other people have tried offering the product or a sum of money in a postal test (although this is more commonly used for concept testing).

These measures tend to relate to the end of the process which most models imply when describing how advertising works. They are measures of propensity to move people towards purchase. Measures at the other end of the extreme are considered equally important by some. The ability of an advertisement to attract attention, sustain interest, imprint a brand name, associate the brand with a specific idea and arouse the informant are all considered important to a greater or lesser degree and included in the many measuring systems.

Not all the measurements are satisfactory, however, and perhaps the most troublesome are those designed to measure the extent to which an advertisement succeeds in attracting attention. Although measures of attention are fairly commonly used in other fields of applied psychology in advertising research there is still great dependence on recall.

Recall is such a complex process, involving perception, memory, suppression and verbalization, that few psychologists feel happy when using it as a measure of attention although the depth of their feeling is dependent upon the precise nature of the measurement (Haskin, 1964).

There was a fashion to distinguish between prompted and spontaneous recall and the two phrases are still in common use although the second, spontaneous recall, seems a strange concept and could be taken to imply a test dependent on free association! It would be more precise to talk about relevant and irrelevant prompting because every question must be a prompt. To ask what brands of dog food a woman can name seems fairly relevant (Axelrod, 1968); to ask what advertisements she saw on the screen earlier in the evening or the day before seems particularly irrelevant but it is extensively done.

There seem to be two current ways of measuring interest. One is to ask people whether they found the advertisement interesting (posing the question with greater or lesser degrees of subtlety), the other is to ask them to indicate their degree of interest in a non-verbal way. A.S.L., for example, have dials marked from 'dull' to 'interesting' which a proportion of their audience are asked to manipulate throughout the test session. It is possible to establish the typicality of the audience by watching its response to cartoons and other matter and to demonstrate that the test is sensitive in that it discriminates between advertisements, but the authors of the test would be the first to admit that they do not really know what it measures: its validity remains undetermined.

Non-verbal Measures

Another attempt in this direction was the construction of a test dependent on the showing of two commercials in parallel, both visible to the respondent at the same time, neither with a sound track. The sound was under the control of the informant who could choose which track to listen to, his choice being automatically recorded. It has been suggested that this is a measure of interest but it might equally be argued that it is a measure of obscurity, the informant switching to the least comprehensible commercial for elucidation!

A test which has been described but not, I think, taken seriously, is one where the clear perception of the advertisement is dependent upon physical exertion by the respondent, in this case manipulating a machine like a bicycle in order to make the commercial more visible! It is probable that such a technique would be more revealing of the personality of the respondent than the effectiveness or interest of the commercial.

Autonomic Measures

The differences between individuals is the main problem with the other group of non-verbal measurements used in advertising research, the measures dependent on the autonomic nervous system and related to emotional arousal. Individual thresholds vary so much that the measurements have to be calibrated for each respondent.

These measurements are all based on the physiological fact that the body reacts to emotional arousal in a way quite beyond our conscious control. Within this category fall measurements of eye blinks, the galvanic skin response (the detective story lie-detector), muscle tension, pupil dilation, breathing rate, heart beat and some others which are less easy to measure.

Apart from the question of individual thresholds these measurements suffer from two other major disadvantages. It is usually impossible to determine the nature or direction of the arousal, whether positive or negative, and to what specifically it is related. Most of these measures involve the respondent in at least some physical inconvenience, although it is true that with recent developments this is much less extreme than it used to be, and has been reduced, for example, to a simple finger stall for the P.G.R. (psychogalvanic skin response) measurement.

Verbal Measures

Measures of the other processes included in the various models of the advertising process tend to be dependent upon a verbal response, either written or oral. Thus people can be asked to write down the brand name or the main message or to tell it to the interviewer who in her turn writes it down.

Beyond the basic measures a great deal depends upon what the advertiser is looking for. Some believe it important that people should like their commercials, others that they should say they believe the message (in spite of experimental evidence that a state of suspended belief may in fact be preferable to either acceptance or rejection). An interesting study by Axelrod has demonstrated the degree to which some of these measures have better claims to usefulness than others.

The Effects of Research

All this produces a confused picture and could cause people to believe that the choice of technique and measurements within that technique does not particularly matter. Nothing could be further from the truth, because the techniques can quickly influence the sort of advertising which is produced. Any good copywriter can quickly learn to improve his score on a given test. If the test is not related to advertising effectiveness the results can be disastrous.

What is clear is that there is still a great deal of development work to be done in the construction of measuring instruments to be used at this stage. This is important because there are dividends to be reaped in using the same technique consistently over time; it makes every additional score more meaningful but to use the wrong technique consistently could be disastrous. At present the only solution is to use the technique which comes close to your beliefs about how advertising works and the peculiarities of your advertising or market.

Using Evaluative Research

The additional benefit which comes from consistently using the same technique is partly an administrative one but also partly due to the diagnostic use of evaluative research. The primary stated use of evaluative research is to determine whether a commercial should run. In practice this is rarely a real decision-point. It is common practice to use the type of measurements described above when the advertisement is in a finished or near-finished form and has already cost several thousand pounds to produce, and when air dates are very close. It is frequently the case that the decision must be how long should the commercial run or how quickly should it be replaced, because not to run it would involve the company in cancellation fees.

It is possible to amend a finished commercial; it is possible to learn from experience and produce a better commercial the next time. In order to do this, straightforward evaluative research must be supplemented by some form of diagnostic research. Some diagnostic measures are included in most evaluative testing, and supplementary research in the form of group discussion is not uncommon. These can often reveal why a commercial is not obtaining the expected response although they will not as clearly show what should be done about it.

The technique recently developed by Clucas is probably more diagnostic than evaluative in nature. It is at the opposite extreme from the autonomic responses in that the audience are asked to say what they were thinking about as each section of the commercial is exposed, and what they thought was being communicated. Although this technique largely avoids measurements based on memory some of its critics are unhappy about the way it breaks down a commercial into parts. While not discriminating between advertisements in a quantitative way the technique may produce insights into consumer reactions for the creative man who has to work with it!

Print Advertising Research

That this chapter so far has dealt so predominantly with television research reflects the emphasis which appears to be placed on research in the different media. Developments in print research have been influenced by the dominance of reading and noting both as a technique for evaluating advertisements and for campaign assessment. This technique is still widely used although it has many critics. Some people question whether the number of people saying that when they previously looked at a magazine they had read a particular advertisement is important or meaningful, others question whether it is accurate. Experiments have suggested a strong tendency for people to claim to have seen an advertisement which is similar to another or a continuation of a campaign.

Dummy magazines in which the editorial or copy are kept constant and the advertisements varied are probably used more extensively in the United States than in this country. They have the advantage of allowing any questions to be asked before and after the placement of the magazines which can be looked at under relaxed conditions in the informant's own home. The extent to which different measurements are used at the second interview is dependent upon the plan of the research.

Non-verbal and physiological measurements are also used to test print advertising. Machines which measure how long people look at each individual page of a marked-up folder or magazine have been developed first in Germany and more recently in this country. Print advertisements are sometimes exposed for very brief periods on a tachistoscope or with varying degrees of clarity to measure brand and message identification and the skin response is also measured on informants while looking at press advertisements. All the measures have the same advantages or disadvantages whether applied to this medium or to television.

Posters are sometimes tested in ways which have a broad similarity to Press, and cinema advertisements in a way not dissimilar from television commercials, but it seems true to say that the more

M

expensive the medium, the more likely is advertisement research to be carried out. Radio commercial research which is used extensively in Europe and to a certain extent in the United States is a rarity in this country, not because the problems do not exist but because the use of the medium and interest in this type of research tends to be low.

Campaign Effectiveness

Development and evaluative research, as they have been described so far, are research into individual advertisements. Some work has been done on the effect of repeated exposure of advertisements and some manufacturers repeat their evaluative research from time to time to try to detect wear out, but in general there is a jump from testing a single advertisement to trying to assess the effects of a total campaign so that future strategy can be modified and the whole procedure repeated.

Isolating the effects of one element in the marketing mix can usually be done only in an experimental situation where the element in question is varied either over time or between areas and all other things kept constant. It is possible in some circumstances to measure the effects of advertising, particularly when the advertising has a specific aim to which a measurement can be related, such as increasing awareness of the brand, changing ideas about a product in a specific direction and so on.

Those who try to carry out a consistent measurement of the effects of their advertising as opposed to the other elements in the marketing mix tend to either carry out annual or other regular surveys into current attitudes to their brands amongst purchasers and non-purchasers, or to carry out a regular index measurement like B.M.R.B.'s A.P.I., which allows them to watch fluctuations in the images of brands and the characteristics of users over time and to relate these to changes in advertising policy.

These types of measurement would normally be used to supplement or complement measurements of sales and other data about the brand's progress in the market. The circle is therefore complete and the continuous process of modification of advertising plans and the development of advertisements reaches the next stage.

This chapter has been an attempt to provide an overall view of advertising research today. It cannot be completely comprehensive but it is an attempt to provide a framework for people lost in the jungle of conflicting claims and opinions.

References

1 AXELROD, J. N. (1968), 'Attitude measures that predict purchase', *Journal of Advertising Research*, March.
2 FOTHERGILL, J. E. and JOYCE, T., *A Continuing System for Planning an Evaluating Advertising Campaign*, A.R.F. Conference, 1967.
3 GREGORY, W. and FANNING, J., *Researching Research — the Market for TV Commercial Pre-testing*, ESOMAR, 1969.
4 HASKINS, J. B. (1964), 'Factual recall as a measure of advertising effectiveness', *Journal of Advertising Research*, March.
5 JOYCE, T., *What Do We Know About How Advertising Works?* ESOMAR, 1967.
6 KONIG, G. and LOVELL, M. R. C., *Measurement of Pupil Dilation as a Market Research Tool*, ESOMAR, 1965.
7 MALONEY, J. C. (1962), 'Curiosity versus disbelief in advertising', *Journal of Advertising Research*.

9 | The Pre-Publication Evaluation (P.P.E.) of Advertising*

MICHAEL J. WEST
Research Director, Benton & Bowles Ltd.

In the previous chapter Ann Burdus has given an overview of advertising research. This chapter concentrates on one aspect of this field of research – the 'pre-testing' of advertising. For reasons which I will trace below, this particular type of research has generated more heated argument than almost any other. Opinions are diverse about what is possible and what is useful in the area of pre-testing; some are even of the opinion that pre-testing of advertising is not possible – and they may be right!

The method presented here is called the Pre-Publication Evaluation (P.P.E.) of advertising. I deliberately do not use the word 'test' because I think it implies a precise measurement of all aspects of the advertisement, that is not yet available to us. The method presented here is one approach, but has proved itself over time as providing, for both the manufacturer who commissions the advertising and the creative group in the advertising agency who supply it, both usable and practical information which *both* find understandable and believable. Even if you cannot wholly agree with either the reasoning behind the method or the method itself, at least it should provide a bench-mark against which to say whether other pre-testing methods you may be offered are better or worse.

The Pre-Test Situation

A fairly typical situation in a large advertising agency where the demand for testing the advertising is likely to arise, is where the

* The P.P.E. is a general term that covers both press and T.V. advertising evaluation.

agency has produced two or three rough advertisements (e.g. storyboard commercials) to the same basic strategy. A choice has to be made between the alternatives and the research man is asked to test the different treatments so that client and agency can decide which is the 'best' one. Generally, decisions about the brand information to be presented in the advertising have been decided; the problem now is to choose the most effective way of communicating this information to potential buyers.

Perhaps this is closer to the ideal situation, but I think it is fairly typical for the larger advertising agencies. It is worth noting, however, that too often research is called for in a situation where the agency has already invested large sums of money and considerable time in producing finished advertising, and with no alternatives to hand. By now, decisions will have been taken prior to the research as to which of the alternative treatments is the best one. In this situation the research comes too late for, where it produces what the client interprets as bad results, the advertising is often rejected or heavily modified, and the whole costly exercise has to be repeated. It is this kind of situation which has often led to distinctly cool relationships between creative personnel and their research departments. The whole situation argues for research at a much earlier stage when changes are much less expensive to make. V.T.R. commercials can be made early on, sometimes for as little as £100 each.

This has the additional advantage of allowing the agency to experiment with different treatments with which the client is not familiar, without committing large sums of money before the research results are in.

Bringing the research man in at an earlier stage has other advantages. Greater involvement in the creative process means he will learn much more, much sooner, about the objectives of the advertising and the creative means by which they are to be achieved. This is important, as in the final analysis only the creative man can give him the basic information on creative objectives which form the criteria against which the advertising can be evaluated as being successful or otherwise.

What follows is an examination of a particular part of the total research contribution towards the creation and evaluation of advertising. For simplicity's sake, and because much of this work has been connected with the creation of television commercials at Benton & Bowles, I shall talk about the P.P.E. in relation to commercials, although the techniques outlined here are often applicable to the testing of print advertisements as well.

What the Client Wants from Pre-Testing

Very often today, as in the past, what the client wants from the pre-test is *precision,* i.e. a series of figures or scores showing how the advertisement has performed on a number of criteria, either in isolation or in competition with other advertisements. This seems to be a reasonable demand; after all, he asks for, and appears to receive, precise research results in other fields, such as distribution (Nielsen) and consumer purchases (Attwood and the Television Consumer Audit). So, when the client comes to assess his advertising he often expects the same degree of precision, and preferably in the form that will predict the change in the sales of his product that is likely to be generated by the advertising.

The problem is not that the request is unreasonable, but that there is no way of producing this information. For those clients who can accept this, the next request is for the measurement of a factor that can be linked to sales, such as a change in attitudes or the degree of brand recall registered by people exposed to the advertising in a test situation. Are these valid tests of advertising or are we still trying to be too precise? What are the limitations to measurement in the pre-test situation?

The Limitations to Measurement

The terms 'measurement' and 'pre-testing', although generally used, imply a precision which is just not available to us at the moment. Among the many factors which limit the range of measurement or the type of evaluation that can be made of advertising prior to transmission or publication, the following are among the most important. These are generally applicable to all pre-packaged household goods advertising.

(*a*) Sales are a function of many factors represented by the total marketing effort, of which advertising is but one. Advertising rarely works in isolation, or even as the single most important factor, to promote sales. The efficiency of the sales force in obtaining distribution, the competitiveness of the retail pricing, the attractiveness of the packaging – all these and many other factors are also instrumental in producing sales. The problem becomes one not of predicting the sales effectiveness of the advertising (this grossly understates the problem), but of isolating the partial effect that advertising has on sales from the multiple and interrelated effect of all the other elements in the marketing mix. Given unlimited time and funds to solve the problem it is extremely doubtful whether a reasonably precise *prediction* could ever be achieved. Within the confines of limited time (often a matter of days) and limited funds (hundreds, rather than thousands) there is no practical solution – at the moment.

(*b*) The prime determinant of a buyer's attitude towards a brand is the 'performance' of that brand when used at home. Only in cases where a new brand is being introduced, and the purchaser has no previous personal experience of using it, is there likely to be an exception to this. (Performance here can be seen as purely physical performance or the degree of emotional satisfaction derived from using the product.) It is difficult to divorce the effect of the advertising on the decision to re-purchase a brand from the effect of previous experience of the brand on the purchase decision – and especially difficult when one is trying to predict the effect.

(*c*) The buyer's involvement with the information offered by commercials is relatively low. For many of the products advertised on television especially, the degree of perceived risk (seen either as an economic risk or an emotional one) is far lower than for many other decisions a housewife has to take on a day-to-day basis.

(*d*) Especially in relation to assessing attitudes towards brands, there is probably a considerable limitation imposed by the inability of the respondent to verbalize these attitudes, either directly or indirectly.

Apart from this, for many what I shall call 'low involvement' products it is probable that no measurable change in attitudes takes place *before* the housewife changes her purchasing habits, but, rather, attitudes tend to change (in a manner that can be talked about by the housewife) *after* the change in brand buying habits takes place.

(*e*) The effect of advertising is rarely so clear cut as in the case where a non-purchaser becomes a new purchaser of the brand (except in the case where a completely new brand is introduced to the market). Most advertising, for existing brands, tends to work by moving people up the scale of buying intensity, i.e. by persuading them to buy *more* of the brand. It is also worth noting that in product fields which have a multiplicity of brands, many housewives tend to buy two or three brands frequently, and it is very often the job of the advertising to move a brand into this 'magic circle' of brands for as many housewives as possible.

If we can accept that, for the time being, because of these and other factors, precision in pre-testing is not currently available to us, this still leaves an area of evaluation which, while being less precise than research measurements in other fields, is yet very useful and valid as a method of assessing the effectiveness of advertising.

The Area of Evaluation

The first step in setting up a P.P.E. is to establish, with the copy group, how both the agency and the client *interpret* the advertising and what they consider the objectives of the advertising are. These objectives are usually written down in the form of a copy brief and contain the following information:

(*a*) The copy strategy which outlines the development history of the brand and the brand information to be communicated by the new advertising.

(*b*) The potential market for the brand and the prime audience for the advertising.

(*c*) A full outline of the copy or the script to be used in the advertising.

The main purpose of the research is to establish whether the housewife's *interpretation* of the advertising meets the criteria laid down in the copy brief. This is basically a method that evaluates the potential communication effectiveness of the advertising: it determines the way in which the housewife *interprets* the information offered by the advertising and the extent to which the information has been *accepted* and correctly *understood*. Most importantly, it identifies areas of *miscommunication* and helps to explain the basis on which this has happened and why.

The research executive would normally have a preview of the advertising (before the test) to establish the accuracy of the copy brief. A special problem is the definition of the brand information to be presented in the advertising. With some commercials where, for example, a presenter talks about the brand, this information is easy to define; in others (what are often termed 'mood' commercials) it is not so much what is said about the brand that is important as what is implied, e.g. by the social class status of the people shown with the brand or the location in which it is being used. The burden of *interpretation* placed on the housewife is often much heavier for this latter type of advertising and this must be recognized in designing and analysing the research.

Before outlining the method used it will be useful to present some of the major assumptions we make about the way in which information is communicated in this type of advertising for pre-packaged household goods.

The Communication Process

The advertising must be seen before it can have a direct impact on the housewife. In order to evaluate it we have to ask the housewife a number of questions after she has been exposed to the advertising; in other words she has to recall what she has recently seen. Some of the information in the commercial will have been 'lost' as the following diagram shows (the various stages are presented here in an arbitrary sequence, for the sake of example):

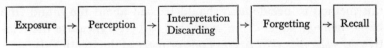

It can be seen that between Exposure and Recall there are more opportunities for information to be lost, other than forgetting. At the stage of *perception* the respondent may not hear or see every detail of the commercial, and what is perceived will vary from one respondent to another. The respondent will *interpret* what has been perceived, and may, during this process, *discard* some information for a number of reasons; e.g. the information is seen as trivial or unimportant or irrelevant.

More information may be lost, quite involuntarily, because the ability of the respondent to remember it is not great enough – i.e. the respondent will *forget* some information that was perceived and not selectively discarded.

Finally, respondents will be asked to *recall* information, and information can be lost at this stage because of their inability to put into words the information they can remember, or because some information which is retained (while being 'important' to the respondent) may not be seen as being 'important' to the interviewer: the skill of the interviewer is crucial here.

In testing the effectiveness of the advertising in terms of its ability to communicate certain information to the housewife, it is important to know:

(*a*) what brand information presented in the advertising is being used by the housewife

(*b*) how this information is being *interpreted*.

The P.P.E. Technique

The test is based on exposure of one of the commercials to the housewife (most usually by using the equivalent of a commercial television set) after which questions are asked to test the degree and nature of the communication that has been achieved.

The starting-point in designing the P.P.E. is the copy brief: the questions that are to be asked, and the areas that are to be probed, should all be located in this document. It is not the purpose of this method to decide *what* should be said about the brand (the basic theme/product claim, etc.), but rather to measure the relative *communication effectiveness* of one or more of the treatments.

Again, the test does not seek to measure a change in *attitudes* – which would be unrealistic after one exposure (even if such a measurement were relevant) – but rather the degree to which the information has been *accepted* and how that information has been *interpreted*. The technique recognizes that an advertisement imparts information in three essential ways, by appealing to:

the SENSES
the REASON
the EMOTIONS

The method is designed to assess the degree to which the housewife

NOTICES about the brand what we want her to
BELIEVES about the brand what we want her to
FEELS about the brand what we want her to.

It is these three basic criteria, and the degree to which successful
communication is achieved for each, that determines the total
communication effectiveness of the commercial.

Research Method

Most P.P.E.s are based on samples of about 50 housewives, each of
whom sees the ad. once.

The exposure of the commercial is normally made in a caravan.
Amongst a number of advantages, being able to take the caravan
into high-density shopping areas increases the ability to interview relevant target groups, which may be more difficult to locate
using other methods. The caravan houses a standard video-tape
recorder playing into a 19″ monitor and loudspeaker. Picture
quality and picture size are, on average, equal to those normally
seen by the housewife on her own set. This equipment gives the
ability to take a double head commercial and produce very
quickly, for testing purposes, a married print on tape of the same
quality as that of a normal transmitted picture.

Once the caravan is parked in the shopping centre or other
location, each member of the team of interviewers recruits one
informant (usually a housewife) and invites her into the caravan.

They are shown the one commercial and then interviewed
individually in depth. For most target groups it is usual to achieve
about fifty interviews per day.

The Post-exposure Interview

The interview takes the form of a series of open-ended questions,
followed by more specific probes on the problem areas which may
be seen by the client/agency as arising from the creative brief.

Basically, the method is a diagnostic one based on the individual depth interview, and is most useful in providing creative guidance.

The first question would probe for the very first thought that came to the respondent's mind while watching the commercial, whether linked to the commercial itself, or some associated subject.

We have found that these first responses often give a good indication of why the set of responses to the following questions take the form they do.

Following questions would cover what is remembered: the brand name, the commercial itself (copy and visual) and any product claims. All responses would be recorded verbatim and interviewers would probe responses fully. These tend to be non-specific at this stage. (The probes seek for expansion of statements, but are non-directional and so have a minimum effect on the structure of the answer.)

The second stage of the questioning would cover the following:

(i) *Comprehension:* (as opposed to rote learning) of claims and of particular visual effects where the possibility of confusion is seen to exist.

(ii) *Believability:* the degree to which the product claims are accepted/rejected. Basically, we would be probing here to find out the degree of rejection (if it occurs) and why the product claim has been rejected.

(iii) *Associative Ideas:* engendered by the commercial, and the reason for them. For example: 'From the ideas the commercial gave you, who do you think would benefit most from the use of...?' 'Why do you say that?'

(iv) *Attitudes:* related to the product. These would include any aspects particularly liked or disliked, the projective appeal of the advertisement and the description of it – all this to relate to the product claims on the one hand and the visual elements (people, situations, used in the commercial) on the other.

Especially when two or more ads. (with the same copy objectives) are being evaluated, a series of scales are sometimes used at the end of the interview to facilitate comparisons between them. The respondent would use these to rate the brand on a number of performance characteristics, e.g., 'I think this brand is very good value for money.'

☐ Agree strongly
☐ Agree
☐ Neither agree nor disagree
☐ Disagree
☐ Disagree strongly

Very often these scales will be available from previous qualitative research completed for the brand.

One of the prime functions of advertising is to *differentiate between brands*. Most of the housewives will already know something about the brand they see in the 'test' ad. Even so, it is important to try and establish whether the 'new' brand 'information' being presented helps them to discriminate the brand from other brands in the product field.

Analysis

The analysis of the questionnaires will cover the following areas of information:

(*a*) the balance of spontaneous versus probed mention of copy points, providing some measure of impact;

(*b*) the balance between mention of particular audio or visual points and of product descriptions or claims. A high degree of product orientation in the responses may be taken as an indication of effective communication of information about the product;

(*c*) the degree to which the product claims are accepted or rejected. The reasons for this. We should be looking for differences between instinctive/emotional rejection, and rejection based on rationalizations;

(*d*) the varying levels of communication of various points and the extent to which the commercial has reached its objectives. Where mis-communication has occurred and the reason for this;

(*e*) the extent to which the product is seen as being different from other brands and whether perceived differences are important to the housewife.

Appendix to Chapter 9
EXAMPLE OF A P.P.E. CARRIED OUT ON A
SINGLE PRESS ADVERTISEMENT

Testing Housewives' Assessment of a Print Advertisement for Maxim Coffee

Introduction

A print advertisement for Maxim was created to the following basic copy objectives:

(*a*) To introduce a new and different A.F.D. coffee to the market.

(*b*) To establish that this brand is different, through association with the concepts of luxury, sophistication and 'being special'.

(*c*) To establish that the brand helps people to get the 'most out of life/out of an occasion', with the slogan 'Maximize with Maxim'.

The test was designed to establish to what degree housewives succeeded in interpreting the advertisement across these dimensions.

During the test fifty-two housewives saw the advertisement.

The following summary of results shows the kind of data that is generated by a P.P.E. carried out for a single print advertisement.

We could not include here the information obtained from the de-briefing session held between the people who carried out the research and the creative group. These sessions are often vital to the success of this method. During this type of interview, answers to the questions are recorded as fully as possible, but abbreviations are sometimes necessary. The interviewer will often learn a great

ADVERTISEMENT I

> Photograph of a group of men and women, dressed in furs, gathered round a fire in the snowy clearing of a forest, drinking hot coffee. Carriages and horses stand in the background.

Make the utmost of those simple get-togethers . . .

MAXIMIZE WITH MAXIM— THE LUXURY COFFEE

Maximize the way you live with the pure luxury of new Maxim. Even the simplest occasion comes off in the highest style. Pure, fresh Maxim, created by a lavish hand to be the smoothest, most luxurious of coffees. Try it. But don't wait for a party. Luxury like this makes its own occasion.

Maxim—pure coffee luxury.

> Picture of cream being poured into a cup of coffee. Next to the cup is an open jar of Maxim.

ADVERTISEMENT II

> Same picture as Advertisement I

MAXIMIZE:

Make the utmost of those little get-togethers by serving Maxim coffee

Maximize the way you live. Serve new Maxim and even the simplest occasion comes off in the highest style. Luxurious new Maxim. Created by a lavish hand to be the smoothest of coffees. Try it. But don't wait for a party. Luxury like this makes its own occasion.

Maximize with Maxim ...the smooth coffee

> Picture of cream being poured into a cup of coffee. Next to the cup is an open jar of Maxim.

deal from the *manner* in which people answer the questions and can often help in explaining why people have not understood something in the advertisement, e.g. the meaning was too subtle or the 'facts' appeared to contradict each other.

Conclusions

The result of this P.P.E. led to a 'strengthening' of the copy, especially the headline. It appeared that a group of housewives were not interpreting the advertisement so much in terms of a luxury product/something rather out of the ordinary, but tended to regard the brand as another instant coffee which would be nice to drink on a cold day, i.e., a highly literal interpretation of the picture in the advertisement. As one of the major elements in the copy objectives was to establish a luxury image for the brand it was decided to *talk* more about luxury in the headline/body copy rather than primarily imply it through the picture. It was thought that this would also help to improve the understanding of the concept 'Maximize with Maxim'. There was to be an associated television campaign as well, which would also be presenting this theme, but using a different treatment, and this was expected to contribute towards the general understanding of the idea.

The first question put to the housewife after she had seen the advertisement was designed to establish the first thoughts that crossed her mind as she was reading the advertisement. These first thoughts can be very important as they often structure all subsequent interpretation/comments on the advertisement.

Question: 'What was the first thought that crossed your mind as you were looking at the advertisement?'

40 per cent commented that the scene was Russian (old Russia/Czarist Russia), or that it was a scene from the beginning of *Dr Zhivago*.

40 per cent said that the scene depicted people/people drinking coffee in the snow/in winter/on a cold day.

36 per cent said that this was an advertisement for instant coffee.

30 per cent commented on the fur coats.

Two syntheses were formed at this stage:

(a) an overall impression of *luxury*
(b) an overall impression of *cold and warmth*.

Grouping these initial reactions across these two dimensions gave the following:

46 per cent formed an initial overall impression of luxury.
46 per cent formed an initial overall impression of cold and warmth.

Of these housewives about 10 per cent were found in both groups.

Some verbatim comments at this stage were:

(i) '*Dr Zhivago*. Warmth on a cold day. Like, the early part of *Zhivago*. Rich and luxurious...'
(ii) 'What a gorgeous coat the woman on the right is wearing...'
(iii) 'Delightful – it brings back a style of living of pre-First World War.'

The next question established what could be spontaneously remembered about all aspects of the advertisement.

On average, each respondent was able to remember at least three items from the advertisement. Total volume of information remembered was high with a large number of details about the picture being mentioned.

The picture aroused a great deal of interest, and helped to offset the ordinary image of the *product* (instant coffee).

Items remembered from the advertisement	Per cent
A cold day/snow/Winter scene	45
Mention of fur coats	45
People around fire/a fire	28
People drinking coffee/instant coffee	30
Forest/woods/trees	20
Mention of horses	21
Mention of dogs	12
Mention of black/coloured man	10
Other details	110

N

Spontaneous mention of the brand name was achieved for 45 per cent of all respondents. On being asked to name the brand in the advertisement the following results were achieved:

80 per cent remembered it was Maxim.
12 per cent mentioned Maxwell House.
8 per cent mentioned Nescafé/no brand name.

In order to test both comprehension and the way the respondent had interpreted the advertisement, the following questions were asked:

Question: 'What was the advertisement trying to tell you about the product?'

Items mentioned	Per cent
It is a warming drink	34
Feeling of luxury—makes you feel luxurious	32
A special drink/for a special occasion	22
High class product/for upper income groups	18
For immediate use/for friendly social gatherings	18
The best coffee/good coffee	12
Smoother coffee	8
Get the most out of life	6
Sophisticated people would drink it	6
Can be drunk anywhere	4

Question: 'How do you think this product is different to other coffees you can buy?'

Differences mentioned	Per cent
More like real coffee	46
Smoother/richer/stronger	36
Better flavour	12
Taste better	8
More expensive	4
No difference	32

The 32 per cent who responded that there was no difference is a response to the product (instant coffee) rather than to the advertisement. As soon as these housewives understood the advertisement was about instant coffee they played back the basic preconceptions about this (to them) ordinary, everyday product.

Question: 'What sort of coffee do you imagine it to be?'

Description of coffee	Per cent
Instant coffee	50
Like Gold Blend	34
Strong coffee	22
Freeze-dried	18
Good coffee	12
Like real coffee	12
Luxury coffee	12
Better than instant	8

There is a distinction to be drawn here between the housewife understanding what the advertiser wants her to think about the coffee and what she interprets the coffee as being – after this one exposure to the advertisement.

These responses are what she interprets the coffee as being, having seen the advertisement once.

As we thought there might be problems with vocabulary in the slogan, and in order to more precisely define its interpretation, the specific question was asked:

Question: 'What do you think was meant by "Maximize with Maxim"?'

Comments	Per cent
Don't need so much/would go further/would be economical	26
You get maximum enjoyment/ pleasure/get most out of it/most out of life	24
Is better/better flavour	22
The best in coffee	18
It would be stronger	12
Improve social position/make life grander	6
People who want luxury coffee	4
Nothing/didn't make sense/don't understand	16

An advantage of this method of evaluating advertisements is the ability to give the creative group the verbatim responses of housewives to a particular question.

Not only does this show them the kind of vocabulary that is used by housewives, but they can see for themselves why a particular piece of copy is not being interpreted as they wished.

'What do you think they mean by "Maximize with Maxim"?'

'It doesn't make sense to me.'

'Overtones of luxury. "Makes the most of what you have." It makes more coffee per spoonful.'

'It could go further, it is stronger. Because it looks darker.'

'I don't know. I didn't understand that.'

'Absolutely nothing. It didn't make sense.'

'It has more coffee flavour than any other.'

'You would get the most out of it. You get a stronger taste of natural flavour.'

'You don't use so much.'

'Something by Maxwell House. You get maximum pleasure out of the taste – strong.'

'Maximum taste, it would be strong. A more luxury coffee.'

'You could mean maxi-clothes while you drink it. Because they did in the picture.'

'Have the best in coffee.'

'Cutting down in the quantity. You don't need so much coffee, it would be economical.'

'To get the best out of the coffee that you buy.'

'Get more of a long drink out of it.'

'The blend of coffee is better, stronger.'

'That it is made on an economical scale. They have economized on the blend and the ingredients to bring out an economical coffee at an economical price. Not really. Minimum amount of coffee is needed for a good cup of coffee.'

'Maximize your flavour of coffee and your enjoyment of the drink. I haven't studied the price so I don't know whether they were referring to costs.'

'Get the maximum taste of coffee. I wouldn't think so, could be maximum value for money.'

'I think they mean you would get the maximum amount of flavour, but I didn't find that. That's what they are trying to put over.'

'Get the most of your "think big". Get the most out of not just your cup of coffee, but the social occasion that goes with it. A positive thought.'

'Make the most of anything – get together, out in the cold. Any situation, any meal.'

'Confusing – doesn't mean anything. Just a pet slogan. Not descriptive, don't understand.'

'Maximum enjoyment out of it probably. Maximum doesn't imply the best, but should do in this case.'

'Mixed – to get that extra flavour, that is like coffee and coffee beans, has to be a good blend. It is the maximum of quality – originates from beans.'

'Make the most of life. Best possible quality – for the money.'

'Make the most of – make your life feel grander.'

'Haven't a clue. Doesn't mean anything, not being clever other than using the reiteration.'

'You would use less coffee for a strong flavour.'

'It annoyed me – thought of the historic film doesn't impress me.'

'They've done as much as is possible with methods available to produce a coffee with maximum flavour.'

'Mixing all the different coffees together. I don't suppose it will be any better than the others. There are so many coffees on the market.'

'Make the most of it and buy Maxim. You're doing yourself good by buying it. It goes a long way.'

'Oh, so it's Maxwell House. I assume they mean minimum price or the middle of the road. It's probably some dreadful ad-man who thought it up, who had some dreadful university course in psychology in America! Middle class, if you could afford it you'd have fresh coffee and someone to make it for you. I suppose it's supposed to make you think what does this mean and you gladly at the end shut your eyes and say nothing.'

'Minimize your time by using Maxim. I think it's very good; it would strike the younger ones – mini and maxi.'

'It points clearly that you'd save time using it; if you used percolated stuff it would take longer.'

'Using a little. Each time you use a little you get this huge cup of coffee. Don't like it particularly. Very ordinary. You've just added a bit to "Max". With all these big brains in advertising they could have thought of something better.'

'Maximize the popularity of your coffee by using Maxim because of it being easy to use and probably its flavour. It's a bit corny. I'd try to think of something better. It's not very striking, but it's perhaps easy off the tongue, but not a very compelling phrase to use. It will suit most people I suppose.'

'It sounds as if they've put some drug in it. Maxim sounds like an additive when it's put that way. Makes it seem as if there's more – I don't know what of. More ingredients are in the blend.'

'Maximize – makes me think of the French *Haute Couturière*. If it's as good as them...Maxim being the most – trying to put something better over. Something bigger over something big. It wouldn't get through to the general public. I liked it – it's different. My gardener and help wouldn't see it, it would be right over their heads. They would understand bigger than big or larger than large. If you're advertising a good class product you want good wording. It gets through to the people who like the good things of life.'

'The full flavour of the best coffee bean. Quite short – Maxwell. Maxim short, to the point, shows that you want the best flavour.'

'Just a gimmick to sell it. Pleasant – it flows off the tongue.'

'Make the most of yourself. Back to the social bit. Sad! I think it's sad this element in people that they need to socialize in that way. Leaves me cold – smart (slick). Typical. You can nearly see the shine on the man's shoes, all slicked up to sell something. It isn't sincere. Doesn't mean anything really. It's used for the alliteration.'

'Goodness knows! Like what! I don't know – doesn't tell me anything.'

'Get the maximum enjoyment out of it.'

'Being the "bestest hostess" – be "one up on your neighbour" – personally I apologize for using instant coffee, one feels it requires an apology.'

'Get more from it – the fact that it must taste better than some-one else's product, more value as well as the taste – value for money – well it would be strong and wouldn't need too many spoons.'

'Do the most – make the most of – have the best.'

'Bring out the maximum flavouring of true coffee.'

'That you get the maximum amount of goodness out of it – the phrase is quite good – it looks good with the cream on top. I would use it for three French boys, they know their coffee – it would be useful then.'

'Get the most out of life.'

'Haven't a clue – not a thing – didn't like it or dislike it.'

'Drink it after.'

References

1 Cox, D. (1961), 'Rational versus emotional advertising appeals', *Harvard Business Review*, Vol. 37.
2 —— (1969), 'The concept of perceived risk', *Harvard Business Review*, Vol. 37.
3 HOVLAD, D., JANIS, L. and KELLEY, H. (1953), *Communication and Persuasion*, Yale University Press.
4 JOYCE, T. 'What do we know about how advertising works?', ESOMAR Conference, 1967.
5 KING, S., 'The Relationship between the researcher and creative people', ESOMAR Conference, 1966.
6 KRUGMAN, H. E., 'The impact of television advertising; learning without involvement', *Public Opinion Quarterly*, Fall, 1965.

I O | Test Market Research

JOHAN AUCAMP
Director, Industrial Facts and Forecasting Ltd.

Definition

In the widest sense of the term, test marketing is a procedure for putting to the test, in the market-place and under normal shopping conditions, the predictions made and targets set when major changes are introduced in the marketing strategy of a product. Test marketing could be relevant when companies are planning to launch a new product or to make changes in the marketing of an existing product. These changes could be in the methods of manufacture, the packaging, the distribution, the advertising, the merchandising effort, etc.

This chapter deals with the test marketing of *new products* since the basic principles to be observed in this case are the same as for such other uses of test marketing as relaunching, repackaging, etc. In addition, the operation is simpler since it is not necessary to introduce all the control factors necessary when one is assessing the effect of changes on an already existing product.

The definition of test marketing for the purpose of this article, therefore, is to introduce a new product to the consumer market in a definable part of the total market for which the product is ultimately being considered, and to measure its performance in this test market.

The test market operation should, of course, be preceded by very thorough product testing, package testing, testing of the advertisements, etc. Failure is too public and too costly to be risked without previous experiment and research.

Though this pre-launch research does not guarantee a test market success, the probability of a failure is at least reduced by having the most acceptable product formulation, the best pack, the best advertising, etc. The test market itself should be the final link in the development chain.

This chapter is divided into four sections:

1 Why test the market?
2 Selecting the test area.
3 Validity of test marketing.
4 Measuring the success of the product.

I. WHY TEST THE MARKET?

More than 80 per cent of new products fail – in fact a failure rate as high as 93 per cent has been quoted. This can be a very costly operation. The rationale of a test market operation is a very simple one – the amount of financial risk involved is much smaller to launch a new product in a limited area than on a full scale. Should the test market results look positive enough, the product might be marketed on an expanded scale in one or more areas or even nationally.

The objectives of a test market fall into two major categories which could be called the mechanical and the commercial objectives (Davis, 1965).

The mechanical objectives are the more tangible, are often of major importance to a manufacturer, but are more often overlooked by those whose main interest is in advertising, marketing or market research. They involve processes such as collecting raw material; labour and equipment; obtaining adequate distribution; delivering the goods to the shops on time and in good condition, etc.

A test market generally offers a valid method of establishing problems in any of these areas so that these can be corrected before a national launch, or before expansion into additional areas.

The commercial aspects of test marketing start to operate after the product has left the factory and are concerned with the way the product is received by the trader and by the consumers. Though not always clearly defined the broad objectives are to assess from results in the test area whether the proposed marketing mix will:

(*a* provide adequate distribution in shops;

(*b*) produce a sufficient number of people trying the new product;

(*c*) produce a sufficient level of sales through repeat purchasing;

(*d*) indicate whether or not the product can be profitably launched in a wider area or even nationally.

In summary, the whole marketing operation is evaluated by the consumer. This covers all aspects of the operation such as: the product itself; the pack; the price; the advertising; the promotion; consumer acceptance, etc.

2. SELECTING THE TEST AREA

Having decided that test marketing should be undertaken, the next step is to select the area. This area can be a number of stores, a town, a sales district, a standard region, a TV area, etc. Obviously, the smaller the area the cheaper will be the operation. On the other hand, the results coming from a small area would, in most cases, be less reliable than those coming from a larger area. The *first* consideration in selecting a test area is therefore size. Other important considerations are: typicality; sales-force capacity; isolation; amount of test marketing taking place in the area; research facilities offered; media.

1 Size

As was seen above, the smaller the area the cheaper the operation, but the lower the reliability. The advice of a specialist should be enlisted to indicate how big or how small the area must be to give the desired answer. Factors such as sales force availability, typicality, etc., could, of course, also be influenced by or influence the size of the area.

2 Typicality

The chosen area must obviously represent, as closely as possible, a microcosm of the national picture. Some of the more important points on which it should conform, are:

(*a*) SOCIO-ECONOMIC. It should have roughly the same proportion of upper, middle and working classes as the country as a whole. This criterion is not very important when a whole TV area is selected as most of these conform reasonably well. It would, however, be extremely important when a test marketing operation is carried out in one town only or in a group of stores.

(*b*) URBAN/INDUSTRIAL. The proportion of urban to rural homes in the area must not be atypical, i.e. the area must not be over-industrialized or too agriculture in nature.

(*c*) DISTRIBUTION. The area must be reasonably typical of the country as a whole as regards channels of distribution and numbers of shops. With the growing importance of supermarket chains, it is particularly important to make sure that the area has a reasonably representative number of these stores. Care should be taken also to ensure that the area is not over-dominated by a local multiple.

(*d*) PRODUCT GROUP. It must not be an area in which the product group – or an individual brand – sells extremely well, or extremely badly, e.g. one would tend not to test a new aerosol furniture polish in Scotland where aerosols already sell at a rate considerably above the national average. Similarly, one would not test a sweet cream butter in an area dominated by lactic butter unless, of course, the intention is to try to sell sweet cream butter to lactic butter users.

Depending on the product concerned, other factors must be considered. It may be necessary to avoid certain difficult-to-reach areas when test marketing cake, which is intended to be fresh when bought; for a soap or detergent, areas with very hard or very soft water should be avoided, etc.

3 Sales-force capacity

The test area chosen should be one that can be covered easily and adequately by the company's sales force. Again, two extremes should be avoided; it must not be an area where the current representation is weak or patchy. Nor should it be the best sales area covered by the best sales force.

Some television companies offer distribution and merchandising facilities. These offers should be approached with great care. They could, of course, help considerably to get good distribution in the test area. But, if this could not be duplicated in a national launch by the company's own sales force or by specially hired contract merchandisers, it will distort the results considerably. Again, the plea is for typicality.

4 Isolation

The test area should also be one that can, with reasonable ease, be isolated from its surroundings, e.g. a town in the middle of the country rather than one in the middle of a conurbation if a town test is to be used. The more isolated the town, or the area, the easier it is to control and evaluate the test.

Wholesale distributors in an area supply shops outside it; consumers outside the area come in to shop there, etc. This leads to the boundaries of the area becoming very difficult to define as it is difficult to estimate how much of the sales are to people outside the area.

The smaller the test area, the more important the isolation factors. In a small test area such as a town, this 'infiltration' can distort the results considerably. The bigger the test area, however, the less important it becomes since the extent of the 'fringe' becomes only a very small fraction of the total area. In using TV areas attention should be paid to the amount of overlap between adjoining areas.

5 Amount of test marketing taking place

Some areas have become very popular as test markets. This is particularly true of some of the smaller TV areas, and this is a development that should be watched carefully and considered as one of the important criteria when selecting a test area. Though there might be some problems in going to some of the larger TV areas, such as London, Lancashire, and Midlands, these might have to be considered more seriously in the future as a number of the smaller areas begin to suffer from 'test-market wear-out'.

6 Research facilities

Test market research can be quite expensive in some product fields. Some of the television companies offer subsidized research facilities, both in the area of retail audits and consumer panels.

Though not one of the most important factors in deciding on a test area, the research facilities available in the area should be considered and could easily become a tie-breaker between two otherwise equally balanced areas.

7 Media

Finally, the test area chosen should have available in it comparable media to those that are going to be used in a national launch. This is often difficult and sometimes impossible, yet an attempt must be made to get it as close as possible to the media situation envisaged for the national launch.

If the national campaign is going to be based on the use of women's weeklies, local press, posters, cinemas, or direct mail then the same sort of operation can be mounted on almost any size of area. If, on the other hand, television is envisaged as the main support for the product, the test should be carried out in a television area.

After this things get less simple, and the test marketer should consult, and rely to a great extent on the advice of, the media expert who could work out for him how to use substitute media to reach the type of consumers he is interested in.

Summary

From the above, therefore, it is clear that a great many things must be taken into consideration when deciding which test market area is to be selected. The final choice would probably never satisfy all the requirements. For each test and each individual product some requirements are more important than others. It is the job of the manufacturer, aided by his researcher, his media man, his sales-force controller, etc., to decide on these, and to balance them one against the other so that the final choice satisfies most of them.

3. VALIDITY OF TEST MARKETING

In his article in *Commentary* (1965), E. J. Davis critically examines the validity of test marketing and concludes:

...In short, test marketing is a complex operation. Its foundation in statistical theory is not particularly sound, but practical difficulties may prevent much improvement in this direction. These are the difficulties of scaling down all the aspects of the national plan to a local level and maintaining a valid replica of the final marketing mix, and there is the frequent failure on the part of the sales personnel to realize the critical need to conduct the test under prescribed conditions, and that any departure from these conditions can throw doubt on the outcome of the whole operation. Many of the predictions made on the basis of test marketing are on too facile a basis, and far more needs to be done to investigate the possibilities of developing improved predictive techniques. In general, test markets are under-researched, with far too many organizations content to measure one aspect of the end result through retail audits, and ignoring the possibilities, and the need to collect other types of data as the test proceeds.

...Against all this, with the ever increasing expense of marketing, there may be even less willingness for a manufacturer to jump directly from pre-testing to national launch. Consequently test marketing is likely to remain. At present it is inadequate in many respects—but so are many research techniques in this and other fields. Even on the present basis, however, test marketing can provide a great deal of knowledge and experience to a new product, and it should give at least a clear indication of a plan which is failing to meet its objectives, even if at present it is not possible to produce a precise national forecast which manufacturers would like...

The one main suggestion that Davis provides for making a test market result more reliable is that more data is needed. The retail audits should not become the one and only measure, but should be read in conjunction with consumer panel data and other consumer data.

A further improvement would be the use of two TV areas so that test measurement can be taken in both areas, again reducing the risk of error.

The A. C. Nielsen Company provides a rather more optimistic picture in an analysis of test market results that they presented in the *Nielsen Researcher* of January–February 1968. In this analysis they state that 56 per cent of brands tested and measured through Nielsen were abandoned, i.e. in the absence of test marketing the odds for a successful national launch is roughly 50/50 or the toss of a coin.

To a large extent a successful prediction of the national share depends on a particular company's own requirements. Assuming that the sponsors of the brands that were ultimately launched would regard the launch as successful if they achieved at least 80 per cent of the final test share at the national level after a similar time-span, the picture shown in Fig. 1 emerges.

National performance 80 per cent of Test Achievement or more.

87%

National performance less than 80 per cent of Test Achievement.

13%

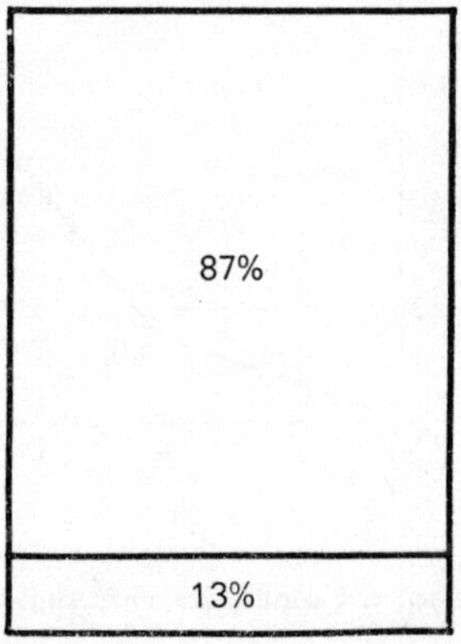

Fig. 1. Division of Test Brands Launched Nationally (Nielson, 1965). (*Composite U.S.A./G.B.*)

It would, therefore, appear that, instead of 50/50 odds, the odds become about 9 out of 10 that a product will aproximate its final test share at the national level after a successful test result. This reduces the risk of a national failure considerably. One of the dangers in test marketing is to take a decision before the product has been tested long enough. The chart on page 209 illustrates that, the longer a product remains in a test market, the greater the chance of a correct prediction from retail audit data; e.g. after four months the probability of a correct prediction is only 15 out of 100, whereas after twelve months this increases to 91 out of 100.

Based on the foregoing analyses, the three most important lessons to be learned about increasing the accuracy of the test operation seem to be:

Take more than one type of measure whenever possible, e.g. both retail audits and panel data.

Leave the brand in test marketing as long as possible before taking a decision.

Use more than one test area whenever possible.

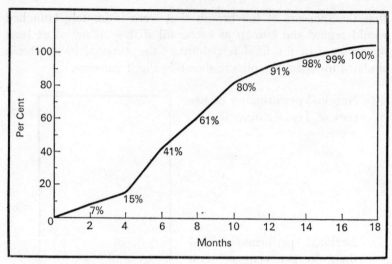

FIG. 2. Cumulative Percentage of 'Correct' predictions (Nielson, 1968).

4. MEASURING THE RESULTS OF A TEST MARKET

The three most frequently used types of test market measurements are discussed below. They are

1 Sales information.
2 Consumer panel data.
3 Usage and Attitude surveys.

1 Sales information

Clearly, the most direct measure of the success of a product is the size of its sales and, on the face of it, it seems logical to measure shipments from the factory. The distributive chain for many products is, however, highly complex and may involve, besides the manufacturer, the wholesaler as well as the retailer. Except in the case of highly perishable goods, therefore, bottlenecks could exist... stocks could be piling up at the wholesaler's, in the warehouse, in the storeroom of the retailer, etc., and what is going out of the factory is not necessarily going at the same rate to the consumer. It could take a considerable time before a seemingly very happy manufacturer, who is relying on shipment data only, finds out that his product is now on the shelves and in the storerooms, but is not being purchased by consumers.

In order to get directly at the retail sales situation, it is therefore, logical to go to the retailer himself. Except in those few cases where the manufacturer is also in the retail trade (e.g. own label), the only link that the manufacturer has with the retailer is his sales force and there are many reasons why the sales representative is not the ideal person to report on his own sales successes and failures.

The first alternative is, therefore, to commission a market research firm to recruit a panel of retailers who will, in return for a nominal fee, allow auditors of the research company to check periodically on movements of stock into the shop and over the counter to the consumer.

The second alternative is to subscribe to the retail audit of one of the specialist market research firms with existing panels of shops. The best known organization in this context is the A. C. Nielsen Company. Two other organizations, Retail Audits Ltd, and Stats (M.R.) Ltd, however, also operate national panels.

Which of these two alternatives is selected for a particular product depends to a large extent on the product type. If a product category is already on the list of one of the specialist firms, the manufacturer can buy very useful back data about the market and can often buy the audit data at very advantageous rates. If, however, the product category is not covered by the specialist firm it could well pay to call in a firm to set up a special audit.

If the test market is to be one of the smaller TV areas, a standard national panel would not have enough shops in the area to make the results meaningful. In this case it would also be important to look into the respective cost of a national audit boosting its shops in the area v. an *ad hoc* panel set up just for the test.

Standard reports on test findings usually contain data about the test brand as well as competitive brands, and would cover the following types of information: sales to consumers; retail purchases; retail stocks; stock cover; distribution – the proportion of shops handling the product and the proportion who actually had it in stock when the auditor called; display material in use.

This information is usually also given by type of shop, enabling the manufacturer to see where his weak points and strong points are in terms of the types of shops handling his product.

2 Consumer panels

Though retail audits are very important in any test market operation – and it is difficult to envisage a test market where retail audits are not one of the measurements – the technique is a relatively blunt instrument. It only tells us how well the product is moving through the shops and nothing about the buyers – who they are; whether or not they come back to buy the product again after their first purchase; how frequently they buy it, etc. To know these things we must go direct to the consumer.

There is one type of consumer research, analogous to the retail panel, which can be very useful in the assessment of a test market – the consumer panel. Two companies, Attwood Statistics and Audits of Great Britain, specialize in this type of research and run very large national panels, and this is the first source of potential information to investigate. If they do not cover a product field adequately (e.g. in the case of say, canned cat food in the Southern ITV area, the number of cat-owners on the panel could be very small), an *ad hoc* panel could be set up. This should, however, be left in the hands of specialists as this type of operation is relatively expensive and fraught with pitfalls. Most of the dangers stem from the very fact that their consumption pattern is under investigation and this could affect their behaviour.

During the past four to five years, a great deal of sophistication has been brought into analysing information from panels. The most important of these is probably the models for predicting the success of a new product considerably earlier in the life of the test market than is possible in the case of retail audit data. The main reason for the earlier prediction is the fact that, in the case of the audit, we do not know how much of the product is still being bought by new trialists and how much by regular buyers. This could, of course, be established very easily in the panel.

The basic method was first described by Baum & Dennis (1961). The same approach, with a number of refinements, was described in detail by Parfitt & Collins (1968).

The raw data used in the analysis is the continuous purchasing records of individual households. From these data three basic components are selected:

(*a*) *Cumulative Penetration* or the cumulative growth in the number of buyers of the brand or product being studied.

(*b*) *Repeat-Purchasing Rate* or how often these new buyers buy the brand or product again after their first recorded purchase. These repeat purchases of the studied brand are then expressed as a proportion of the total purchases in the product field by these buyers; this is called the Repeat-Purchasing Rate.

(*c*) *Buying Level Index* is a comparison between the amount that buyers of the product under study spend in the product field and the amount that all buyers in the product field spend. This enables us to establish whether they are heavy, light or medium buyers (by volume) in the product field. This is expressed as a Buying Level Index, with the average buying level for the field being 1·0. For example, if on average all the people who buy cat food buy 100 units per month, and those who buy the test brand buy 120 units per month, their Buying Level Index $= \frac{120}{100} = 1\cdot2$.

Cumulative Penetration

To illustrate: assume that a brand-share prediction analysis covers newly launched Brand F in an established and relatively static product field (for example, canned dog food). The first requirement is to persuade households who own a dog to try Brand F. If the advertiser does not succeed in doing this on a reasonable scale, there will be no future to predict. The chart below begins with the brand's launch. As each new Brand F buyer is picked up from panel records, she is recorded on the

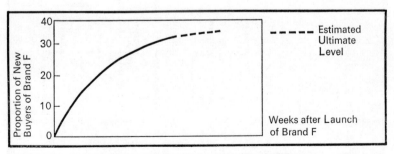

FIG. 3. Cumulative Penetration of Brand F(a).
(a) Total buyers of canned dog food = 100 per cent.

cumulative penetration curve. It is not necessary to wait until the total cumulative penetration has been completely observed before predictions can be made. Once the shape of the curve is determined and a declining rate of increase is observed, it is possible to project the curve to make a reasonable estimate of the ultimate likely penetration. (See Fig. 3.)

Repeat-purchasing Rate

The ultimate success of any brand depends on the willingness of consumers, once having tried it, to continue buying it. In perhaps oversimplified terms, persuading a consumer to try a brand is a function of advertising, promotion and distribution, but getting her to keep on using it is a function of her acceptance of the product as such. The success or failure of the product's acceptance in the market-place is expressed by the repeat-purchasing rate.

As each new buyer of Brand F appears on the panel records, her purchasing behaviour in the product field is isolated as a continuous record over time. This is shown in Fig. 4 in a hypothetical buying pattern in which Brands P and K represent the existing competitive brands.

In the example, the first-time buyers of Brand F accumulate to 7 in the first three weeks of the study. The repeat-purchasing rate

Weeks	1	2	3	4	5	6	7	8	9	10	11	12	13
Buyer No.													
1	F	F		F	K	K		K		K			
2	F	K	F		K	F		K	P		P		
3		F	F			F	F			F	F	F	
4		F		F	P		K	K				K	
5		F	K		F	K	K	F	P		P	K	
6		F	F	P	F		F	P	F	F	F	F	
7		F	F	K	P	F	F	P	K		F	K	
Cumulative Buyers	2	4	7										
Repeat-Purchasing Rate				6/10 =60%		5/10 =50%		5/10 =50%		4/10 =40%		4/10 =40%	

FIG. 4. Repeat Buying Rate.

is calculated from the period after the first purchase of Brand F, here in two-week periods. It is not an expression of calendar time because calculation begins for each buyer from the date of entry into the market, i.e. buyers 1 and 2's first opportunity to re-purchase is in weeks 2 and 3, but buyer 7's first opportunity is in weeks 4 and 5. In each of the two-week periods these 7 buyers made 10 purchases in the product field of which successively 60 per cent, 50 per cent, 50 per cent, 40 per cent and 40 per cent were repeat purchases of Brand F (see Fig. 4).

This pattern of a declining repeat-purchase rate is normal because second, third, fourth, etc., purchases of a new brand still tend to be exploratory and are also often still a benefit from pro-motional activity connected with the launch.

The critical point for the prediction of the ultimate brand share comes when the repeat-purchasing rate begins to level off as in Fig. 5. At this point it is possible to calculate what the brand share will ultimately be.

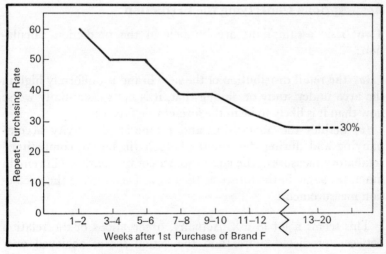

FIG. 5. Repeat-Purchase Rate for Brand F.

It is estimated in Fig. 3 that Brand F is likely to reach about 30 per cent of potential buyers (a potential buyer here is a buyer of tinned dog food). In Fig. 5 the repeat-purchasing rate for these buyers has levelled off near the 30 per cent level. With the assumption that households having tried Brand F purchase tinned dog food on average at the same rate as the average of total buyers in the market, the predicted share for Brand F would be:

SF = Estimated penetration × repeat-purchase rate × buying rate index
SF = 30 per cent × 30 per cent × 1·0 = 9 per cent.

The buying level of buyers of Brand F could be a very important element. If, for example, they were to a large extent made up of heavy buyers in the product category, the buying rate index could be as high as 1·2 or 1·3, changing the estimated share of Brand F to:

30 per cent × 30 per cent × 1·2 = 10·8 per cent.

Assumptions Underlying the Prediction

Two basic assumptions are implicit in the prediction calculation:

(a) the retail distribution of the new brand is uniformly high in the area under study or, failing that, it is not substantially worse now than it is likely to be in the foreseeable future;

(b) besides the advertising and promotional activity accompanying and during the brand's launch (including competitors' retaliatory measures), the circumstances of the market will remain much the same in the future as they have been during the prediction measurement.

This seems a lot to ask. Actually, observations of the relation between predicted shares and the actual shares achieved over periods of up to two years suggest that the predicted shares tend to be a reliable guide to likely ultimate shares in almost all cases unless a *major* change takes place in the market – e.g. a new brand is introduced. In these cases the prediction will not be valid any more.

The experience that Attwood and A.G.B. (the T.C.A. Panel)

have had so far using this method of projection has been very satisfactory and, in conjunction with the general retail audit measure, enhances the accuracy of test market results considerably.

3 Usage and attitude surveys

The purpose of advertising and promotion is to persuade the potential consumer to try the new product. Once this break-through has been achieved, the advertising should keep the product in the consumer's mind so that she can buy it again.

The manufacturer probably wants to find out two basic types of information:

(i) whether the advertising is making an impact among potential buyers;

(ii) how buyers use the product, and what they think of it.

These surveys are often called 'Advertising Awareness' and 'Usage and Attitude' surveys and should probably be done as two separate surveys, rather than one combined survey. The reason for this preference for two surveys is a very practical one: if the advertising awareness questions are asked first, the attitude data could easily be contaminated; if the usage and attitude questions are asked first, it would probably influence the answers respondents give to the advertising awareness questions.

Two separate surveys need not increase the cost by a great deal as the advertising questions could often be attached to one of the many omnibus surveys now available in this country. These surveys are conducted at regular intervals – often weekly – by research companies. A client can buy space on the questionnaire at a fee per question. Since a number of clients buy space on a particular questionnaire, the overheads are shared between them and the cost per client considerably reduced. Each client has access to the answers to his questions only.

The information usually obtained from the awareness survey include:

awareness of the product and main competitors;
awareness of advertising for the product and main competitors;
what the advertising is saying of the product.

This survey could be done at, say, three-monthly intervals to measure build-up in awareness of the product and the advertising, or once a year. The exact timing depends on the research budget available and the use the figures can be put to.

The Usage and Attitude survey concentrates more on the product and consumer experience and satisfaction with the product. By interviewing a cross-section of consumers one can usually divide them into three groups:

buyers of the product;
those who have heard of it but who have not (yet) bought it;
those who have never heard of it.

The first group – the buyers – can be questioned in considerable detail about their experience with the product. The areas generally covered include:

extent of purchase and repeat purchase;
frequency – quantities purchased;
reasons for purchase;
points liked about the product;
points disliked about the product;
intention to buy again, and reasons for buying/not buying again;
brand images compared with competition.

A note of warning here: the frequency of buying answers often disagree with those of a diary survey. This is particularly true for products which are bought infrequently but it also happens with frequently bought products. This is to a large extent due to memory failure. People tend to 'telescope' the last purchase, i.e. they say it was a week ago, rather than two or three weeks ago; they overclaim the number of times they have bought a product, etc.

Here again, the frequency of conducting the survey depends on the product, the budget and the use that the results can be put to. It is far more useful to have trend data than data from a once-off survey. In the latter case all one gets is a figure expressing a point of view at one point in time. Trend data tells one whether attitudes, purchases, etc. are increasing, decreasing, or stable, e.g. 90 per cent satisfaction looks very good on a once-off survey. If, however, 85 per cent liked the product in January, 80 per cent in March and 70 per cent in May, this 70 per cent is seen as a danger signal rather than a good high satisfaction figure.

References

1 BAUM, J. and DENNIS, K. E. R., *The Estimation of the Expected Brand Share of a New Product*, ESOMAR Congress, 1961.
2 DAVIS, E. J. (1965), 'The validity of test marketing', *Commentary* (The Journal of the Market Research Society), Vol. VII, No. 5, July.
3 'Measuring the odds in test marketing', *The Nielsen Researcher*, Oxford Edition, January–February 1968.
4 *The Nielsen Researcher*, Oxford Edition, January–February 1965.
5 PARFITT, J. H. and COLLINS, B. J. K. (1968), 'Use of consumer panels for brand share prediction', *Journal of Marketing Research*, May.

11 | Research at Retail Level

C. J. WALLIS

Associate Director, A. C. Nielsen Company Ltd.

Shop Audits

It is a fair guess that most people, when asked to define 'marketing research', would, if they were able to answer at all, conjure up first a picture of an interviewer asking a string of questions!

Yet shop audit research, which is one of the most widely used techniques, provides manufacturers in twenty-one countries with a completely factual intelligence service. There are no questions and answers, no opinions whatsoever, but actual sales.

This is because the basic data are obtained by skilled auditors who personally check retailers' invoices, count stocks and observe retail prices, etc.

This factual approach, and the location where the research is carried out – at the point-of-sale – are the most important characteristics.

The scale on which shop audit research is conducted makes it exceedingly complex but the basic principle is quite simple:

1 An accurate national sample of retail stores (chemists' or grocery stores, for example) is selected – something much more easily said than done!

2 The owner of each store is asked – in return for cash payments and/or other forms of compensation – to co-operate in the research project by (a) saving all his purchase invoices and (b) allowing an auditor to check these invoices, once every two months, and also take a detailed record of stocks – and observe prices, displays, etc.

3 Having ascertained, for each brand, (a) the quantity purchased during the bi-monthly interval and (b) the increase or decrease in stock levels, it is a simple matter of arithmetic to compute (c) the quantity sold to consumers.

4 From these and certain additional facts obtained by observation (e.g., displays and retail prices), many vital types of marketing information are ascertained, for every package size of every brand of hundreds of commodities sold in the types of stores selected.

5 All figures obtained from the sample of retail stores are expanded, by a complex mathematical procedure involving the use of computers, so that the figures reported to manufacturers represent estimated totals for all stores of the types audited in the entire country.

Since audits are made at regular intervals a pattern results from the findings. Trends are revealed which enable a manufacturer to observe the effect of his marketing strategy on his brand's sales. Moreover, shop audits furnish research facts about competing brands so that each client can observe, and learn from, the results of competitors' marketing tactics.

The principal types of information derived from shop audit research for each brand are as follows:

Sales to consumers (in money value, number of packages, weight, etc.).
Purchases by retailers.
Retail stocks.
Retail stock-turn or number of days' supply.
Retail distribution (i.e. per cent of stores handling the brand).
Per cent of stores that are out-of-stock (on the average day).
Retailer's selling price.
Displays of various kinds.

The information is collected in such a way that a number of special analyses are possible in addition to the normal provision of breakdowns by shop type and size and by region.

Each product may be audited separately by package size, type, colour or other characteristics provided this information appears on the retailers' invoices.

Shop audit research is widely used in Great Britain, U.S.A., Western Europe and in Australasia and South Africa – and for a great many reasons. Here are a few examples:

To decide on the products to be produced, including questions of design, colour, flavour, etc.

To select the most saleable package sizes and types.

To select the most effective channels of distribution.

To apportion promotional efforts most effectively by seasons of the year, by shop type and by region.

To test new products in the market-place.

To appraise foreign markets – and determine the most effective methods for use in such markets.

In summary, shop audit research is a reliable and accurate marketing tool which allows manufacturers to determine their policies on the basis of factual information collected at the last link in the distribution chain – the retail shop.

Test marketing is a subject in itself and the value of shop audit research in this field is widely acknowledged. Less well known, however, is the application of the shop audit technique in Controlled Store Testing, so this is dealt with at some length in the following section.

Controlled Store Testing

Until the early 1950s it would have been true to say that relatively few – and only large – companies devoted substantial sums of money to new product development. Staple brands rarely changed. A well-established range could, perhaps, count on a steady market for many more years. So why the increasing emphasis on the investment in new products since then? Why are many more companies engaged today in the 'new products race', spending, in the food sector alone, at the rate of about £90 million a year to develop acceptable new lines and bringing out as many as 1,000 new or improved brands, types and pack sizes?

The simple truth is that there is no longer such a thing as product security. All available evidence suggests overwhelmingly that the consuming public has continually changing tastes. And not only tastes but habits, attitudes and aspirations change; composition of markets change, conceptions of convenience change, and just as fashions change, so more and more products contain an in-built element of fashion.

The record of home laundry products demonstrates the extent to which manufacturers have sought to cater for the changing requirements of housewives – by offering wider choice and greater convenience of use. In 1947, the housewife had a choice of some ninety-two home laundry products. Twenty years later, she had 288 choices, each with its own varying blend of convenience, efficiency and economy. Moreover, none of the long-established products over this period had remained the same. The market had grown and developed on the strength of continually updated products, new variations and especially innovation – in consonance with changing demands, changing technologies and the exploitation of new raw materials.

Just try to categorize the technological changes that have activated this field: from soap powders through detergents to enzymatic detergents; new types of dissolvents, scourers; the industrial chemist has produced an almost unbelievable change in the products. The marketing man and salesman have produced almost as many changes in pack shapes and sizes from the carton to the aerosol. In any field of industry, from motor-cars to foodstuffs, a similar pattern of change is repeated.

So today, more than ever, the growth of any company depends upon the effective introduction of new products whilst maintaining a nucleus of successful lines. But it takes time to develop a new product and time is scarce when new products are needed to bridge the gap between projected profit requirements and estimated profit returns from current lines. Clearly the bigger this 'profits gap' then the greater is the pressure to rush through new lines. On the other hand, if this gap can be kept to a minimum by ensuring that existing products are as profitable as possible, there is less pressure on the new product developers and a greater likelihood of their being given time to plan efficiently.

This situation puts the spotlight on existing products. In a series of case studies in both the U.S.A. and Great Britain, the A. C. Nielsen Company has demonstrated how essential forward planning is on what may be termed 'going' brands. They found that the beneficial effects of product improvements are lasting for shorter and shorter periods of time – averaging only a year – so that contingency planning is necessary to reactivate brands at more frequent intervals.

In other words, keener competition is forcing manufacturers to place greater emphasis on keeping their products up to date. They know that existing products contribute most to profits in the short-term and provide the investment required for long-term objectives. By the same token, any change to existing products which is wrong carries a much more severe penalty than an unsuccessful new product. All of which makes it important that significant change designed to update a 'going' product is right.

Because there are many changes available to a manufacturer, the possibility of a wrong or indecisive change – both of which could be expensive – is that much greater. What is required, therefore, is a method of reducing the possibility of a wrong decision being made.

Consumer interviews can go some way towards eliminating non-starters but they leave an area of doubt when an interviewee is faced with the question of whether or not he or she will buy. Surely the best guide is obtained by the sales achieved when the change is introduced in a real life situation.

Controlled Store Testing is a technique which measures the effect of product changes in actual selling conditions. This technique does not replace test marketing but it does provide a valuable way of testing the viability of a product change before committing resources to it. Controlled Store Testing also offers a way of testing the effectiveness of increasingly costly promotional aids to ensure they do the job for which they were designed.

Any salesman will recognize the difficulties of obtaining distribution for new products, let alone an alternative to a current line, but the Controlled Store Testing technique replicates ideal selling conditions where the problems of variable distribution are replaced by perfect availability and continuous shelf-stocking. This method of research can and does show quickly whether the proposed product change can be expected to have a significant effect on sales. It is an aid to management in taking the right decision, at an early stage, on changes aimed at maintaining or improving the profitability of existing product lines.

Since a management decision is to be made upon the basis of

this research, which in practice is conducted over a short period of time and in possibly no more than forty shops, it is essential that technique is at maximum efficiency. To be so, it must be effectively controlled.

The control is exercised in these areas:

1 Experimental Design.
2 Collaborating Stores.
3 Results and Interpretation.

1. EXPERIMENTAL DESIGN

The essence of successful controlled testing is in deciding what precisely the aim of the test is. This may seem to be obvious but a common fault within this sphere of research is trying to obtain too much information from a programme designed specifically to answer one question.

Once the objective has been fixed, the design to use depends upon costs, time available, and the product field in which the test is being conducted. Costs and time available, whilst closely related, must be two separate considerations. The period of time, especially, varies from test to test and depends upon the complexities involved.

It would be impractical to enumerate all of the experimental designs that can be used in this type of research and, since there are books which deal with the subject in detail, only two of the designs available will be dealt with here.

A. *Latin Square designs*

This type of design is used when a shop can receive only one treatment (subject of a test) at a time. If, for example, the marketing department of a company had devised four different types of display material and could not decide which one to employ, an experiment using the Latin Square technique could be indicated. An example of the design, in which there are four treatments (A, B, C and D), four time-periods and four shop groups, is given on the next page.

Every treatment appears in every shop group for equal periods of time and the number of periods is equal to the number of treatments. This is the unique feature of a Latin Square design.

TABLE I

| | Four Treatments | | | |
| Periods | *Shop* | | | |
	1	*2*	*3*	*4*
1	A	B	C	D
2	B	C	D	A
3	D	A	B	C
4	C	D	A	B

Time-periods and shop groups need further explanation:

Sales will be the criterion upon which the display material will be judged. Since the sales data will be subjected to statistical analysis a reasonable volume of sales will be required. The period of time over which the test is conducted will therefore be a function of the rate of sale of the product. This may be four weeks or four months. It will always be a multiple of four if the time-periods are to be equal to the number of treatments.

The shop groups in this particular example could be four shops or four hundred shops. Practical problems of organizing innumerable stores, and the cost of doing so, usually determine the number of stores involved in such tests. There must be, however, sufficient to obtain a statistically significant result.

B. *Factorial experiments*

This design is used when it is possible to put two or more alternatives in the shop, such as two different banded pack offers, so that the consumer may exercise a choice between the alternatives confronting her for a product she has decided to buy. The design therefore 'spots the winner' by comparing the relative sales performances of the alternatives placed in store.

The same kind of considerations concerning the duration of the test and number of shops needed apply to this experiment as they do to Latin Square designs.

2. COLLABORATING STORES

One of the problems of conventional test marketing in a town or an area, besides selling the product into stores, is maintaining the shelf-space and stock levels for the product under test. If the product is out of stock or is not given sufficient display it can only add to the duration of the test.

If a quick concise answer is required this distributional problem has to be eliminated. The stock placement and maintenance of stock levels on the shelves should therefore be taken out of the hands of store personnel and carried out either by an independent organization or the research company involved. Whichever concern undertakes this task must ensure that nothing upsets the test conditions, and this can only be done by regular visits to the stores.

3. RESULTS AND INTERPRETATION

It is from these regular visits that sales data on the product under test can be collected. At the same time other information relevant to general store activity can also be obtained. This is important since promotional activity on commodities other than those under test could influence total store traffic and therefore influence the results of the test.

The sales data collected are subjected to an analysis of variance. This must be done because the number of stores participating is usually small for administrative reasons as well as cost. This type of analysis therefore eliminates the risk of drawing the wrong conclusion from the test. The interpretation that is placed on the statistical results may be influenced by other information that has been collected from the stores over the period of time the test has been conducted.

A justification for Controlled Store Testing is to be found in the results of actual case histories. Examples of some of the problems confronting management are:

(*a*) Can production costs be reduced by removing the protective carton from a product – without reducing the sales volume?

(*b*) What would happen to a brand's total sales volume if an additional size were added?

(*c*) A new packaging technique will produce significant production and machine cost savings. Can this new type of package be introduced without endangering sales volume?

The A. C. Nielsen Company, which operates not only in the U.K. but in many Western European countries as well as in

P

America and Australasia, has provided two examples of their Controlled Store Tests. One is from Sweden, where the Controlled Test is operated in shops in the Stockholm area; and one from England, where the service is based upon large self-service shops in the London conurbation.

Case History I – a jam jar with or without the carton?

Our client had a jam which we will call Alpha. It had been on the market for years and had a share of about 15 per cent. Alpha was packed in a jar with the brand name on the plastic lid. The jar was wrapped in a carton which had various fruits printed on it.

In the course of a Nielsen presentation, mention was made of representatives' reports that dealers were taking the cartons off and selling the jar as it was. The trade was convinced that the product was more saleable like this. This came as a complete surprise to the manufacturer, but it was seen that new possibilities would be opened up if it was found to be true. Above all, the elimination of the rather expensive carton would mean a better margin for the same selling price. Given steady or increased sales, a reduction in price could be made without prejudicing profits. Since the Swedish market was comparatively price-conscious at that time, a price-cut was imminent.

We suggested that our client should use the controlled testing service with equal quantities of Alpha in jars alone and in jars with cartons, set up in each shop next to each other. A control was introduced which ensured that all the shops had carried the brand before the test and had sold Alpha only in the carton pack (i.e. they did not take it out of the carton to sell it). The test was only intended to measure whether Alpha sold better in its original form or without its carton.

It would obviously have been unrealistic to offer both packs nationally, so it was decided that a control period at the beginning was not necessary and that the absolute sales figures would not be significant.

SALES INCREASE WITHOUT CARTON

Even during the first week of the experiment it was apparent that Alpha without its carton was beating the original pack two to one.

The same thing happened in the three remaining periods. In addition, the results were very consistent, and if we take each shop and each period as one observation, we reach the conclusion shown in Table 2.

TABLE 2

Week	1	2	3	4	1–4
Number of Shops:					
With higher sale of jars *without* carton	9	9	6	10	34
With higher sale of jars *with* carton	1	—	1	—	2
With equal sales of both types	—	1	3	—	4
Total	10	10	10	10	40

In no fewer than 34 cases out of 40 the plain jar beat the carton pack.

It was agreed that this experiment was not sufficient to judge the effect of the change at the national level. So our client decided to take Nielsen test marketing service in an area which covered 2 per cent of the total population of Sweden. This fully prepared test permitted a detailed study of the effect on sales caused by the elimination of the carton.

Case History II – a new size?

The British case study concerns a fairly common situation – the example of a food manufacturer with a brand packed only in one size. Naturally interested in maximizing sales, the manufacturer considered the possibility of introducing an additional size, but wished to test the effect on total brand sales as a result of this move. In order to evaluate such a change a 2 × 2 Latin Square design was used.

The four weeks' test in Panel A and Panel B stores showed a fairly dramatic increase in overall sales, following the introduction of the new size, as Table 3 demonstrates.

The test indicated not only that the new size would add significantly to total brand sales volume, but that in terms of

TABLE 3

		2 Sizes		1 Size	
Panel A	Sales	27·4	28·0	17·7	18·1
		1 Size		2 Sizes	
Panel B	Sales	15·7	18·4	23·2	29·6
		Week 1	Week 2	Week 3	Week 4

consumer acceptance, when both sizes were sold alongside each other, the new size was purchased one in four times.

Other facts were discovered about the new size during the test operation such as the retail reactions both to the change and its wider implications, factors which were invaluable to the manufacturers involved.

In the light of this encouraging evidence, Nielsen recommended a larger-scale test.

Both of these brief case studies show how valuable it can be to introduce a check between the product testing and test marketing stages, particularly where changes to an existing product are planned.

I2 | Research into Consumer Durables— with Special Reference to Electrical Appliances

M. SIMMONS
Joint Managing Director, G.S.R. Ltd.

Introduction

This chapter is concerned with the applications of market research to domestic electrical appliances and, in part, is relevant to other consumer durables such as cars and furniture. The following areas are covered:

1 Market characteristics.
2 Information needs.
3 Available information.
4 Product development.
5 Monitoring consumer demand.
6 Identifying potential customers.
7 Distribution to the trade.
8 Forecasting consumer demand.
9 *Ad hoc* research.
10 Non-domestic demand.

1 Market Characteristics

The U.K. electrical and radio goods market was worth about £600 million in 1968 at retail selling prices. This represents 2¼ per cent of total consumer expenditure.

Expenditure in 1968 was 22 per cent above 1963 at current prices; and 10 per cent above 1963 at constant prices. Electrical appliances now take up a lower share (2·25 per cent) of total consumer expenditure than in 1963 (2·40 per cent).

TABLE 1
ELECTRICAL and RADIO GOODS

| | Expenditure in £ million | |
	Current prices	Constant 1958 prices
1963	497	544
1964	515	552
1965	528	556
1966	523	544
1967	558	574
1968	609	596

Source: Monthly Digest of Statistics.

The two salient features of the electrical appliance market over recent years have been:

Price competition. Prices of electrical appliances have become relatively cheaper than other goods and services, partly owing to increased competition both here and from abroad. Since 1958, prices of electrical and radio goods have increased by only 2 per cent compared with 30 per cent in ten years for the general consumer price index.

TABLE 2
ELECTRICAL AND RADIO GOODS

	Price index 1958 = 100
1963	91·3
1964	93·3
1965	93·1
1966	96·1
1967	97·2
1968	102·2

Source: Monthly Digest of Statistics.

Rationalization. Against a background of fluctuating consumer demand, static prices and smaller profit margins, there has been a move towards rationalization both at the manufacturer and retailer end. Several large manufacturers now dominate certain sectors of the market; and the number of retailers handling these goods has contracted.

TABLE 3

RETAILERS STOCKING

	Number of outlets	
	Jan. 1963	Jan. 1968
Washing-machines	12,600	10,400
Refrigerators	12,800	9,500
Radios	13,800	13,100
Television sets	12,100	10,600
Tape recorders	11,100	10,400

Source: Gallup Quarterly Dealer Survey.

N.B. Includes radio; electrical dealers, department stores and electricity board showrooms.

2 Information Needs

The impact of these market trends should be a growing acceptance of the need for thorough knowledge of the market to back up management judgement and expertise.

Millions of £s are spent annually in the consumer durables market on all aspects of production and marketing – from initial design and tooling to final distribution and advertising. The cost of failure is high and is increasing as the market becomes more competitive.

Market research, at a fractional cost of the total investment, can provide the necessary facts to reduce the risk of failure. The essential information requirements of durable manufacturers are:

To assess consumer needs so that their products are designed to meet them.

To know the current demand for their products and for competitive products as an aid to tactical marketing.

To identify their potential customers so that promotional efforts can be directed with maximum effect.

To have comprehensive knowledge of the trade pipeline as an aid to efficient distribution.

To forecast consumer demand quarterly over, say, the next five years, as an aid to production scheduling and strategic planning.

Any durable manufacturer embarking on a market research

programme should work closely with the researcher to ensure that the project is based on a comprehensive, unambiguous and accurate brief. He should only carry out research that can be used and is relevant to his problem. Too much money can be wasted on non-actionable irrelevancies. He should get the researcher involved in the interpretation of the findings and so obtain the maximum research contribution to business decisions.

Initially, he should ensure that he really needs market research to answer his problem. Sometimes the answers are available from published or from his own sources.

3 Available Information

There are three main sources of available data on the electrical appliance market; the manufacturer's own information, trade statistics and guarantee cards.

The manufacturer knows his own deliveries to the trade and, if he is dealing direct, he can use his representatives to feed back marketing intelligence. When using reps for this purpose, the manufacturer must ensure that reports are free from bias; and that the real cost does not exceed that of commissioning a research company.

A second source of information is that on industry deliveries compiled from individual manufacturers' returns by their trade associations – BEAMA and BREMA. This is supplemented by import statistics from the Board of Trade.

From these sources, a durable manufacturer can regularly ascertain his own share of total industry deliveries to the home trade including imports. He can further examine these by type, for example by cubic capacity of refrigerator or by twin-tub, single-tub and automatic washing-machine.

This does not give the manufacturer any information about consumer sales and, as is demonstrated later, there can be a vast gap between deliveries to the trade and sales to the final consumer.

Guarantee cards, returned by the consumer, can be analysed to provide information on the manufacturer's own sales. However, the procedures must be correct to avoid misinterpretation.

Many consumers do not return their guarantee cards. The rate of return varies according to the product and model. A relatively low-price durable which requires little after-sales service (such as electric irons) would have a low return – perhaps one-third of buyers. A higher priced item requiring regular service (such as an automatic washing-machine) would have a high return, probably over two-thirds. The rate of return is also dependent on the design and content of the guarantee card. Any change in the card is likely to affect the level of returns.

The lessons are:

Make guarantee cards clear, unambiguous and easy to complete. Keep them as short as is compatible with the required information.

Once that has been achieved, resist any change.

Calculate return rates separately for each model relating the number of cards sent back to ex-factory deliveries.

Make this calculation over a sufficiently long period to allow deliveries and consumer purchases to equate.

These procedures restrict the use of guarantee cards. A period of at least one year, free of any change in the card, is required to compute the rate of return. *Ad hoc* additions or amendments cannot be made to information recorded.

Within these limitations, guarantee cards can provide estimates of model sales, stock turn, characteristics of the consumer and source of purchase. The names and addresses can be used for follow-up inquiries to obtain consumer opinion on installation, product performance and servicing problems.

Two final comments on guarantee cards: they provide no information on the competition, and their handling can be costly if not properly organized. In practice the cards are normally stored away, and hand sorted and counted when required – a messy, space-consuming operation. A manufacturer intending to make effective use of guarantee cards would be well advised to investigate possible computer applications for data recording, storage and retrieval.

4 Product Development

Product development in the appliance market often means placing a large capital sum at considerable risk. Investment in tooling and plant is high. Many new products fail.

Market research at a marginal addition to the total investment can reduce the risk of producing a new product or model which does not meet consumer needs.

A comprehensive research programme on new product development would include the following:

1 An appraisal of the task the appliance is to perform: the conditions under which the task will be carried out: the characteristics of the user: and the important features in the buying decision.

2 This would be followed by the testing of concepts, covering *only* those points where action can be taken, with a sample representative of the demand for the appliance.

3 As soon as prototypes are available, in-home tests should be carried out so that performance and consumer reaction can be assessed under actual working conditions *before* full-scale production is undertaken.

4 The tests should include instruction manuals, which are normally written by engineers and are often incomprehensible to the user.

5 Consumer reaction to the product should be re-assessed every few years. The capital cost of major design changes may be inhibitive but innovations can be introduced into new models of the old product.

The initial appraisal study would usually be carried out in two stages: firstly, unstructured depth interviews or group discussions to probe the areas to be explored; and secondly, an activity study with a larger representative sample of housewives.

A quantitative study for washing-machines would cover:

Activity. For example, how housewives go about their washing; the garments washed; the fabrics; the weight of wash; the water temperatures used; the number of rinses, and so on.

Environment. The size of the kitchen; the space available; is the washing-machine moved around; water and electricity supplies.

Buying decision. The relative importance to the consumer of appearance, design, function, reliability, initial cost, running costs, servicing.

This would guide the designer on the magnitude of the task his machine must cope with – the load capacity, the number of loads, the washing action, the water capacities, the operating temperatures; and on the buying considerations that must be emphasized in the design brief.

The activity study could also reveal needs that have not been fulfilled (e.g. washing-machines on castors) or design features that are never used (e.g. time clocks on cookers).

5 Monitoring Consumer Demand

Once the product is launched, regular information on total market and brand sales can be used by the manufacturer:

1 To gauge the success of his present marketing activities. Is he gaining, losing or maintaining market share?

2 To pinpoint weaknesses in his market share – by area or by type of outlet so that appropriate remedial action can be taken.

3 To adjust production targets. This is essentially an exercise of adjusting supply to meet effective demand. Actual consumer sales can be plotted against set targets. Research in this context is used as a warning signal.

4 To provide information on the competition. If a competitor has invested a considerable sum in product development and advertising, a check can be kept on his achievements.

5 To assess the effect of specific promotions – his own or competitive.

6 To trace the changes in consumer acceptance of product types. An example can be found in the washing-machine market where manufacturers have to decide on the allocation of resources between the different types: automatic, twin-tub and wringer machines. Further examples are small or large capacity refrigerators, pump or gravity spin dryers, upright or cylindrical vacuum cleaners. The manufacturer has to decide on which types to concentrate his efforts. Should he get out of small-size fridges and attack the large capacity market in order to gain share of an expanding sector? Research, by showing the trends, can guide the manufacturer on these decisions.

7 To appraise consumer acceptance of a new variation of a product, such as fridges with built-in freezers.

8 To examine the trend in retail selling prices. What price ranges are becoming more popular?

9 To detail the growth, for example, of stencil (retailers' own) brands and the progress of cheaper imported machines such as 'Indesit'.

Few of these points can be efficiently monitored from trade statistics or guarantee cards. Statistics on deliveries to the trade are insufficient to guide the manufacturer on market movement and his own standing in the market. This is because in the short term ex-factory deliveries and consumer sales can vary substantially. Many durables spend as long as five months in the trade pipeline – perhaps two months with wholesalers and three months with retailers. Stock turn is much slower than in most non-durable markets.

One manufacturer of twin-tub washing-machines had twenty weeks' supply at the current rate of sale in the retail trade during 1968, compared with an average of ten weeks' supply for his main competitors. Ex-factory deliveries were buoyant but consumer demand had fallen and retail stocks were piling up. The manufacturer, unaware of consumer sales, was probably optimistic about his 1968 performance. Knowledge of the true facts would have enabled him to cut short-term production before creating ill-will with the retail trade which had piled up nearly half a year's supply.

Similarly, in 1959 a breakthrough in the refrigerator market was generally anticipated. Many fringe dealers began to stock. Retail demand increased and ex-factory deliveries went up. Manufacturers took this as a sign to increase their capacity. Unfortunately the increased demand was from the trade and was not reflected in consumer demand. What followed is now well known; over-production, price reductions, falling profit margins and a general manufacturing slump.

How then can continuous estimates of consumer demand be obtained from research? There are two possible methods: the retail audit and household surveys.

The traditional technique for securing continuous market size data in non-durable fields is the retail audit, which involves checking sales among a national panel of stores. The retail audit claims its strength from its mechanical nature which removes interviewer/respondent bias from market measurement and gives a relatively high yield of information per £ spent on sampling.

There are several disadvantages in applying this technique to the consumer durable field:

1 There are difficulties in obtaining co-operation from certain retail organizations.

2 A very diverse sample of outlet types would be required to cover the extensive range of durables that can be included on consumer research. This would considerably increase the sample size and the cost of the operation.

3 Certain important sources of purchase would not be covered on a retail audit, for example, mail order.

4 Finally, whilst useful data such as retail distribution, stock levels and display can be obtained, the retail audit provides no information about the buyer or about the replacement market, which among durables is an important element in any forecasting model.

For all these reasons consumer demand is monitored in this country from household surveys.

Consumer acquisitions over a defined period are recorded either from independent household surveys or from a panel. The main disadvantage of this method is the small pick-up of recorded purchases. Assume a market where 750,000 units are sold per annum, then the approximate sample yield in a purchase quarter would be:

Sample of households per quarter	Number of recorded units in a purchase quarter
10,000	110
25,000	275
50,000	550

This small base is sufficient to provide a national estimate of demand, but even on a 50,000 quarterly sample is clearly inadequate for providing such information as quarterly brand shares within regions. The answer is to accumulate such analyses over a longer period – and to accept that the tactical use of the research is thereby limited. The alternative of increasing the sample size would be prohibitively expensive.

These limitations in estimating consumer purchases from the household approach are largely offset by the vital ancillary information yielded, which can be used to identify potential customers and to forecast demand.

6 Identifying Potential Customers

Buyer profiles, built up from continuous consumer research, are an essential aid to media planning and advertising strategy. Recent buyers can be analysed by class, age, region, household composition as well as other characteristics. These profiles can be compiled for the product group, for the main types and for the leading brands in the market.

To illustrate this point, the washing-machine market in 1952 was predominantly ABC_1. These were the people who were buying and where manufacturers should have been concentrating their immediate efforts.

TABLE 4

WASHING-MACHINES, 1952

Total consumer purchases	100
Class:	%
AB	58
C_1	31
C_2 DE	11

Source: Gallup Monthly Purchase Index.

Now the situation has changed completely:

TABLE 5

WASHING-MACHINES, 1968

Total consumer purchases	100
Class:	%
AB	19
C_1	25
C_2 DE	56

Source: Gallup Monthly Purchase Index.

This swing to the lower social classes is highly correlated with the level of penetration achieved by the product. In 1952, only

9 per cent of households owned a washing-machine compared with two-thirds in 1968.

Historically, the majority of appliances show a rapid increase in sales as ownership passes from 10 per cent to 20 per cent of all households. This is known as the 'take-off' stage. The AB social classes lead the way in the acquisition of a new durable. Then it begins to be acquired by the C_1s and C_2s. Eventually it is the role of the C_1 C_2 groups, because of the high proportion of households they represent, to produce the take-off for the durable.

Profile data should be concerned with the *type* of appliance, where relevant, not just the product group. For example, buyers of large capacity refrigerators differ from buyers of smaller sizes.

TABLE 6

REFRIGERATORS, 1968

	Under 5·5 cu. ft.	5·5 cu. ft. and over
Consumer purchases	100	100
Class:	%	%
AB	15	31
C_1	28	35
C_2	38	25
DE	19	9

Source: Gallup Monthly Purchase Index.

And buyers of automatic washing-machines are different from twin-tub buyers.

TABLE 7

WASHING-MACHINES, 1968

	Automatic	Twin Tubs
Consumer purchases	100	100
Class:	%	%
AB	32	15
C_1	29	24
C_2	28	42
DE	11	19

Source: Gallup Monthly Purchase Index.

This information aids the advertiser in planning his media scheduling, particularly when most of his expenditure is on print as in the electrical and radio goods market. About £15 million was spent in advertising these appliances in 1968: two-thirds on press and one-third on television.

Profiles can also be a useful guide to advertising policy as distinct from media placement. For example, if a market depends mainly on replacement buyers the advertising can more usefully concentrate on features which may mean little to people without experience of the product. Large capacity refrigerators appeal mainly to replacement buyers. It is therefore sensible to highlight product features such as automatic defrosting in advertisements. The advertiser is aiming at people who already know the chore of defrosting a fridge.

These market segmentations, properly utilized, can guide manufacturers on their promotional efforts so that they can be directed to achieve maximum effect.

7 Distribution to the Trade

A durable manufacturer, particularly if his products are largely sold through wholesalers, is unlikely to have comprehensive knowledge of the retail pipeline. Regular checks with a sample of retail outlets can provide information on:

> the number of retail outlets selling the product group
> the number selling each brand
> brand distribution patterns
> the progress of new models
> the number of weeks' supply of stock held by the retail
>   trade
> retail selling prices by brand
> display at the point-of-sale.

Regular retail research primarily tells the manufacturer how many outlets sell his brand compared with the competition. The level of distribution should bear some relation to advertising policy. A national campaign loses its effectiveness if a potential buyer has to visit say ten outlets in order to find the brand he wants. Such a policy pre-supposes a degree of brand loyalty which rarely exists and underrates the sales persuasiveness of the first nine outlets called on. Awareness of the level of distribution can determine whether national or local advertising tied up with stockists is likely to be more effective.

A guide can be given to the optimum retail distribution for a manufacturer; and also which outlets his direct selling force should deal with and which should be left to wholesalers.

There are about 19,000 traditional outlets – radio; electrical dealers, electricity board showrooms and department stores – for electrical appliances in Great Britain. This excludes fringe outlets such as furniture stores, chemists and hardware stores.

Few of these outlets warrant direct attention. Typically for these appliances the retail trade is highly concentrated. A small proportion of stockists account for a high proportion of stocks. Also this means a high proportion of sales since the larger stockists keep at least as favourable a stock ratio as the small outlets.

This concentration of stocks – and sales – is illustrated below. For washing-machines, one-quarter of stockists account for 55 per cent of all stocks and one-half of stockists account for 81 per cent.

TABLE 8

SHARE OF TOTAL STOCKS, OCTOBER, 1967

	Largest 25% Stockists	Largest 50% Stockists
	%	%
Washing-machines	55	81
Vacuum cleaners	52	80
Radios	58	81
TV sets	55	80
Spin driers	60	84
Refrigerators	63	84
Tape recorders	60	83

Source: Gallup Quarterly Dealer Survey.

These larger outlets have to be defined in a meaningful way for action by sales forces. Taking the example of washing-machines:

TABLE 9

WASHING-MACHINES, OCTOBER 1967

	Stockists
All stocking washing-machines	12,000
Stock size: washing-machines	%
1–2	20
3–4	20
5–6 – – – – – – –	16 ⎤ – – –
7–8	11 ⎬ 25%
9–10	8
11–12	6 ⎫
13–14	4
15–18	6 ⎬ 25%
19–25	5
26+	4 ⎭

Source: Gallup Quarterly Dealer Survey.

The largest 25 per cent of stockists carry 11 or more washing-machines. The largest 50 per cent carry 6 or more washing-machines. When the data was collected those carrying 5 machines were counted with those carrying 6 machines. The 50 per cent line therefore runs somewhere between 5 and 6, hence the line going through the 16 per cent.

Now what are the implications for the manufacturer?

The marginal cost of getting into the smaller outlets may well exceed the profit that arises from them.

In the appliance field, the manufacturer can set his sights on say the 25 per cent largest stockists and still compete for about three-fifths of the market.

These large outlets can be defined to representatives in terms of stocks held at time of call.

The distribution pattern for a brand can be examined by sales area, type of outlet and size of outlet (defined in terms of stock held). This research enables the manufacturer to check strengths and weaknesses. He can assess his efforts to achieve a high distribution among the larger stockists. He can use the area results to set targets and check performance.

Over time, he can see whether his brand is losing or gaining distribution, and in which sector of the trade. He gets a warning sign when distribution is falling below an accepted level.

He can also watch the progress of new models, normally initiated in a regional launch. From this, realistic marketing targets can be set nationally. Additionally, the development of competitive launches can be followed.

Information on stock levels enables the manufacturer to ensure that a satisfactory number of weeks' supply at the current rate of sale is being maintained within his outlets. This research provides an early warning of any build-up or decline of stocks. A manufacturer with this information can take action to run down stocks of his brand if total stocks are rising to a dangerous level. It also provides a basis for adjusting short-term production targets.

Another use of retail stock data is to determine policy on obsolete models. The number of stockists and their average stocks can be calculated. If a deal is being considered, the manufacturer can estimate the cost to him of taking these stocks from the dealers.

8 Forecasting Consumer Demand

A great deal of attention is currently being paid by manufacturers and researchers to the prediction of consumer demand for durables.

The objectives would normally be:

To forecast short-term, say quarterly over the next twelve months, as an aid to efficient production scheduling.

To forecast long-term, say annually over the next five years, as an aid to strategic planning.

To forecast not only total consumer demand for the product group but also the types and ideally the brand shares.

Management decisions on whether to develop an existing market or enter a new one all involve making an estimate of future demand, for example:

What is the long-term demand for colour television?

What share of washing-machine sales will automatics take up in five years' time?

Does the dishwasher market warrant investment and development?

Which has more potential: fridges with built-in deep freezers or separate deep freezer units?

No forecast can be compiled without comprehensive knowledge of previous trends. The past has to be studied in order to assess the future. Accordingly, the first and major requirement of any forecaster is an extensive, continuous and consistent series of the relevant input data, whether it is manufacturers' deliveries, purchases by different sectors of the population or household ownership levels. This indicates the way a market is developing and the likely course the market will take if prevailing conditions continue.

The next requirement is the correct technique. Most durable forecasts would separate demand into three components and treat each separately:

Initial demand. People buying the product group for the first time.
Replacement demand. People buying a replacement for a previous durable.
Additional demand. People buying an additional durable, e.g. multiple ownership of cars or TV sets.

Initial demand can be predicted by the use of techniques such as curve fitting previous ownership levels to project the future trend. The 'take-off' phenomenon, where initial demand tends to accelerate between 10 per cent and 20 per cent levels of household ownership, is relevant to such projections. Another important issue is the likely level of market saturation. Forecasters are concerned with the maximum number of households who will ever buy an appliance and the time-period over which demand will approach saturation. For example, in estimating initial demand for washing-machines, it may be concluded that ownership will rise from 66 per cent in 1969 to a saturation level of 80 per cent in 1979. That is, initial demand over the period would involve about $2\frac{1}{2}$ million washing-machines.

An important factor in estimating saturation levels for certain appliances is the average size of a kitchen in this country, which is about one-third the average size of kitchens in the States. Two-thirds of U.K. households have kitchens of less than 100 sq. feet. This restriction of space in which to accommodate these appliances affects their long-term potential as well as their design.

With scarce resources of money and space available to the

consumer, research into the order in which durables are acquired can provide useful supplementary information to assess initial demand. Research of this type indicates the priorities of consumers and which markets are likely to achieve quicker saturation.

The importance of *replacement* demand depends on the level of household penetration achieved by the durable, and its average life.

TABLE 10

REPLACEMENT DEMAND, 1967

	Replacement Demand as a proportion of total demand	Percentage of homes owning
	%	%
Washing-machines	64	63
Refrigerators	23	53
Vacuum cleaners	68	82
TV sets	79	91

Source: Gallup Monthly Purchase Index.

Replacement demand takes up over three-quarters of the TV market. The appliance has a high household penetration and a short life compared with other durables. Conversely, initial demand accounts for over three-quarters of the refrigerator market. Refrigerators are still not in nearly half of British homes and they have a relatively long life.

TABLE 11

AGE WHEN REPLACED, 1968

	TV Sets	Refrigerators
All replacement purchases	100	100
	%	%
Under 3 years	13	5
3–5 years	25	16
6–10 years	26	41
Over 10 years	36	38

Source: Gallup Monthly Purchase Index.

Forecasts of replacements can be made as follows. The numbers of a particular appliance which have been in use for

1, 2, 3, . . . X years can be estimated. The probability of an appliance being replaced at 1, 2, 3, . . . Z years can be obtained, again from continuous research. This data is used to assess the number of appliances 'at risk' of being replaced in following years.

The third component – *additional* demand – is already important for cars. About 10 per cent of car-owning households possess a second car. Multiple ownership is increasing for appliances such as radios and TV sets. Where this component is significant, it must be incorporated in the forecasting model.

A number of forecasting models have been developed on the above basis and highly sophisticated statistical and mathematical techniques have been employed to take account of all the inter-relationships involved. The forecasting methods based on this approach have been referred to as the 'segmental method' as they require the use of data collected from various groups and segments of the economy.

Other methods for forecasting durable demand have generally expressed expenditure as a function of a number of factors, such as disposable income, relative prices, index of hire purchase control and total stock of durables, in the form of econometric forecasting models. It has, however, been found from experience that there is often a significant amount of individual durable expenditure which cannot be explained using these variables.

Another approach to forecasting is based on the premise that purchases of durables tend to be planned some time in advance of the actual purchase. The use of survey data on consumer purchasing intentions for forecasting of consumer durable goods has been pioneered by the Survey Research Centre at the University of Michigan since 1953. More recently, quarterly surveys have been conducted by the U.S. Bureau of the Census.

There are conflicting claims on the predictive ability of anticipatory data. Used alone this data does not produce reliable forecasts. Further experimentation is necessary to assess whether consumer intentions improve the traditional models which incorporate other data.

A recent approach has been to collect consumers' attitudes to their economic environment and prospects. The aim is to build up an index of consumer attitude which would predict expenditure more accurately than intentions. All of these approaches warrant more attention to establish the optimum technique.

Even the best forecasts are based on assumptions and these assumptions change. Appliances have been a target for monetary and fiscal action by the government. In recent years there have been frequent changes in purchase-tax rates and in hire-purchase controls through variation in the minimum deposit allowable and the period of repayment. There have also been wider measures such as restrictions on bank advances and increases in the Bank Rate which affect demand. Forecasting is now very dependent on assessing the next steps that might be taken by the government.

9 *Ad Hoc* Research

The information needs described earlier apply to most durable manufacturers. Additionally each manufacturer will have particular requirements dictated by his own circumstances.

He may be losing brand share and need to explore why consumers buy a competitive product rather than his.

Research can indicate the important factors in the consumer's purchase decision; and the relative influence of price, advertising, product design, product performance, reputation and recommendation either by acquaintances or retailers. The manufacturer's standing on each of these points can be compared with the competition. An appraisal can be made of the necessary action required to reduce any competitive advantages and so secure a larger share of the market.

A variety of related marketing problems can be probed. How important is after-sales service in determining what make is bought? What policy should he adopt: handle it himself or rely on local dealers?

What loyalty do consumers have to his products? When they replace, will it be with his brand? This is a key question in developed markets where a manufacturer's prospects largely depend on his share of replacement purchases.

If buyers are going away from his brand, what are the major reasons? Once the manufacturer knows, he can begin to take appropriate remedial action.

What is the manufacturer's standing in the retail trade? How can he secure better penetration among the important larger outlets? Trade research can provide a framework for effective distribution policies.

How important are leaflets and brochures at the point-of-sale? Are they displayed? Do potential buyers pick them up? Is the manufacturer's expenditure warranted? Should he spend more on this form of promotion?

Should a multi-product company advertise its brands singly or together?

These examples illustrate a few of the many marketing problems which can be investigated through individual *ad hoc* research studies on durables.

10 Non-Domestic Demand

There are about $1\frac{1}{2}$ million non-domestic establishments in Great Britain made up approximately as follows:

Retail outlets	600,000
Restaurants: canteens	50,000
Other service trades	100,000
Wholesalers	50,000
Factories: offices	250,000
Hotels: boarding houses	100,000
Other establishments	350,000
	1,500,000

The remaining units include licensed clubs, hospitals, schools, universities, public authorities and places of entertainment.

These non-domestic outlets represent a source of demand for many durable goods.

This is largely an unexplored field where the research problems are complex but not insoluble. The main problems in the non-domestic sector relate to sampling and for certain categories locating the correct respondent.

Standard piloting procedures can overcome these difficulties and surveys can be mounted which provide useful information on usage and purchasing behaviour for all relevant durables in specified categories of outlet, either on a regular or *ad hoc* basis.

References

1 BROWN, D. A., *Some First Results Using a Forecasting Model for Consumer Durables*, ESOMAR-WAPOR Conference, Dublin, 1965.

2 ——, BUCK, S. F., and PYATT, F. G. (1965), 'Improving the sales forecast of durables', *Journal of Marketing Research*, August.

3 BUCK, S. F. (1966), 'Problems and procedures in continuous sampling', *Commentary* (The Journal of the Market Research Society), August.

4 CORLEY, T. A. B., *Domestic Electrical Appliances*, Jonathan Cape, 1966.

5 E.I.U. RETAIL (1969), 'Conditions for growth in electrical appliances', *Business Special Report*, 133, March.

6 HEALD, G. I., *The Relationship of Intentions to Buy Consumer Durables with Levels of Purchase*, London Business School, London, 1969.

7 I.C.I., *Short Term Forecasting*, Monograph No. 2.

8 —— (1966), 'Consumer buying intentions and purchase probability: an experiment in survey design', *Journal of the American Statistical Association*, September.

9 LYNN, J. A. and SIMMONS, M. (1966), 'Consumer durables: continuous market research', *Commentary* (The Journal of the Market Research Society), October.

10 PYATT, F. G., *Priority Patterns and the Demand for Household Durable Goods*, Cambridge University Press, 1964.

11 SALTMARSH, J. A., *The Special Dangers of Incomplete Information in the Field of Consumer Durables*. Unpublished paper, 1956.

12 —— (1963), 'Market research and design', *'Design for Profit' Symposium*, February.

13 STONE, J. R. N. and ROSE, D. A. (1965), 'The market demand for durable goods', *Econometrics*, July.

14 TREASURE, J., *Forecasting the Demand for Consumer Durables*, J. Walter Thomson, 1967.

13 Industrial Research—with special Reference to Research in the Textile Industry

ANDREW McINTOSH

Managing Director, Industrial Facts and Forecasting Ltd.

The important thing about marketing research is not what it is, but what it can do. This chapter, though not a case study in the true sense, discusses how the industrial market researcher can help the manufacturer in the textile industry. It is loosely based on two papers given by the author in 1968, the first at a Senior Management Seminar of the University of Bradford Management Centre, and the second at a session of the Textile Marketing Forum organized by the same university.

The User's Approach to Marketing Research

By marketing research we do not mean merely the collection of data. Green & Tull (1966) suggests two definitions:

1 'The systematic and objective search for, and analysis of, information relevant to the identification and solution of any problem in the field of marketing.'

2 'A cost-incurring activity whose output is information of potential value for marketing decision.'

For the purposes of this paper, the second definition, which sees marketing research from the standpoint of management, is more relevant. Marketing research does cost money, and the cost is related to the availability and complexity of information gathered, not to the value or usefulness of the information. The cost of research is only justified if it produces *useful* information, which helps management to assess alternative policies and the pay-off from them.

Let us first dispose of one problem which often worries the manufacturer of industrial goods, whose immediate customers are in industry rather than among domestic consumers. The differences between consumer and industrial market research are – or ought to be – differences in degree, not in kind. Both of the Green & Tull definitions apply equally to consumer and industrial research.

From the manufacturer's standpoint, the techniques used to produce the required information – provided they are sound – are of little interest. The manufacturer of industrial goods is normally in closer direct contact with a limited number of customers.

In order to be persuaded that he can get value from marketing research, he must be persuaded, first, that the market researcher can get different, or better, or more useful information from customers with whom he is in regular contact than he can himself, and make better use of that information in guiding marketing decisions. Second, he must be persuaded that the theory of probability sampling, which he may accept as valid for assessing voting intention, or TV audience measurement, is applicable to the study of his own products.

Marketing Decisions Based on Fact

The textile industry in itself runs the complete gamut of marketing problems. Many manufacturers or converters have customers who can be counted on the fingers of one hand; others are selling to a highly fragmented wholesale or retail trade. Part of the textile industry is directly dependent on fashion trends; part on technical developments which are occurring at an accelerating pace; and part is in a business which appears not to have changed significantly since Arkwright and Shuttleworth.

The textile industry does not need a special kind of market research; it needs the whole range of marketing research skills to be applied to solve some of the most intractable and challenging problems in British industry.

But it is important to be fully aware of the conditions which are necessary for marketing research to do an effective job. These can be summed up as ability and willingness to take marketing decisions arising from the research.

Ability to take decisions in turn depends on the recognition that marketing decisions are being taken all the time, based either on fact or on assumptions. Before research can even be designed, let alone used, these assumptions must be made explicit, so that the manager can assess how good or how bad the information is on which he is making assumptions.

Willingness to take decisions based on research is more difficult to assess. It is nothing to do with the size or resources of the company; and it may be enough for one influential man to have the drive to influence decision-making throughout the company. But it is unlikely that a company will be making fact-based marketing decisions, using marketing research effectively, if decision-making in other parts of the organization is completely dependent on unquestioned assumptions from the past, with no analytical approach to the assessment of new conditions.

Information Requirements

It is common to discuss marketing information requirements in terms of the source of the information. I prefer to categorize it in terms of the way in which the information will be used.

Costs and Margins

The marketer makes his living as a juggler with margins. In order to assess his margin he needs to know his product costs, his sales and marketing costs, and the revenue available. The revenue available will be discussed in a separate section on pricing policy. Cost information will normally come from within the company: it is at least as important as statistics on volume and value of sales.

The marketer is interested in more than just the cost figures, which go into his periodic calculations of margin. The whole essence of the marketing approach is to make meaningful comparisons and analogies. One of the most useful sources of comparison, especially in the textile industry, is the Centre for Interfirm Comparison Ltd, which makes available, on a confidential basis to those who assist in providing the information, data on a variety of very critical elements of cost.

A certain amount of information on the build-up of costs is also available from the Census of Production, which gives data on such important elements as stocks of materials and stores, work in progress, goods on hand for sale, wages and salaries, and capital expenditure. However, Censuses of Production appear at infrequent intervals, and very late: piecemeal volumes of the 1963 Census started becoming available only in 1969.

Market Size and Characteristics

This information area is perhaps the hard core of marketing research: the original 'market research'. Every marketing man will have, as a basic tool, statistics on his own sales, though he may have to adapt the classification and method of reporting to get information which is of more value than the financial ratios required by his accounts department.

His potential market will be the total market value of his own and competitors' sales. This will frequently be available on a regular basis from his trade association, which will act in this respect in the same way as the Centre for Interfirm Comparison. All member firms will submit delivery figures, which will be issued in total to those participating, usually on a monthly or a quarterly basis.

These figures must be distinguished from data on sales to the ultimate consumer, which are beyond the power of the individual manufacturer to supply. It is therefore dangerous to place too much reliance on a simple analysis of changes in 'market share' arrived at by comparing one's own deliveries with industry deliveries. Variations may very well arise from changes in trade stocks rather than in final demand for the firm's products. And changes in trade stocks themselves are almost always impossible to obtain from statistical sources.

The problem with internal statistics and trade association statistics is that the categories which must be used are *product* categories not *market* categories. External information, on the other hand, will be categorized in terms meaningful to the customers, which will very seldom be the same. A given man-made fibre, for example, may sell under a national or international brand name to fabric manufacturers who may either use it by itself, or together with other fibres, to make fabric. It may then go either direct to retailers for sales as fabric, or to makers-up of a wide variety of clothing and furnishing goods.

Finally, a certain proportion may be sold as sewing thread to retailers for home use. Suppose, then, that the manufacturer of the man-made fibre is interested in his share of the market. From Volume 75 of the 1963 *Census of Production* he ascertains that the gross output of the eight enterprises (twenty-seven establishments) in the industry was £211 million. This gives him his crude market share, but there is little he can do with it in terms of marketing action unless he knows how he is doing in each of the intermediate markets to which he sells. To do this he needs to go to no fewer than nine other Census volumes, which I list simply to show the complexity of 'desk research':

76 Spinning and doubling of cotton, flax, and man-made fibres.
77 Weaving of cotton, linen and man-made fibres.
81 Hosiery and other knitted goods.
82 Lace.
83 Carpets.
84 Narrow fabrics.
85 Household textiles and handkerchiefs.
87 Textile finishing.
89 Miscellaneous textile industries.

And this is only the start. Even if our manufacturer can sort out the place of his own product in the very wide variety of materials used for each of these types of product, he is still totally ignorant of the final wholesale or retail distribution pattern for his product. The *Census of Distribution*, of which the most recent relates to 1961, gives the number of outlets stocking carpets, bedding, furnishing fabrics, men's and boys' wear, women's and girls' outerwear, other women's and girls' wear, infants' wear, dress materials, and haberdashery. But there is nothing to say how much, in volume or value, of each of these categories of goods goes through each of the types of outlet; no indication of the importance of man-made fibres in each category; and no information at all on the ultimate consumer.

It will now be apparent how much is missing, even in the most simple factual analysis, from non-survey sources. If our manufacturer of man-made fibres is to make the most elementary assessment of his market he must carry out research, using sample survey techniques, on his final customers – who they are, what they want, and what influences them–on the relative importance of the various channels of distribution, including the margins available at each stage, and on many other subjects.

Survey research on market size and characteristics has two principal functions: to add knowledge which is not available from other sources, and to enable all sources of knowledge to be brought together in a way which makes sense, and can be acted on.

The first has already been discussed. Non-survey sources almost always start from the position of the manufacturer, and fail to give information about the customer. The second function is the more significant. Information is frequently available from survey sources about the right products; it is sometimes available about the right distribution channels; it is occasionally available about the right markets. But it is almost never available in a form which brings the three together to enable the marketer to take any real decision about how to formulate or promote or sell a given product to its proper market.

The Product

Marketing research has been used for many years to provide customer reaction to a product. An original ancestor of this technique is the Hollywood sneak preview. After the producer's lackeys had proclaimed their enthusiasm for the new masterpiece, it occurred to the men who actually had to sell it to the distributors that inside opinions might not be wholly objective. So audiences in certain selected cinemas in Southern California became accustomed to the advertised film being replaced by a new film before it had been publicized. Actors and actresses, producers and writers, heavily disguised, sat in the audience, winced at each groan and sneer, and warmed to each laugh and sob. This too was unsatisfactory: audiences in Glendale and Beverly Hills were not easily comparable with the Bronx or Hamtranck; and there was some dis-agreement on occasion about whether the audience was absorbed or bored, amused or contemptuous.

Nevertheless, something very like the sneak preview technique is used with great success by Marks and Spencer Ltd, who use the Pantheon and Marble Arch stores in central London to try out new lines, judging in the end, solely by sales, whether to order in quantity and sell throughout the country.

Marketing research introduced representative sampling, to ensure that the audience was typical of the movie-going public, and the questionnaire, to ensure that the same questions, meaningful questions, were being asked in all cases. This technique is applicable, with the necessary amendments, in a wide variety of fields. Milk chocolate, instant coffee, washing-machines, cigarettes, detergents: all of these can be offered on trial to a representative sample of consumers, and reactions recorded after a suitable period.

If the product is a variation on one already marketed either by the research sponsor or by a competitor, the placement test may be paired. The housewife is asked to try two or more different versions of the same type of product, and to record her opinions in comparative form. This is easier to do, since it does not require absolute judgement, and it corresponds in some part to the actual condition of choice in the buying situation.

Such a technique has been used for many years by some firms in the textile industry. Manufacturers of stockings may maintain panels of women who receive free samples of new designs, and report on their experience of them. This is also possible for a variety of low ticket items of clothing where utility is perhaps of more significance than fashion.

But it will be evident that these techniques are not suitable for a great deal of the clothing industry, and thus for the textile industry behind it. The reason is quite fundamental to marketing research, and misunderstanding of it is a common source of disenchantment with research findings.

However good the sample, and however perceptive and unambiguous the questions, the situation in which the respondent finds herself in a market survey is always to some degree false. It is impossible to simulate exactly the conditions of the market-place, where a choice has to be made, with limited resources, between alternatives which differ not only in product formulation (which, for a new product, will not be known in advance).

Products also differ in price, in packaging, in the reputation of the manufacturer, in the amount of money and skill spent on advertising and promotion. Their success in the market-place is affected by their availability in the retail distribution network, location in the shop, and other less rational factors.

None of these can be satisfactorily simulated in a product test: if they could, the launching of new products and designs would be a much less risky business than it is. Marketing research in this sphere tends to be valuable as a spur to killing off the sickly new product more quickly than would otherwise be the case. This in itself may be a source of very considerable saving of money and effort.

The use of field surveys should not be allowed to replace other methods of inquiry. In the textile industry, particularly those sectors in which technical development is taking place, a close study of competitive patent registrations is essential, from both a technical and a marketing viewpoint. Even if patents or registrations of applications are cryptic in themselves, they indicate the lines on which competition is working, and provide indications of future market trends.

Attitude Research

It has been pointed out that the product itself is only one of a number of factors which influence success in the market. No textile manufacturer needs to be reminded of this. A considerable proportion of total expenditure on market research is on the way in which the product is presented to the market; the importance of the manufacturer's reputation, and how it can be enhanced; packaging, sizing, and formulation of the range; and, most important and expensive of all, advertising and sales promotion.

The problem for the textile manufacturer is immensely more complex than for the manufacturer of detergents or confectionery. Fashion changes take place at very great speed, and apparently at the whim of forces outside the control of any industry. Even industrial espionage is not successful in getting audience information on

Paris fashions; above-board market research is hardly going to improve the position.

However, there is scope for some improvement in the study of which of many new styles shown at fashion shows are going to be popular. It is well known that women are not able to forecast what fashions they themselves will be wearing in six or twelve months' time; but the mini-skirt survived for years all the top designers' attempts to outdate it, and public opinion plays some part in this process.

In other fields – such as men's and children's clothing and soft furnishings – fashion is less overpowering, and market research can be used to establish preferences in colour or design, to study trends in attitudes to different garments and different types and styles of furnishing.

The most common use of attitude research will undoubtedly be in the field of advertising and communications. In an industry where fashion and style is so important, the good reputation of a manufacturer and a brand name is a most valuable asset. The commonest form of research here is recognition of a brand name, and how accurately it is related by the public to the correct product field. Much advertising expenditure is intended to produce precisely this recognition and awareness, even before a particular garment, carpet, or fabric is to be promoted. There are innumerable examples of this, but perhaps the best are the major branded man-made fibres, and the leading makes of stockings and lingerie.

A typical market research project of this type will obtain reaction to brand names, and to the products it covers; attitudes to the products themselves, in terms of design, quality, price, etc., knowledge of the manufacturer and his reputation.

Direct advertising and media research involving assessment of the penetration of advertising media among the target audience, awareness of the advertising and its message, and comprehension of copy points, are covered elsewhere in this book.

Pricing

This will be a very short section: marketing research has not, to my mind, evolved satisfactory methods of assessing the acceptability of different price levels. There are good reasons why this should be so for all industries: price is the final element in the marketing mix, or in the total buying situation, and unless this buying situation can be simulated effectively by research, the critical decision to buy or not to buy at this price cannot meaningfully be made.

The situation is more difficult still in textiles, when the same product may be sold at totally different prices by a chain store and a draper's next door to each other in the High Street. Indeed, the textile industry not infrequently delights the academic economist by producing examples of reverse price elasticity of demand, where demand increases with an increase in price. In other words, the consumer is buying much more than a product when she buys clothes or furnishing: she is buying a way of life, self-respect, and the admiration of her family, friends and neighbours. Price may, in certain circumstances, be a minor element in the assessment of costs and benefits.

Distribution Research

In its classical sense distribution research consists of factual assessment of the number, type and location of retail outlets selling a given product. The next stage is the retail audit, where throughput and stocks of a given product and the brands of that product are physically checked at regular intervals.

These techniques, which are described in more detail elsewhere in this book, are applicable in theory to the textile industry: but the practical problems are very considerable.

The first problem is one of defining a product and a brand. Most grocery and household products, such as soup or soap, are recognizable as such, and can be clearly defined. The same is true, though with more complexity, of a pair of stockings, or a pair of men's shoes. But even the (to the researcher) notorious complexity of the biscuit and sugar confectionery markets is outstripped by ladies' shoes, or hats, or underwear. A garment may have one label, or labels indicating the shop, or the manufacturer, or the type and manufacturer of the material. It will be readily seen why classification problems have deterred the retail audit firms effectively from work in textiles.

*   *   *   *   *

The second problem is one of use, rather than of research technique. With so little vertical integration in textiles the customer who matters is very often not the ultimate consumer, whose needs are affected by policy decisions outside the influence of the manufacturer of the fabric, or the converter of the raw material. Retail research is in this case irrelevant to the manufacturer's research needs, since his promotion and product development are determined immediately by a much smaller number of direct customers. This manufacturer requires instead information about changes in the whole pattern of wholesale and retail distribution: the growth of mail order, the incidence of closed markets resulting from mergers and takeovers, and the often complex structure of discounts prevailing.

Competition

Market researchers have been schooled for many years to answer the question 'What is my share of the market?' The only proper answer is 'Why do you want to know, and what will you do if you know?' Unless it is related to a systematic study of alternative policies available to the company, research on brand share may be no more than a boost to the ego, or a twinge to the ulcer, of the chief executive.

However, information on brand share may, though meaningless in itself, lead a company to ask better questions of its market researcher. Suppose that brand share is declining in a rising total market – a not uncommon situation for an established firm in a technologically advancing industry. The rise in the total market could be simply due to demographic changes, such as an increase in the number of families with young children, which give no real clue to appropriate marketing strategies.

On the other hand, it could be due to a widening penetration of the product field among the population as a whole. And it is here that the question must be asked: 'Is my market share declining because competition is attacking the new market more effectively?' If so, how? Because in these circumstances, unless remedial action is taken, the company is doomed to a continued decline in market share, and is vulnerable, as competition acquires a healthy base among new buyers, to direct attack in its own area of strength.

Market research is also – if we rule out industrial espionage – one of the most effective sources of information on competitive plans and developments.

A company salesman may be on very friendly terms with his customers, and yet not be told what his competitors are doing or planning or promising. A market research interviewer, on the other hand, especially if he is working anonymously for a consultant rather than directly for a manufacturer, may be given a good deal more information.

There is nothing suspicious or underhand about this. A market researcher should always operate within the Code of Standards of the Market Research Society, or some comparable code, which ensures that the interview is not conducted under false pretences, and that the source of information will not be revealed unless explicit permission is given.

Under these conditions, the market researcher is enabled to build up, piece by piece, information which in aggregate gives a pattern of competitive activity not available from any other source. He is able to assess the way in which the development of his company can be related to the real world of his customers, and the likely effects of given marketing activity on his business and his profits.

Conclusion

All aspects of the activity of an enterprise in the textile industry are in need of contact with the market, and feed-back from the market. The role of market research, as one of the major sources of marketing information, is to provide this contact and feed-back, as a control on marketing and promotional activity, as a guide to product development, and as a basis for setting realistic targets and objectives for corporate development.

Reference

1 GREEN, P. E. and TULL, D., *Research for Marketing Decisions*, Prentice-Hall, New York, 1966.

PART THREE
Case Histories

14 | The Industrial User and His Marketing Research Needs: Three Case Studies

P. G. ANDERSON
Marketing Research and Analysis
Manager, Kodak Ltd.

The extent and nature of the use of marketing research techniques by an industrial company can depend upon a number of factors. These include:

1 *The size of the company*. Marketing research is one of a number of management techniques. The ability to employ any one such technique on a thoroughgoing scale depends partly on the size of the company. For the benefit of a substantial market research department to be economic the company usually has to be large.

2 *The susceptibility of the marketing problems which arise to market research techniques*. Companies whose products consist largely of fast-moving, heavily advertised products bought by the general public have at their disposal a number of techniques likely to be of value: product testing, advertising research, continuous panel techniques, motivation and other types of direct research on the consumer. On the other hand, a company selling small numbers of large and expensive pieces of capital equipment to a narrow and specific list of customers is not likely to find market research of much value. Most industrial companies lie somewhere on a continuum between these two extremes. The more they approach the former the more likely they are to be able to use the techniques of marketing research.

3 *The degree of sophistication of the marketing organization and its members*. Some managements are conservative in availing themselves of new techniques for increasing their efficiency. Other managements are more aggressive and more eager to exploit new

tools of management which become available for helping them increase their profitability. Today's professional manager would not think of taking any major action without basing himself on data provided by a specialist information system.

4 *Inevitably, the calibre of the marketing researcher and his staff.* It is as true of this area as of any that the best practitioner is not only a good technician but also a man who can see the assignment through his client's eyes and bring his expertise to bear at exactly the relevant points.

The marketing research department typically is a component within the marketing division of a company. Alternative positions are in the financial organization (perhaps when there is a particular desire to ensure that findings are in no way influenced by those with an immediate interest in the results) or reporting direct to the managing director. There are also one or two other alternatives but typically the marketing division is the place and certainly the results produced are by their nature the information basis for marketing activity.

Given that the marketing research department has been established, where do the demands for the department's services arise? Obviously in the problems which marketing people inevitably come up against. In a company where marketing research naturally has a large contribution to make, the executives of the marketing division are likely to be aware of the type of problem that marketing research can help in solving. This means demand from the marketing division to the marketing research department. Perhaps a rather more usual pattern is one where projects are also generated by the marketing research department's ability to appreciate marketing problems and how marketing research techniques might be able to solve them. The most efficient organization is undoubtedly where the marketing research department really is an integral part of the marketing division, where marketing people know what market researchers have to offer and where researchers make themselves sufficiently aware of what is going on in the selling 'front line'. Where this degree of integration prevails, the research done is a mixture of surveys requested *from* the marketing research department by the operating division and surveys initiated *by* the marketing research department where they see they can solve a problem. About six years ago in my own company the work carried out by my department was probably 50 per cent from each of these sources. The pattern today, after a considerable development of the marketing organization, is that much more than 50 per cent of the work is generated by demand on the department from the marketing group. This undoubtedly is a healthy sign and the right way for things to develop.

What type of problems arise? They are of all sorts and sizes. The three following case histories are typical for an industrial company and range widely in their complexity from relatively simple to quite sophisticated.

Estimating Size of Market from Published Statistics

Obviously, one of the most fundamental facts any manufacturer wishes to know about his business is the size of the market he is engaged in. One way is to carry out a survey of all or a sample of the firms in an industry, asking the firms selected the size of their annual output. This is likely to be very expensive to the manufacturer (although this is not necessarily a bar if the information is very valuable). There are also technical reasons why it may be difficult to obtain the necessary information with which to devise a sample precise enough to be able to obtain a sufficiently accurate answer. Another method would be to use a syndicated continuous panel service. The main limitation here is simply that such methods are restricted to fast-moving consumer goods. The best way it could possibly be done would be for members of the industry to exchange their sales data. This in fact is done in, for example, the motor-car industry. Nothing could be more accurate, nothing more up-to-date and it costs virtually nothing! It is an ideal, however, which is hardly ever reached.

The first choice of the marketing researcher would be to examine published information. Economists, statisticians and marketing researchers have always grumbled at the shortcomings in availability of statistics in the U.K. They still do although the statistical sources in the U.K. have improved greatly since the last war. There are now innumerable statistical series published by the Central Statistical Office, the Board of Trade, the Department of Employment and Productivity, H.M. Customs and Excise and many

other government departments, not to mention foreign govern-
ments, a whole host of trade associations, the United Nations and
other bodies. The setting up by the Board of Trade of the Business
Statistics Office in January 1969 was a development which is
undoubtedly going to have a profound effect on the quality and
quantity of data available to business and is likely to be of
immense value to marketing researchers. These various sources
contain data of a national accounting nature and on imports,
exports, population, production, distribution, and many other
subjects. The first gambit of any marketing researcher in virtually
any problem is to find out what data already exists on the subject
in mind and to do desk research. The first and most obvious course
in attempting to estimate the size of a market is to go to the published statistics.

'Size of the market' can be expressed in a number of ways. The
quantity and/or value of the product concerned coming on to the
market year by year is one very meaningful way. A simple model
for this could be expressed as 'production in the U.K. plus imports
minus exports'. Provided one has the components of this model, the
market size can be worked out very simply. Data on production is
contained in a Board of Trade publication known as the 'Business
Monitor'. This publication covers a number of industries. Exports
are also included in the same document. Import data is contained
in a publication of H.M. Customs and Excise called 'Overseas Trade
Accounts of the United Kingdom'. The size of the amateur still
camera market in the year 1964 is found by using this model to be:

	Quantity ooo's Units	Value £ooo's
Production	1,434	2,682
Exports	−630	−1,015
	804	1,667
Imports	+1,362	+6,326
	2,166	7,993

The simplicity, cheapness and accuracy of this method are
appealing. There can, however, be some disadvantages:

(a) *Availability.* This method can of course only be used if the
products you are interested in are included in published sources.

In fact a very wide range of products is included but many are not.

(b) *Detail*. Apart from availability of data on the actual product group, there is also a possibility that information is not included in sufficient detail. For example, in the above instance, import data divide the totals into miniature cameras and other cameras. Had this distinction not been made, the data would have been far less meaningful. As it is, the category 'miniature cameras' is defined as 'cameras taking film of 35mm width'. Within this definition there are at least three sub-categories, failure to distinguish between which is a severe drawback. In this instance, we are fortunate enough to have access to further information which enables us to make the necessary segregation. It may well be possible, incidentally, to come to an agreement with the government department concerned for the supply of additional data not included in regular publications.

(c) *Definition*. In any statistical work definition is tremendously important. The quantities in which data are stated (e.g. value, numbers, square or linear measure, etc.), the time or period covered, the universe to which data apply (e.g. the U.K., England, an industry only, etc.) and other factors must be defined for valid use. Similarly, it is absolutely essential that the categories dealt with (e.g. products) should be sharply defined and that it is clear what is included and what is not included under any heading. Even when there is this clarity, headings sometimes 'wear out' over time perhaps through development or innovation. For example, the heading 'cameras' over time came to include various extraneous pieces of equipment like some types of photocopying apparatus. This was due to the fact that a new invention appeared and was classified in the then existing category in official sources which seemed most appropriate. This tends to falsify the original definition. In the instance mentioned the photocopiers, having grown considerably in importance, now have the separate heading they merit. It is important to be aware of such irregularities when using published data.

(d) *Speed*. The speed with which this class of data becomes available is not always as great as could be desired. Regular series of data are often available fairly quickly. On the other hand data from censuses can take a number of years to become available. Whilst such material remains valuable, it inevitably suffers from the defect that it is out of date even at the point at which it first becomes available.

Despite these objections, the use of published statistics has an obvious appeal. In addition, such data collected over a number of years provides trend data to which statistical treatment can be applied for further purposes, such as forecasting.

Use of Customer Index for Basic Marketing Information

Knowing the size of the market you are in is a good start. Armed only with this knowledge, however, a manufacturer would feel a little bereft of hard facts on which to plan his marketing operation. The next major need is to find out about his customers – who they are and how they use his products. Where the customer is the consuming public, the marketer has at his disposal a range of well-established consumer marketing research techniques for finding the answers to this type of question – *ad hoc* surveys, retail audits, consumer panels and product testing procedures. On the other hand, the manufacturer producing goods for industrial or commercial consumption has a less easy task. There is, of course, little trouble if he is selling to a very small number of known customers. The majority of manufacturers, however, sell to relatively large numbers of customers. Some manufacturers produce goods with a single use in a single industry, but the majority of products have multiple uses in a number of different industries. The manufacturer needs, for the efficiency of his own operation, to know the uses to which his products are put, the industries they are used in, the size of the companies using them and any trends in these factors. For example, it is important for the marketer to know that A per cent of his business goes to industry X, B per cent to industry Y, and C per cent to industry Z, etc. This information is greatly increased in value if he further knows that, say, percentages A and B are increasing and percentage C is decreasing. When, from published sources, he adds to his knowledge that industries X, Y, Z are expanding or contracting, as the case may be, he has a tremendously strong feel of the market he is working in.

It would be possible to find out this type of information by a series of *ad hoc* surveys. This however could be extremely expensive and probably not particularly accurate. There is no agency service of a continuous nature that I am aware of which collects this type of information. The accounts department will have a large amount of useful information, for example, on the breakdown of customers by size of order or annual turnover and, of course, the actual trend of sales volume. This information is very valuable but still the marketer would like more. The industry of the customer or end use of the product are likely to remain unknown quantities if this source is available. Names like I.C.I. or The Steel Company of Wales are indicative enough (although the former covers a number of industries). A name like A. Smith Limited conveys nothing whatsoever.

In reality, a lot of this very desirable information is already available in a manufacturer's own company, particularly if he has a sales force selling direct to users (the situation is not so easy if a substantial proportion of his goods are sold through wholesalers). This source is the representative. He actually *calls* on A. Smith Limited and therefore knows perfectly well what industry they are in. He also knows the use to which the product is put and he can probably make a guess as to the size of the company in terms of number of employees, provided the classification you ask him to make is not too fine. It is possible to develop a system which collects this data held in a dispersed and unusable way and turn it into a systematized marketing information flow of great value in marketing operations.

Kodak Limited has a number of such surveys in continuous operation, known as customer indexes. A typical procedure for these surveys is as follows:

1 A survey card, as small and simple as it can reasonably be made, is devised. This contains in tabular form the specification of the type of information required. This specification is defined by the operating marketing division in agreement with the marketing research department. In an advanced, but not final, form the card is piloted with two or three representatives to check feasibility and completeness. The information asked for is typically the industry of the customer, his application for the company's products, his size (e.g. in number of employees), his use of other manufacturers' products, etc. Sales data can be added at a later stage (e.g. 4).

2 At the same stage a follow-up card is also designed. The purpose of this is to accommodate information obtained subsequently to the initial survey (see 3) so that the records (see 4) can be updated.

3 The survey forms are then issued to the sales force, each representative filling in one form for each customer on the next call he makes on them. In theory, a complete set of survey forms should be available at the end of the first complete journey cycle after the survey is initiated. In practice, due to journey cycles not always including every customer on the territory, human failing, etc., the survey usually takes more than one journey cycle to complete.

4 The data from each survey card is then coded for incorporation into a data-processing system for permanent record and analysis. The original card is returned to the representative, so that he has a record of his own customers and the information he has given about them.

5 On each subsequent call (after the one on which the initial survey form was completed), the representative fills in a follow-up card, which enables him to record any *change* in the information about his customer. In the event such changes tend to be few.

6 This follow-up card is then used to amend the master record, thus keeping it up to date.

The data-processing methods used in the past have consisted of conventional card punching, sorting and tabulating machinery and even of edge-punched card records (which have proved the most flexible and effective of any but have size limitations). Most records currently are fully computerized.

By way of examples of the type of data collected and the way they are ordered for informational purposes, the following table sets out the overall analysis of the business of the Industrial Sales Department for the period 1959–64. The type of activity of the customer and the rate of increase of business from each of these types of activity over the five-year period is analysed. (The figures have in fact been falsified but the illustration remains valid.)

It is of basic importance for the marketing manager concerned to know that 56 per cent of his business comes from five types of activity only out of a total of twenty. It is even more important for him to know that engineering and aircraft and missiles customers, together accounting for 25 per cent of the business, have expanded

Analysis of Industrial Sales Department's Business, 1959–64
By Activity of Customer

Activity of Customer	% of Dept's Business	% Increase over Period
Engineering	14	+ 51
Aircraft and missiles	11	+ 37
Metal manufacture	11	+166
Public services	10	+ 9
Food, drink and tobacco	10	+172
Electrical goods	8	+ 75
Distributive and other services	7	+100
Teaching	5	+185
Chemical and extractive	5	+123
Technical and scientific	5	+173
Vehicles	2	+255
Nine other activities	12	—
All customers	100	+ 83

over the period under review at a rate very much less than the average rate for all customers. He will also note that in public services, a substantial proportion of the business, the expansion has been virtually nil. On the other hand, sales to metal manufacture, technical and scientific and food, drink and tobacco, together accounting for a quarter of the total business, have expanded at rates at least twice as fast as all customers on average. In addition, the much smaller areas of teaching and vehicles are obviously expanding at a tremendous rate. Here indeed is material which is vital in formulating marketing policy which an uncritical statement total figures from the accounts department would completely ignore.

Similar analyses can be carried out for size of customer, area of the country or representative's territory. An analysis by size of account can be illuminating. (See p. 274.)

Whilst the situation prevailing today is very different, at the time of the analysis 49 per cent of customers in this illustration accounted for 4 per cent of the business whilst only 7 per cent of the customers accounted for 60 per cent of the business. This is a compelling pointer to distribution and trading policy.

This index also produces data helpful in routing and customer calling policy and could be used to produce lists of customers of a particular specification where these are needed, e.g. for mail promotions or sales activity concentrated on a particular sector of

ANALYSIS OF A TYPICAL SALES DEPARTMENT'S BUSINESS
By Size of Account

Size of Account	% of all Customers	% of Business
Under £100	49	4
£100–£249	22	10
£250–£999	22	26
£1,000–£1,999	4	14
£2,000 and over	3	46
	100	100

the market. It is valuable in the administration of other marketing research surveys because it is a major aid in designing and locating samples. It also has other research advantages, particularly in relation to forecasting.

The great advantage of this method is that it is relatively straightforward and can often be carried out with a company's existing resources. This is certainly true if data processing equipment is already installed in the company. Even if it is not, hand analysis methods are possible. The results, whilst simply obtained, are tremendously valuable for a basic understanding of the market and for guiding marketing policy.

Investigating a Market by Sample Survey in Preparation for a Product Launch

Cases 1 and 2 are fundamental and therefore extremely important. A sound basic informational background is necessary for any worthwhile marketing operation. They are also relatively elementary in concept and require no great expertise to execute them. It is often necessary to carry out studies of a considerably more sophisticated, deeper and far-reaching nature.

Published data tend more to contribute to the basic outline of a market than to describe its function or its dynamics. Sales data, whilst very important and often a good guide in forecasting, are otherwise very limited. It is often necessary to find out much greater detail about the structure of an industry, the practices used in it, the attitudes and motivations of its members – a lot more about 'what' and not only that but also 'why'. In these cases much more complex methods are needed.

A case which illustrates this more demanding requirement is the need to investigate an existing but unfamiliar market prior to launching a new product in it. For security reasons it is not possible to identify the product field (although the industry involved was one of the sectors of the printing industry) but the purposes of the study and the research techniques used are nevertheless clearly demonstrated.

The progress of the survey followed five clearly distinguishable stages:

1. DESK RESEARCH

All surveys start with desk research. A few – like case 1 – finish with it. It is always just possible that the information we want to find out is already available somewhere. One would look extremely foolish if one devoted substantial resources to discovering something that was already known. Existing sources rarely suffice to answer the whole inquiry but at least they can give a valuable background, help in an understanding of the assignment and delimit the areas where information is to be found.

There is a certain amount of published data on the printing industry. The Censuses of Production contain a certain amount of basic data and a number of limited studies have been carried out, notably an economic survey of the industry of a few years ago and a statistical study by one of the magazine publications in the industry. However, at the time the survey was carried out (1965), 1963 Census of Production data was still not available and consequently data from the 1958 and previous censuses had to be used. These tended to give not very helpful data about the number of establishments, and certainly gave no information about the actual product field we were interested in. The other studies available were no more than useful background. Original research had therefore obviously to be undertaken.

2. DEVISING THE METHOD

The terms of reference for the survey were:

(i) To obtain a reasonably accurate estimate of the size of the market expressed in quantity terms for the type of product in question.

(ii) To obtain an intimation of the likely rate of development of the market.

(iii) To study the structure and functioning of the market in terms of users, suppliers, equipment owned, marketing and distribution methods and brands available in the immediate product field.

(iv) To study the technical and working practices within this segment of the industry.

Answers to qualitative aspects do not normally require highly representative or precise samples. Quantitative measurements of any precision certainly do. Thus, the requirement in the present case was for an orthodox sample survey, with a well-designed sample of a size sufficient to yield an acceptable degree of precision in the quantitative results.

Probably the most difficult element in the plan was to find sufficient information about the universe of printing firms to enable a study of anything like sufficient accuracy to be carried out. A frequent frustration in industrial marketing research is the lack of a sampling frame of all firms in the industry being surveyed. Our search for a sampling frame yielded a fairly good approximation in the form of a Trade Directory. This purports to list the majority of firms in the industry and the edition currently available at that time listed something like 8,000 firms. Various other well-informed trade estimates of the actual total number varied between 9,000 and 11,000. There was little doubt that the firms not included in the directory would be the 'tail' of very small companies which are characteristic of many industries. Even armed with this frame, there was still no indicator as to the number of firms coming within each of the three sectors of the market – letterpress, lithography and gravure – let alone characteristics, e.g. by size or type of business, within each sector. The scheme conceived to enable us thus to define the shape of the industry was to carry out a simple random one-in-three sample of the names in the directory and send them a very simple mailed questionnaire to discover the type of work carried out. Answers from those in the sector in which we were interested would then act as a sampling frame from which to draw a sub-sample for a more detailed inquiry by personal interview.

With this concept in mind, the question naturally arose as to whether to carry out the work with the resources of the department or to buy the services of an agency. The financial requirement would have been fairly substantial. Even when giving a job to an agency, much internal staff effort is required in the way of indoctrination, compiling the questionnaire, and generally liaising and supervising the progress. On the other hand, our own staff had the requisite technical background. The mailed questionnaire phase to study the shape of the industry would not in any case cost a great deal. The personal interviewing requirements were well within the capacities of the department and it was felt desirable for the department to acquire the valuable additional knowledge which would be obtained in personally doing the interviewing. It was thus decided to make the project an internal one rather than to buy the services of an agency.

The plan thus became:

(a) A phase to study the universe itself (described above). It was also decided to 'hitch' on to this phase a simple inquiry into the volume usage of the class of product under study. Such a quantitative measurement would require a much larger sample than would otherwise be needed or could be mounted in the personal interviewing phase, although the latter would also be used to obtain quantitative information to supplement the mailed survey phase.

(b) To draw a sample of the sector of the industry being studied, for the purposes of the personal interviewing stage. This was carried out on orthodox statistical sampling principles.

(c) The development of a fairly heavily structured questionnaire to elicit the information required in the study.

(d) To administer this questionnaire to the sample selected in (b).

(e) To process the results so obtained by hand methods, analyse these and write an interpretative report.

3. ASSESSING THE INDUSTRY

The phase to identify the firms in the sector of our interest and to study its shape went reasonably satisfactorily. It is a characteristic of mailed questionnaires that the response can be very low. I was interested particularly in this phase for technical reasons; I hoped that the questionnaire would be short and simple and that the direct approach from a large company with a very well-known name and a good industrial image would net a good response. In fact it turned out to be 47 per cent. In terms of the usual yield of this method this was good. However, it was still too low from the point of view of eliminating bias in the subsequent work. We therefore carried out a supplementary phase of telephone interviewing asking exactly the same questions of the non-responding firms. This resulted in a final response of 73 per cent.

4. FIELD WORK

Having identified the sector of the industry of our interest, a sub-sample of 190 was designed for personal interviewing (see (b) above). This phase was carried out satisfactorily. Quantitative information was obtained to supplement the information from the mail phase. In my experience, interviewing of this variety yields a very high response rate and there is rarely any reluctance to provide the information required. In this type of interview, the subject-matter the interviewer is discussing with the respondent is the respondent's day-to-day business concern and is therefore of high interest. Interviews tend to be technical discussions which flow easily and it is doubtful whether there is any conditioning or biasing such as can occur where attitudes are concerned or where opinions of consumer brands are being sought or where a great deal depends upon the exact wording of a question. Nevertheless, a lot of attention is still required in devising the questions for the structured part of an industrial interview.

5. PROCESSING AND ANALYSIS

Although the initial phase involved something like 2,000 questionnaires, the information on each was so little and so simple that hand analysis was the appropriate method to use. With the lengthier personal interviews, the number was so small as to make hand analysis again appropriate. There was nothing in any way atypical about this concluding phase of the survey.

These three cases show a variety of techniques. They are typical of the marketing research needs of a large manufacturer. They also demonstrate that a very great deal can be done with the resources normally found within most industrial companies of any size.

15 Using Data from Consumer Diary Panels to Evaluate Consumer Promotions, etc.

J. H. PARFITT
Managing Director, Mass Observation Ltd.
and
DR T. I. McGLOUGHLIN
Director, Attwood Statistics Ltd.

The essential requirement for an evaluation of advertising and promotional expenditures is to have an accurate and reliable measurement of the effect of these activities.

Since the ultimate purpose of advertising and promotion is to sell the product it is logical to define 'effect' as effect on consumer sales, whatever intermediate measurements (consumer reaction, advertising awareness, etc.) may be legitimately employed to increase understanding of the stages of the complex process between advertising and sales.

Even if the sales effect of advertising and promotion is measured, this can be a barren activity unless the results can be correctly interpreted to aid decisions about future action. The evaluation of the past is interesting but only useful in marketing terms if it can be used to predict what is likely to happen in similar circumstances in the future.

On the whole, marketing research has not been very successful up to now in opening up this area of potential knowledge, despite the big prizes to be gained from doing so. We still live in an age when an experienced marketing man steering by the seat of his pants and armed with a minimum of relevant research data fixes next year's advertising and promotional expenditure with one eye on what his competitors are likely to do and the other on what he and they spent this year – and who is to say he is wrong? This paper does not supply the complete answer – it merely tries to throw light on the problems of research, and the ways in which it might develop, using the techniques available in continuous Consumer Panels.

What part can Consumer Panels play in evaluating advertising and promotion?

A priori, Consumer Panels are well situated to play an important part in the problems of evaluating advertising and promotional expenditures for consumer products, by measuring the effect they have on purchasing behaviour.

(*a*) They measure consumer purchasing behaviour accurately and sensitively.

(*b*) They measure this behaviour on a continuous basis, and this is important because the effect of advertising and promotion needs to be observed over time preferably in the same consumer sample.

(*c*) They also measure some of the principal ingredients in the advertising/promotional mix; they can measure exposure on the part of the consumers to Press and TV advertising (and to radio and cinema also) and they can determine when purchases are made involving promotions (most types of promotions, at any rate).

Despite all these advantages, however, the resulting measurement of the relationship between advertising/promotion and consumer purchases can be elusive and even when successfully measured is often difficult to interpret as an indicator of future action. Why this should be, and the type of measurements available from Consumer Panels are discussed in the next sections.

The complexities of the evaluation of advertising and promotions in terms of its effect on consumer purchasing behaviour

Despite the evident advantages of continuous Consumer Panels for measuring the immediate sales effect of advertising and promotion, there are in reality a number of practical difficulties that sometimes make the clear evaluation of these activities very elusive, particularly the evaluation of advertising. There are three principal difficulties and these spring from the complexity of the problem itself rather than from the Consumer Panel techniques as such.

(i) THE SHEER COMPLEXITY OF CONSUMER PURCHASING BEHAVIOUR

Even in product fields of relative marketing tranquillity where total purchases and brand share hardly vary over time, there is usually considerable change in individual purchasing behaviour concealed beneath the surface of this stability. This can complicate the interpretation of the simple relationship between exposure to advertising or promotion and purchasing.

Although in aggregated data the increases and decreases in purchases made by individuals balance out in a stationary situation, purchases made by individuals can show relatively large changes. In an actual example, the purchases of 350 households in seven product fields (of high purchase frequency) over two consecutive eight-week periods increased from 21·3 to 21·5 packages. However, 49 per cent of households' purchases changed by more than 20 per cent. This can complicate the interpretation of the simple relationship between exposure to advertising or promotion and purchasing and puts a premium on samples of adequate size.

(ii) THE COMPLEXITY OF ADVERTISING AND PROMOTIONAL ACTIVITY IN SOME PRODUCT FIELDS

In Great Britain, in particular, there are a number of product fields where promotional activity is the rule rather than the exception and for each brand one promotion overlaps the other in steady progression and a very high proportion of total purchases are made with one type of offer or another. The following example (Fig. 1) from a washing powder brand is by no means an exception.

Many of the competitive brands had a similar level of promotional activity and, in addition, advertising is widely used by these brands. Whilst the immediate effect on purchasing behaviour of the total activity can be observed, it would be extremely difficult to isolate the effect of any specific promotion. The measurement of isolated promotions or advertising campaigns which can be usefully provided in many fields (and a number of examples of which are given in this paper) would not be relevant in this situation.

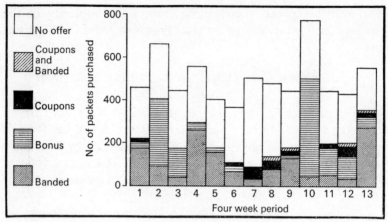

FIG. 1. Example of Overlapping and Complexity of Promotional Activity—Washing Powders.

Source: All figures and tables in this chapter are based on data from the Attwood Consumer Panel, Great Britain, unless otherwise indicated.

Here we are interested in the marginal effect of adding or subtracting a promotion and this complicates the analysis.

(iii) ADVERTISING DOES NOT NECESSARILY HAVE THE EFFECT OF INCREASING SALES

The purpose of an advertising campaign may be to prevent or arrest a decline in the brand's sales and indeed in most product fields this must be the primary purpose—either that or many advertising campaigns are not as successful as they were intended to be. This is also true of promotions, but promotions can be directly related to consumer purchases and therefore the immediate effect of the promotion can be observed more directly than for advertising. Advertising is one stage removed from the act of purchase and therefore cannot be as explicitly related. This complicates the interpretation of the measurement of the sales effect of advertising where the result is a negative or nil change in purchases.

In most product fields and most of the time only a minority proportion of advertising expenditure actually results in a positive increase in consumer purchases, i.e. in the sense that, in total, consumers can be seen to be purchasing more of the product after

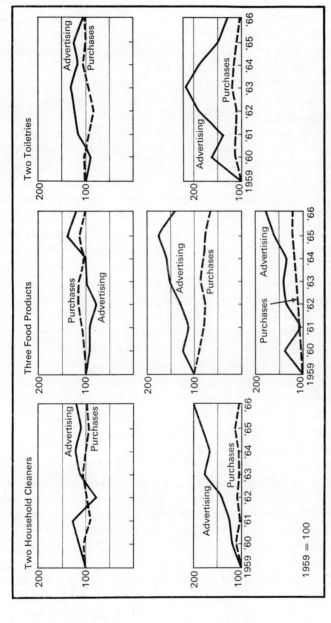

FIG. 2. TV and Press Advertising and Purchase Trends: Relatively Static Fields, 1959–66.

Note: A growth of about 5 per cent would be expected in each product field if the *per capita* consumption remained constant.

an advertising campaign than they were before. Most advertising is in fact defensive. This can be illustrated, by inference, in the relationship between TV and Press advertising expenditure and market growth or decline in a number of consumer product fields in Great Britain between 1959 and 1966.

These fields are all frequently purchased household consumer products: packeted foods, household cleaners and toiletries. In all the fields the competition is fierce and generally increasing. Comparable expenditure figures are not available for promotional activities but in none has promotional activity decreased and in most it has substantially increased. In every field the nationally advertised brands represent the dominant share of the market (in some virtually the total share) and the advertising expenditure does *not* represent a total growth of advertised brands at the expense of unadvertised brands. In some fields new brands have entered the market and taken share from existing brands (notably the two toiletry fields) and in most there has been a significant shift of brand shares in this period among the established brands and these activities are reflected in the advertising expenditures.

In only two of these fields has there been any increase in the total market. All this adds up to a high and increasing proportion of defensive advertising, as distinct from advertising resulting in a measurable total increase in consumer purchases.

Even in product fields which are expanding substantially where advertising expenditure is associated with increasing purchasing volume (and these are a minority of household consumer fields) there is still a great deal of defensive advertising.

Figs. 2, 3 and 4 illustrate expanding fields.

In the first two of these fields the fastest growing part of the market has been the developing 'own label' brands, which account for virtually none of the advertising shown here. In the first field the mainly 'own label' sector of the market has increased in volume from 100 to 417 between 1959 and 1966 as compared with 100 to 245 for the advertised brands. In the second field the 'own label' volume increase has been six-fold compared with a volume increase from 100 to 220 for the advertised brands. Clearly this is a battle being fought on a price basis and much of the advertising (and the increasing promotional expenditure) is designed to combat declining share, but not so far declining volume.

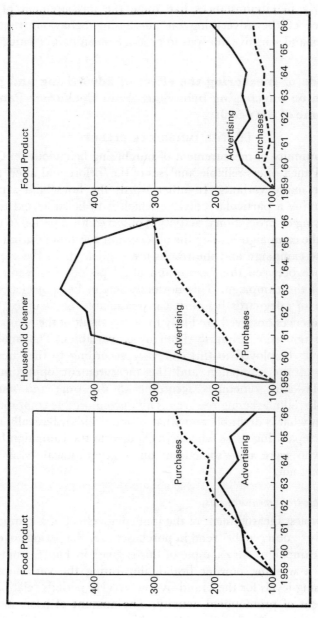

FIG. 3. TV and Press Advertising and Purchase Trends: Expanding Fields, 1959–66.

Clearly in circumstances like these the measurement of the influence of the advertising on purchasing behaviour requires complex and sensitive analysis to produce meaningful results.

Methods of measuring the effect of advertising and promotion on purchasing behaviour from Consumer Panels, and some of the result

(a) THE IMMEDIATE EFFECT

The continuity of measurement of purchasing behaviour on Consumer Panels offers reliable analyses of the 'before and after' type in their many variants. In other words the household sample representing a particular universe which is to be subjected to an advertising or promotional activity is observed for a period of time before the campaign breaks; the observation continues during and after the campaign and the results are compared. In theory, the difference between the 'before and after' periods represents the effect of the campaign. This normally has to be subjected to a number of safeguards before it can reasonably be assumed that the differences observed are likely to be the result of the campaign and do not arise primarily from other variables. The analysis techniques employed to this end vary according to the circumstances of the campaign and the measurement opportunities available – and sometimes according to the time and money available (all marketing research is an uncomfortable compromise between what is desirable and what is practicable). Basically they involve separating those who were exposed to the campaign from those who were not – sometimes on a geographical basis and sometimes not.

(i) *Simple trend measurements*

The simplest measurement of the immediate effect of a campaign is merely to observe the trend in purchases over the period covered by the campaign. An example of this is given in Fig. 1, from the case of a washing powder brand, illustrating the variations in purchasing levels for the brand by four-weekly periods relating to the extent of promotional activity. The amount of promotional activity is complex, but the relationship to purchasing behaviour is clear. It can be argued, however, that other variables (e.g.

variations in advertising expenditure) may have accounted for the changes and some form of control for these other variables is often introduced into this analysis.

(ii) *Area control samples*

The two following examples, one for a coupon promotion and the other for an advertising campaign, make use of geographical control areas, i.e. simultaneous measurements before and after the campaign in areas not exposed to the campaign. The coupon example concerns a mildly seasonal packeted food product and the coupon was applied in February at the beginning of the peak season in an area where the brand was relatively weak (the North). The control area where the brand was strong (the South) did not receive the coupon.

The conclusions from this analysis are that the coupon had a substantial effect on buyers and expenditure in February and retained a substantial part of this in the three following months, even after allowing for seasonal increases that would occur at this time anyway. This is particularly well illustrated in the improvement of the brand's share of the total market in the North.

The advertising example using a geographical control area produces a negative result in the long run after a slight (but not statistically significant) advantage in the period of the advertising campaign. This example involves another food product where *increased* TV advertising was used in one area and the results are compared in areas where the TV advertising was not increased. A twelve-week control period was used (the product measured has a high purchase frequency) before the increased advertising began, to compare the purchasing levels in the experimental area and the control areas.

TABLE I

AREA CONTROL MEASUREMENT FOR AN ADVERTISING CAMPAIGN
Volume of Purchases (Control Period = 100)

	Pre-Campaign Control Period 12 weeks	Campaign Period 12 weeks	Remainder of the year 36 weeks	Same Period in 1966 36 weeks
Experimental Area	100	105	102	98
Control Areas	100	103	107	101

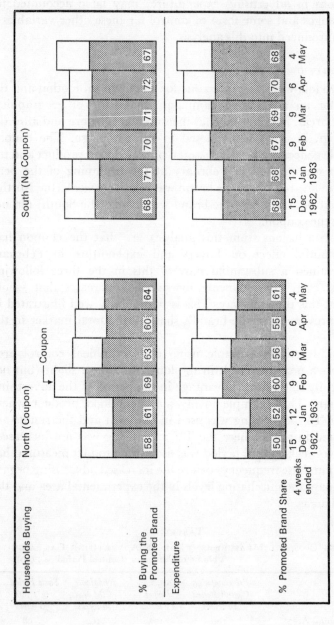

Fig. 4. The Influence of a Coupon on Purchases: Control Area Comparison.

It is likely that the interpretation of the results of this analysis would have been enhanced had the households in the experimental area been analysed by their degree of exposure to the increased advertising.

(iii) *Control samples within an area*

On the whole, the use of geographical control areas is not considered ideal since so often there appear to be differences in purchasing behaviour between areas, which are not removed by establishing a base period to iron them out before the campaign begins. Therefore, the establishment of controls *within* the area of the campaign is more generally favoured for this type of measurement – and clearly this is vital if the campaign is on a total national basis.

Some examples of this type of analysis are drawn from the A.I.M.A. Panel in Germany involving a coupon promotion, a free sample promotion and an introductory offer promotion; all are detergent brands, one new and two established brands. The analysis method used was to isolate the households who took up or received the particular promotion and to measure their purchases for thirteen weeks *before* this and for thirteen weeks *after* and to compare the results. The control sample was obtained by taking the next Panel household (in numerical order) to each household taking up the promotion – provided, of course, that they did not also take up the promotion – and making a similar analysis of their purchasing behaviour.

The first fact which emerges from these analyses is that, not surprisingly, promotions tend to be taken up more strongly by those who are already buying the brand. The ideal promotion would be one where the non-buyers of the brand were persuaded to take up the promotion leaving the existing buyers to buy in the normal way – an ideal, needless to say, which is difficult to achieve in reality. The extent of the existing buyer bias in these examples is shown in Fig. 5. The number of buyers and the volume of purchases of each brand prior to the promotion in the sample that took up the promotion are taken as 100. The comparable levels in the non-promotion sample are then calculated on this index basis.

In all three examples the brand purchasing levels of the housewives who took up the respective promotions were higher than in

T

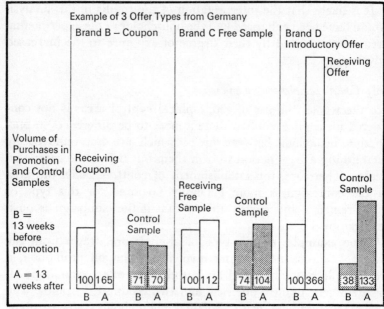

Example of 3 Offer Types from Germany

| Brand B – Coupon | Brand C Free Sample | Brand D Introductory Offer |

Attwood Institut Für Marktanalyse Gmb H

FIG. 5.

the control samples. Brand D had been launched in the period prior to the promotion and therefore the absolute purchasing level at this time was comparatively low (as will be seen by the after-promotion index). The presence of a control sample certainly modifies the conclusions to be drawn about the effect of these promotions in two of the three examples.

The simplest example is that of Brand B. Here the coupon has had the effect of increasing the number of buyers of the brand and the volume bought and the additional buyers are buying at the same rate per household as the pre-promotion buyers.

In the case of Brand C, however, the control sample suggests that the increase in volume of purchases of the housewives who used the coupon would probably have occurred anyway, and the additional buyers brought in after the coupon promotion are buying the brand at a lower rate per household.

The analysis of Brand D is complicated by the fact that the promotion occurred shortly after the brand was launched. The promotion produced a greater increase in the number of buyers of the brand (probably mainly new buyers) compared with the control sample – which was presumably one of the main objects of the exercise – but the rate of increase in volume of purchases is much the same between the promotion sample and the control sample (although at a different absolute level). This declining repeat purchasing rate as the penetration is pushed up is an expected phenomenon in the launch of new brands as will be seen later.

(iv) *Advertising exposure control samples*

Once again, the isolation of the purchasing behaviour of housewives exposed to a campaign, from those who are not, is employed in this example of the effect of an advertising campaign. In this particular example, involving a food product brand, a Press advertising campaign spread over a two-year period has been superimposed on the normal TV advertising support for the brand. A common sample of Panel housewives who were reporting their purchases over the full two years has been selected and these have been classified according to their likely exposure to the advertising (based on readership of the publications used in the campaign) into heavy, medium, light and non-reader categories.

The purchases of the brand (in volume and market share) were measured in the quarter-year prior to the start of the Press campaign and in the same period in the two succeeding years – as shown in Fig. 6.

After the first year of the advertising campaign the volume of purchases and share indices have a consistent relationship with the amount of exposure to the Press advertising – those not exposed showing a decline in purchases, those most exposed showing the greatest increase in purchases. By the end of the second year there had been an absolute control of this particular Press campaign. The only group whose purchases have not fallen below the 1964 level are the heavy and medium reader groups. It would seem that in the second year light readership was not sufficient to counteract the tendency for purchases to decline.

We have in this second year an example of a method of measuring advertising effectiveness when the advertising is engaged in resisting a decline in sales (see page 282).

There is a further measurement which can be extracted from

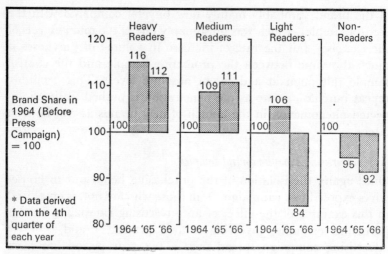

Fig. 6. Two-year Press Campaign—Food Brand I: Purchases Related to Advertising Exposure.

this study and this relates to the relative effectiveness of the Press advertising on housewives who have (or have not) been exposed heavily to the TV advertising for the same brand. The TV advertising is a relatively common element running through the whole period of the study, including the period before the Press campaign began (Q.4 1964). Fig. 7 illustrates this analysis. The readership groups have been split into two (rather than four) in the interests of sample size.

Almost all the increase in purchases among the heavy and medium reading groups is confined to those who had *not* already been exposed heavily to the TV advertising. The implication of this is that the TV advertising had already raised the level of purchasing of its heavy viewers as far as it was likely to go before the Press campaign began. Certainly the general level of purchases of the heavy and medium ITV viewers was some 10 per cent higher than that for the light and non-ITV viewers before the Press campaign began.

There is some hint here of a phenomenon that has been observed before and this is a 'saturation' level for the absorption of an advertising message, i.e. a limit on how far absorbing the message can be translated into purchasing action merely by increasing the number of messages sent.

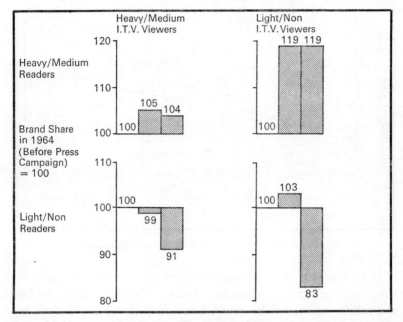

Fig. 7. Two-year Press Campaign—Food Brand II: Purchases Related to Advertising Exposure.

(v) *Demographically matched control samples*

The last of the examples of measuring the immediate purchasing effect of a campaign involves the complete demographic matching of the 'control' sample against which those exposed to the campaign are measured. The campaign involved a door-to-door promotion of the product in one area, and *within* this area a demographically matched sample was selected as the control. The object of the promotion was to increase the penetration of the brand in the market, in the belief that if housewives could be persuaded to try the brand they would like it and go on using it. The purchasing behaviour of the two matched samples was observed for a period before the promotion began and the cumulative penetration of the brand was measured, i.e. every time a household bought the brand for the first time, since the analysis began, they were recorded on a cumulative penetration curve. The result of the promotion was observed as shown in Fig. 8.

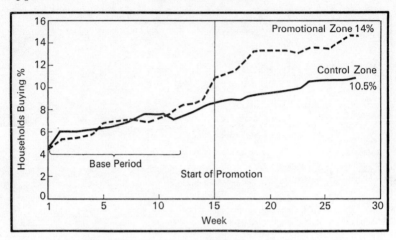

FIG. 8. Matched Panel Study: Week-by-Week Penetration.

It is estimated from this analysis that as a result of the promotion some 33 per cent more housewives tried the product within the period covered than would have done if there had been no promotion. It might well be asked: Did they go on using the brand after their first purchase? This question is the subject of the next section of this paper.

(b) THE LONGER-TERM EFFECT OF ADVERTISING AND PROMOTION

So far the examples chosen have illustrated the measurement of the immediate effect of advertising and promotional campaigns – although the term 'immediate' can be stretched over long periods as far as advertising campaigns are concerned. We have observed the changes in the trends of purchasing behaviour which appear to be the immediate effect of particular campaigns.

In reality, although the immediate effect is clearly important, there is a longer-term objective in advertising and promotion, and that is to bring about some advantageous change in the purchasing behaviour of those who are induced to buy at least once by the advertising or promotion. The pay-off is in the repeat purchasing which follows from the initial purchase resulting from the campaign, whether it is new buyers persuaded to go on buying or existing buyers persuaded to buy more.

(i) *Share prediction analyses for campaign measurements*

These longer-term behavioural changes can be studied in the analyses developed for brand share prediction purposes. The methods and feasibility of these analyses have been described in detail in a paper (Parfitt & Collins, 1968) presented at the 1967 Conference of the Market Research Society.

The basic formula for the prediction of share is:

Estimated Penetration of the Brand	×	Repeat Purchasing Rate	×	Buying Rate Index[1]

The particular use of the analysis in this context is to relate the repeat purchasing rate and buying rate index of buyers brought into the market for the brand, by advertising or promotion, to the characteristics of existing buyers, and to assess the effect of the campaign on the ultimate brand share. It also throws more light on the underlying purchasing changes that occur from the influence of advertising or promotion.

An example to illustrate this concept is taken from the launch of a toiletry brand (Brand F). The penetration of Brand F was estimated to reach ultimately 27 per cent of buyers in the market. Heavy promotional activity was introduced at this point and this increased the penetration to 39 per cent. This study is illustrated in Fig. 9.

(ii) *Related effects on different promotions*

Among the following cases of promotion activity associated with the launch of new brands, there are two examples (Brand A and Brand S) where the repeat purchasing rate of the buyers brought in by the promotion is in fact relatively high, in relation to the repeat rate of the existing buyers – and a further example (Brand F illustrated in Fig. 9) where the promotion buyers showed a very healthy repeat rate, even if it is substantially lower than that already prevailing. The fourth example (Brand C) is perhaps more normal, at least as far as price-cutting promotions are concerned.

It is important at this stage to recognize an almost invariable rule which emerges from this type of analysis. This is that the

---

[1] Buying Rate Index is a measure of whether the buyers are heavy, medium or light buyers in the total market against the average of the market.

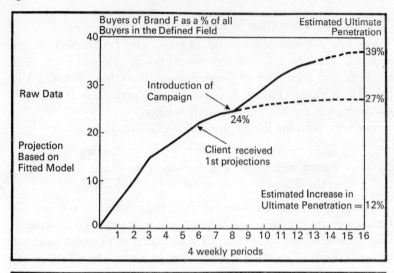

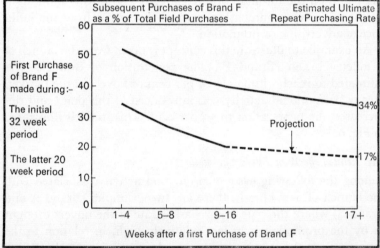

FIG. 9. The Effect of Additional Promotions on the Launch of a New Brand—I.

earlier the date a buyer enters the market for a particular brand the higher, on average, will be that buyer's repeat purchasing rate.

For newly launched brands this may have an important bearing on the timing of certain types of promotions, e.g. free samples. It also means that by the time a promotion is used to increase the penetration of the brand beyond the level at which it appears

TABLE 2

THE CONTRIBUTION TO THE ULTIMATE BRAND SHARE MADE
BY BUYERS INTRODUCED BY PROMOTIONS

Detergent Brand A (Gift on pack offer)	Ultimate Penetration $\times$	Repeat Purchasing Rate $=$	Ultimate Brand Share	Buying Rate Index
Before introduction of the promotion	6% $\times$	10% $=$	0·54%*	(0·9)
After introduction of the promotion				
— Buyers before promotion	6% $\times$	10% $=$	0·54%*	(0·9)
— Buyers after promotion	4% $\times$	8·5% $=$	0·31%*	(0·9)
			0·85%	

Source: Attwood Statistics (Nederland) N.V.

Toiletry Brand S (Coupon)				
Before introduction of the promotion	26% $\times$	38% $=$	9·9%	
After introduction of the promotion				
— Buyers before promotion	26% $\times$	38% $=$	9·9%	
— Buyers after promotion	12% $\times$	25% $=$	3·0%	
			12.9%	

Toiletry Brand F (Price cut)				
Before introduction of the promotion				
— Buyers already in	24% $\times$	34% $=$	8·2%	
— Expected further buyers	3% $\times$	25% $=$	0·75%	
			8·95%	
After the promotion				
— Buyers already in	24% $\times$	34% $=$	8·2%	
— Buyers after promotion	15% $\times$	17% $=$	2·6%	
			10·8%	

Food Brand C (Price cut)				
Before price cut†				
— Buyers already in	20% $\times$	19·5% $=$	3·9%	
— Expected further buyers	5% $\times$	18% $=$	0·96%	
			4·86%	
After price cut				
— Buyers already in	20% $\times$	19·5% $=$	3·9%	
— Buyers after the price cut	16% $\times$	10% $=$	1·6%	
			5·5%	

* Share calculated after allowing for buying rate index.
† Penetration estimate excluding expected new buyers.

otherwise to be stabilizing, the repeat purchasing rate associated with these additional buyers is likely to be considerably lower than that obtained from the buyers already brought in.

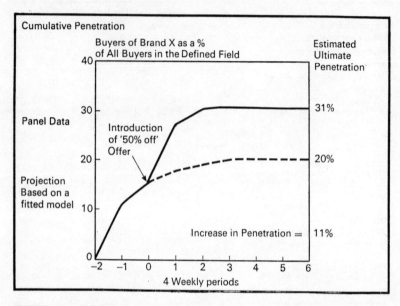

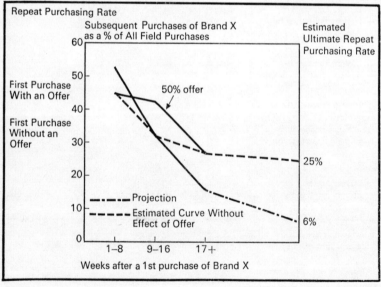

Estimated Ultimate Brand Shares				Ultimate Brand Shares	(Buying Rate Factor)
	Ultimate Penetration	× Repeat Purchasing	=		
Before Introduction of Offer }	20%	× *25%	=	<u>5.15%</u>	(1.03)
After Introduction of Offer }	Buyers of Brand X Without an Offer				
	*20%	× 25%	=	5.15%	(1.03)
	Buyers of Brand X With an Offer				
*Based on separate calculation	*11%	× 6%	=	<u>0.65%</u>	(1.01)
			Total	<u>5.8%</u>	
	Apparent Effect of '50% off' offer = + 0.65% (Or 12½% increase)				

FIG. 10. The Effect of a 'Deep Price Cut' on an Established Brand – I.

So far the examples have all been of newly launched brands. In this type of example the promotion has a special task to perform, i.e. to introduce buyers to the brand for the very first time. This differs only in degree from the effect of promotions on purchasing of established brands, however, and calls for no basic difference in analysis methods – the share of an established brand is just as much a compound of penetration, repeat purchasing rate, and buying rate index as is the ultimate share calculation for a new brand. The only technical provision is that to provide such an analysis for a going brand it has to begin at an arbitrary point in time (there being no convenient launch date to start from) and this point of time must be long enough before the start of the campaign to allow the penetration curve of 'first-time' buyers to flatten out, i.e. it must allow for the average frequency of purchase of the product.

An example of such an analysis is taken from an established brand of detergent (Brand X). In the normal way the brand would penetrate about 20 per cent of the buyers in the market and achieve a repeat purchase rate of 25 per cent (which would be normal in a highly competitive relatively disloyal market with five or six major brands to choose from) – thus indicating that its market share is around 5 per cent. In this example a 50 per cent price cut promotion was introduced with the effect illustrated in Fig. 10.

The effect of this price cut was to increase the brand share by 12½ per cent, which is very much in line with the other two price cutting examples we have – Brand F: 20 per cent, Brand C: 15 per cent. There is some suggestion from this that price cutting may have the effect of greatly increasing the penetration at the time but not achieving too much repeat purchasing in the long run.

It is possible, therefore, that some promotions which show less immediate effect than price cutting may show more long-term effect. It must be emphasized that this is only a suggestion, not yet a proven fact.

(iii) *Free sample promotion*

Free sample promotion is often used, particularly with new product launches and for food brands. The following three examples show that their effect can vary considerably, presumably dependent on the degree of product acceptance and the choice of targets for receipt of the free sample.

In the first example, of a food brand (Brand B), the sample was distributed selectively purely on a limited geographical basis.

In the second example (Brand K) the free sample was aimed at a special and dominant group of buyers in the field who had not so far chosen to try the brand to any great extent. The free sample was distributed in a magazine (selected by analysis of the buying behaviour of the readers) and succeeded in reaching a substantial number of the target group.

In the third example (Brand L) we have an entirely new washing product and the free sample was distributed right at the beginning of the launch to increase knowledge of the product.

The results of the three analyses are shown in Table 3.

The limited penetration achieved by the Brand B free sample was a direct result of the limited geographical distribution. The repeat purchasing rate was low and so too was the buying rate index, which reflects the large number of complete non-buyers picked up by the free sample. A similar conclusion applies to Brand K, despite the attempt to aim directly at the market potential. The timing of the Brand L free sample at the start of the launch, dictated by the need to get the product into homes where there would otherwise be no experience of it, clearly worked.

The ratio of the repeat purchasing in the free sample homes to those in the purchase homes (36 per cent) is also higher for Brand L than for the other examples (24 per cent and 18 per cent). It is

TABLE 3

THE CONTRIBUTION OF FREE SAMPLES TO THE ULTIMATE
MARKET SHARES OF THREE BRANDS

Method of Introduction to the Brand		Penetration	×	Repeat Purchasing Rate	×	Buying Rate Index	=	Ultimate Brand Share
Brand B	Free sample	3%	×	6%	×	0·59	=	0·2%
	Purchase	15%	×	33%	×	1·07	=	5·0%
								5·2%
Brand K	Free sample	14%	×	5%	×	0·5	=	0·35%
	Purchase	13%	×	21%	×	0·97	=	2·65%
								3·00%

Method of Introduction to the Brand		Penetration	×	Repeat Purchasing Rate	Estimated Ultimate Sales*
Brand L	Free sample	29%	×	3·0	0·9%
	Purchase	23%	×	8·3	1·9%
					2·8%

* With a new product there is no market on which to base share and therefore the ultimate level of sales is calculated in quantity terms. For this reason also there is no Buying Rate Index and the repeat purchasing rate is calculated as packets bought per four weeks.

perhaps merely a truism to conclude that a free sample campaign is likely to be at its most efficient when the product is likely to have a wide appeal (as distinct from a sectional appeal – unless the sections can be isolated) and when having a product 'in the hand' is more effective to demonstrate its advantages than more indirect methods. Brand L meets these requirements more than the other two brands, and Brand K got more directly at its target than Brand B, and this is reflected in the results.

(iv) *Advertising effectiveness in prediction analysis*

The final example in this section concerns the measurement of advertising effectiveness. The example has already been published in part and concerns an established food brand (Brand H). Promotions and advertising were used at the point where the penetration curve for the brand was flattening out and produced a substantial (and 'unseasonal') increase in penetration.

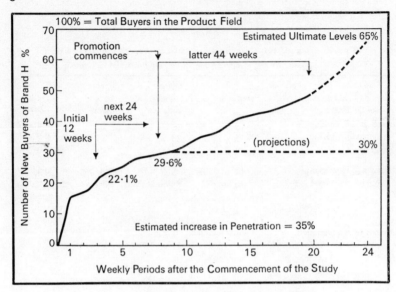

Fig. 11. Cumulative Penetration of Brand H.

The repeat purchasing rate of the buyers brought in before and after the promotions respectively are shown as follows:

TABLE 4

EFFECT OF PROMOTION ON SHARE OF BRAND H

Brand H	Ultimate Penetration		Repeat Purchasing		Buying Rate Factor		Ultimate Brand Share
Before the Promotion							
— First 12 weeks	22·1%	×	50%	×	1·29	×	14·3%
— Next 24 weeks and expected further buyers	7·9%	×	29%	×	0·85	×	2·0%
	30·0%		46%		1·18		16·3%
After the Promotion							
— First 12 weeks	22·1%	×	50%	×	1·29	×	14·3%
— Next 24 weeks	7·5%	×	29%	×	0·85	×	1·8%
— Latter 44 weeks and expected further buyers	35·4%	×	20%	×	0·90	×	6·4%
	65·0%		34%		1·03		22·5%

Apparent effect of the promotion of the ultimate brand shares = 6·2% (or 38% increase).

The various promotional and advertising campaigns added a considerable number of new buyers at a healthy repeat purchasing rate.

In this example a small part of that activity – a burst of Press advertising – is examined in more detail in order to study its contribution to the total effect.

The burst of Press advertising was of limited duration. The total Panel sample was classified according to whether they had been heavy, medium or light and non-readers of the particular publications used.

Two questions arise from this study:

(i) What was the effect of the campaign on purchasers of the brand?

(ii) Did the campaign produce new buyers or increase the purchases of existing buyers?

The number of new buyers coming into the market in the period during and immediately following the advertising burst is shown as follows both in terms of the absolute number (i.e. the contribution to the penetration curve) and the net increase (after allowing for lapsed buyers).

TABLE 5

INFLUENCE OF PRESS ADVERTISING FOR BRAND H

	Total	Heavy Readers	Medium Readers	Light or non- Readers
Buyers in the twelve weeks prior to the campaign	100	100	100	100
New buyers entering the market during and after the campaign	+38%	+44%	+40%	+28%
Net increase in the new buyers	+ 7%	+12%	+21%	−11%

Certainly, the increase in the absolute number of new buyers appears to be correlated with the degree of exposure to the advertising campaign, and the total net increase in new buyers is to be found among the medium and heavy readers.

The extent to which the existing buyers increased their purchases after the advertising burst is shown as follows:

TABLE 6

EFFECT OF ADVERTISING BURST ON EXISTING BUYERS OF BRAND H

	Total	Heavy Readers	Medium Readers	Light or non-Readers
Volume of purchases of existing buyers in the twelve weeks prior to the campaign	100	100	100	100
In the twelve weeks after the campaign	101*	109	108	86

* This represents an increase in repeat purchasing rate from 70% to 74%, due to a decline in total market purchases in the second period.

Again, the effect of the campaign, in terms of purchase volume of existing buyers, appears to be confined to the heavy and medium reading groups.

The total increase in volume of purchases over the period measured was 9 per cent, but this resulted from increased buyers and increased volume from existing buyers offsetting a net loss among light and non-readers. Thus, the campaign contributed to the total growth of the brand illustrated in Fig. 11 and Table 4 by the contribution made by households exposed to a greater than average proportion of the advertising.

The Long-term Use of this Type of Data

The effect of advertising and promotions on consumer purchases can be measured. So far, however, this has been done primarily to pursue specific and limited objectives. Important though these objectives are, the long-term use of this type of measurement is to learn a good deal more than we know at present about the likely effect of advertising and promotional campaigns *before* they begin. In fact we need to begin to draw up some rules, along the lines of those already being compiled for brand share prediction in test marketing. It is highly likely, however, that this is an area less susceptible to simple rules than is brand share prediction.

Basically, we need far more case histories than we have and they need to be analysed in a more standard way — along the lines set out in the last section. Only with a data bank of examples will we

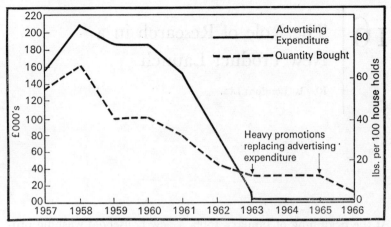

FIG. 12. Effect of Advertising Expenditure on Purchasing.

begin to see the common elements which run through these studies and use this information to influence future action. Already there is some suggestion of a common pattern emerging with regard to the effectiveness of certain types of promotions. One rule, however, has certainly emerged from the observations of Consumer Panel data and that is that no amount of advertising and promotion will support a brand which has lost consumer acceptance or indeed never obtained consumer acceptance. This principle is clearly illustrated in Fig. 12 showing a declining brand which heavy advertising and latterly heavy promotion was unable to resuscitate.

Reference

1 PARFITT, J. H. and COLLINS, B. J. K. (1968), 'The use of consumer panels for brand share prediction', *Journal of Marketing Research*, May.

16 | The Role of Research in a New Product Launch

Royds (London) Ltd.

At the beginning of January 1966, a new household washing product was launched on a test market basis in the Anglia ITV area. The brand name of this product was Bio-Tex. The launch of this product, Bio-Tex, introduced a new concept into the household washing practice of British housewives, as it was the first enzymatic-soaking product introduced into the United Kingdom, although it had been successfully launched in Holland in 1963.

The purpose of this chapter is to describe the role played by market research in the marketing and promotion of this new product Bio-Tex, from the start of planning in the summer of 1965 right through to the spring of 1967 when Bio-Tex finally achieved national distribution. It is our intention to discuss the wide variety of research techniques employed in connexion with the introduction of Bio-Tex and to show how research was used in the planning and development of the new product. This will be done by describing the use of market research during four separate stages in the development and introduction of Bio-Tex.

Phase 1   Planning the Launch
Phase 2   The Anglia Test Market Operation
Phase 3   Extension into the London and Southern ITV Areas
Phase 4   Extension of Distribution to Other Areas

Phase 1: Planning the Launch

In the early summer of 1965 Nicholas Products Limited, who were to manufacture and sell Bio-Tex in the United Kingdom, briefed the advertising agency Royds on the Bio-Tex product concept and outlined their plans for the launch of the product.

The Bio-Tex concept was entirely new to the U.K., taking the form of a detergent powder, with enzyme additives, specifically formulated for the soaking process. In order to pre-empt competitors who were expected to enter the U.K. market with similar products, Nicholas Products Limited wished to launch Bio-Tex with a minimum delay.

For various reasons (including the urgent timing, trade mark registration, printing and manufacturing arrangements) the brand name Bio-Tex, a 4 oz. pack size, pack design, product formulation and a retail selling price of 1s. 2d. had already been decided.

Although the advantages of an early launch were fully appreciated, it was also recognized that careful planning was essential to ensure a successful introduction into the highly competitive U.K. washing product market. It was, therefore, agreed that the initial launch would be confined to a single test area, Anglia, commencing in January 1966.

Market research was an important element in the planning of the launch, and in June and July 1965 a number of *product researches* were initiated.

(a) LABORATORY TESTS

A series of tests, carried out in the research laboratories of Nicholas Products Limited, confirmed the superiority of Bio-Tex over existing washing-powder brands in removing proteinaceous stains *just by soaking* – and showed a performance equal to existing washing powders in removing ordinary dirt and grime *by the normal washing process*.

But Bio-Tex was shown to be inferior to the leading washing powders in imparting whiteness or brilliance to the garments processed.

(b) PLACEMENT TESTS

A panel of 2,000 housewives was used for a placement test of Bio-Tex in plain packs. This test demonstrated that the concept of a specialist soaking product was acceptable to housewives and confirmed the performance findings of the laboratory tests – including some dissatisfaction with the 'brilliance' achieved in the final result.

(c) HOME ECONOMISTS

Two experienced Home Economists experimented with Bio-Tex in a series of tests, employing a variety of soaking and washing procedures, involving also a range of washing-machines.

Their reports were favourable to Bio-Tex as for the soaking process but warned against over-claiming on end-wash results from use of Bio-Tex *alone*. The Home Economists provided recommendations for terminology of pack instructions, leaflets and so forth. They also recommended that a larger pack size should be provided for regular users.

As a result of this body of research, it was decided that an optical dye should be included in the product formulation to improve optical brightness in the end-result. This decision was implemented in the launch programme.

It was also agreed that in addition to the 4 oz. pack a 9 oz. pack would be marketed at a later stage if test market results were favourable.

This research also provided guidance to the creative team and essential evidence for the I.T.C.A. copy committee regarding the claims made for Bio-Tex in TV commercials.

In September 1965, a Consumer Survey was carried out to investigate the basic household washing habits of housewives. The survey comprised:

(i) A national quantitative study amongst 505 housewives. Undertaken by Marketing Advisory Services Ltd.

(ii) Qualitative work involving five group discussions in London and Leeds and sixty-nine intensive interviews in Tyne-Tees and Anglia carried out by Royds Consumer Survey Unit.

The findings provided a broad and detailed background on household washing habits and the attitudes of housewives towards household washing.

What was immediately relevant to the planning programme was the finding that only a small percentage of housewives regarded soaking as an essential part of the washing process. Whereas 75 per cent of housewives soaked some items *sometimes*, only 11 per cent soaked most of the wash on a regular or fairly regular basis. Sixty-four per cent soaked some items more or less regularly for specific reasons mainly associated with real or imaginary staining problems: perspiration, blood, nappy and handkerchief stains, body and food stains in general.

The regular, heavy soakers believed that the soaking process was essential for a good end-result to all the wash. The light or irregular soakers – the majority – believed that soaking was necessary only for specific staining problems.

Sixty-six per cent of the housewives who soaked used their regular detergents for the soaking process; the remainder variously used bleach, salt, soda or disinfectant.

The findings of this survey proved to be vital in deciding on the positioning of Bio-Tex in the market for the launch operation and in finalizing the creative approach for the advertising campaign.

Although Bio-Tex had achieved over 15 per cent of the total Dutch *washing powder* market in only two and a half years, adequate consumer research information was not available. Royds therefore obtained consumer data in Holland to provide a basis for comparison with the U.K. research findings.

The Dutch data immediately disclosed an essential difference between the two markets. Soaking all or most of the main wash was an established tradition in Holland: and before the introduction of Bio-Tex, most Dutch housewives had used soda for this process.

Following analysis and evaluation of the U.K. and Dutch data, the agency advised Nicholas Products Limited that the *per capita* potential – at least in the short-run – must be taken as significantly lower in the U.K. than in Holland.

For preliminary planning purposes, it was therefore agreed that the first-year target in the U.K. would be set at a 2½ per cent market share (£1·5 million on a national scale) and that subject to test market results, the three-year target would be unlikely to exceed 7½ per cent (£4·5 million).

The decision had been taken to use television (plus door-to-door couponing) for the test market launch of Bio-Tex in Anglia. The actual creative strategy was determined by the following four principal considerations, of which the last two were derived directly from the consumer research:

(i) The *product* was a new concept: a specialized soaking product with a *unique* enzyme ingredient.

(ii) There was no direct *competition*. There was no other specialized soaking product – no competitor with enzymes.

(iii) The primary *target* was heavy soakers – 11 per cent of housewives. The secondary target was the light or irregular soakers – the majority of housewives, 64 per cent. In total, 75 per cent of housewives.

(iv) The *advertising objective* was to persuade all these soakers to try Bio-Tex for the first time.

To fulfil this objective one had to find an outstanding advertising proposition that would sell itself to *all* soakers. It was known from research that regular heavy soakers had a number of different reasons for soaking; but that there was *one* basic reason common to both regular and irregular soakers. They all soaked articles that suffer from difficult food stains and body stains – the proteinaceous stains that are removed by the biological action of enzymes.

This led to the launch theme: 'Bio-Tex soaks stubborn stains away.' This theme was to be used throughout 1966 on all advertising material – TV commercials, packs, leaflets and display material.

It was decided that the product description should be 'Soak and Pre-wash powder'; and that the enzyme content should be described as 'Biological Action'.

The advertising themes, the product description, and 'Biological Action', all positioned Bio-Tex as a unique product specially formulated for the soaking process. In this way Bio-Tex avoided a direct confrontation with the big washing-powder brands which together were spending at a rate of £9 million per annum in advertising and promoting 'whiteness' and 'brightness' claims.

A thirty-second launch commercial and a thirty-second continuity commercial were produced, based on the theme 'Soak stubborn stains away'; two seven-second commercials were produced at the same time.

The two thirty-second commercials were both pre-tested in storyboard and finished form. Pre-tests were carried out in London and in Norwich amongst representative housewife audiences in theatre test conditions. The pre-testing programme was carried out by Royds Creative Research Workshop in conjunction with Advertising Assessment Limited. In Norwich, studio facilities were provided by Anglia TV.

Shortcomings evident in the pre-testing of storyboard versions were remedied and the test results for the finished versions indicated that both commercials would effectively communicate the Bio-Tex concept.

Phase 2: The Anglia Test Market Operation

Selling-in of Bio-Tex in Anglia commenced as planned at the beginning of January 1966. In addition to the television advertising, there was house-to-house distribution of a 10d. coupon leaflet. Eighty per cent of homes in the area received a coupon and 38 per cent of these coupons were eventually redeemed.

The major research requirements involved in the test market operation were the provision of retail audit and consumer purchasing information.

(i) Retail audit data – distribution, consumer off-take and stock levels – were provided by Nielsen with a boosted sample of grocery outlets in the area.

(ii) Data on product penetration in Anglia homes, and repeat purchasing by housewives was obtained from a panel of 800 housewives specially set up by K.B.M.S. for Nicholas Products.

In addition, at the beginning of April 1966, Marplan carried out a survey amongst housewives, in Anglia to determine awareness of Bio-Tex, and initial attitudes towards the product.

The most important findings from these various researches were:

(i) By the end of March, data from the K.B.M.S. panel indicated that 50 per cent of housewives had purchased Bio-Tex at least once. It also indicated that about 11 per cent of housewives were making regular repeat purchases.

(ii) Nielsen data indicated that consumer off-take was in line with the planned target equivalent to a $2\frac{1}{2}$ per cent sterling market share of washing-powder market.

Nielsen also showed grocery distribution of more than 70 per cent, with Bio-Tex on display in 47 per cent of outlets at the end of March.

(iii) Marplan findings indicated that, by the beginning of April, 80 per cent of Anglia housewives had heard of Bio-Tex and nearly 70 per cent could correctly recall advertising detail.

These research findings, in conjunction with the known volume of factory deliveries and the enthusiastic support of retailers and salesmen alike, provided evidence that Bio-Tex was an acceptable product and the initial test marketing procedures had been effective. The decision was, therefore, taken to proceed with the next stage of the Bio-Tex launch into the London and Southern ITV areas.

Phase 3: Expansion – London and Southern

The marketing and promotion of Bio-Tex in London and Southern generally followed the procedures which had been successful in the Anglia test market.

Basic research information was provided from the Nielsen Food Index and from the Attwood Household Panel in these two areas.

The London area launch, which commenced on 1 July 1966, was extremely satisfactory. The data from Nielsen and Attwood showed that levels of distribution, the extent of product penetration and repeat purchasing, reflected the Anglia pattern.

The launch in Southern was, however, less successful than in London or Anglia. The Southern launch had originally been planned to start on 1 July, but was advanced by one month when information was received that another enzymatic wash product was to be introduced into this Southern ITV area on 1 July.

The Southern area launch was a deliberate test of a quicker and cheaper distribution programme.

The Nielsen data showed that after eight weeks Bio-Tex had only gained 45 per cent distribution in Southern area grocers compared with 70 per cent in Anglia and 65 per cent in London after a similar time lapse. The relatively low level of distribution for Bio-Tex in Southern was an important reason why coupon redemption was only 18 per cent – half the rate achieved elsewhere.

In September 1966, three months after the launch, a consumer survey amongst 300 housewives was conducted in the Southern area by Royds Consumer Survey Unit. The main results from this Southern area survey showed Nicholas Products that:

(a) Only 48 per cent of housewives were aware of Bio-Tex compared with 63 per cent aware of its direct competitor.

(b) There was considerable confusion between the two products on the part of housewives. Both products were identified as special stain removers and this belief tended to inhibit frequency of use.

As a result of this research, Nicholas Products and Royds decided that a change would be necessary in the advertising in order to differentiate more clearly between Bio-Tex and its competitor. Up to this point in time the advertising claims of the two brands were very similar:

'Bio-Tex soaks stubborn stains away.'
'... soaks off stains.'

The need for differentiating Bio-Tex from its competitor was extremely urgent, because in mid-August 1966 the latter went into national distribution.

Phase 4: Expansion into National Distribution

During the period of six months from Autumn 1966 to Spring 1967, Bio-Tex was launched in the remaining television areas and was in effective national distribution by the summer of 1967.

Retail audit and household panel data – the latter from both Attwood and the Television Consumer Audit – continued to provide checks on distribution, stock cover, consumer off-take, product penetration and purchasing level. This standard data kept Nicholas Products informed on the progress of their main competitor.

Apart from this continuous market trend data, the main research effort was directed towards the development of a new advertising platform for Bio-Tex.

The first step in this research programme was a series of concept tests amongst a national sample of housewives. The concepts were presented in the form of advertising-style headlines and included the original Bio-Tex concept – 'Soaks stubborn stains away'. Housewives were questioned as to their understanding of the alternative concepts and their attitudes towards the relevance and credibility of these concepts. The concept which emerged as most relevant and believable was 'Soaks away stains – loosens dirt'. It was believed that this new claim would differentiate Bio-Tex from its rival, but, additionally, evidence from the concept testing indicated the new claim would have a broader appeal than the 'stubborn stains' claim which had led housewives to think of Bio-Tex (and its competitor) as special stain removers rather than general pre-wash soaking products for everyday use.

Royds then produced a number of television commercials in storyboard form based on the new concept. These commercials were pre-tested in order to determine which of the alternative treatments appeared to communicate the new concept most effectively.

The pre-testing of the storyboard commercials provided a clear indication that the most effective treatment would be based on the use of a well-known character actress, Thora Hird, as presenter. Miss Hird, through her television roles, was well known to housewives and, as further consumer studies showed, was readily identifiable as a sensible, straightforward 'ordinary' housewife.

A series of commercials were produced by the agency based on the presentation of the new Bio-Tex concept by Thora Hird. The commercials were pre-tested in London and in Manchester, where Granada TV provided the studio facilities with the actual testing being carried out by Royds Creative Research Workshop in conjunction with Advertising Assessment Limited.

The pre-testing confirmed the credibility and authority of Thora Hird as a presenter as well as the clarity and acceptability of the new Bio-Tex concepts. On this evidence, the Thord Hird campaign was used to launch Bio-Tex in the Northern ITV area in February 1967. This campaign was also extended at the same time to the existing Bio-Tex areas – Anglia, London, Southern and Midlands – and was subsequently used in new areas as Bio-Tex went into national distribution.

Summing-up

The use of market research in connexion with Bio-Tex, of course, did not stop once the product went into national distribution by the summer of 1967. During the subsequent two years there were a series of market surveys, attitude studies and regular advertisement testing. Product tests were undertaken against its national competitor and against a third brand, which was test marketed in the Midlands and Tyne-Tees from the summer of 1967. This *ad hoc* research was additional to continuous market trend data from Nielsen, Attwood and the Television Consumer Audit.

However, the purpose of this chapter was to show how Nicholas Products used market research to assist them in planning test marketing and subsequent, phased, national introduction of Bio-Tex. The important lessons to be drawn from this particular case history are, in the authors' views, as follows:

1 Every item of research was undertaken to deal with a specific information requirement. None of the research was carried out because somebody thought it might prove interesting.

2 The research techniques employed were designed to provide answers to specific problems. Inevitably, some individual researches could have been improved technically in the light of subsequent knowledge, but in no instance was the problem bent to match a particular technique.

3 Nicholas Products involved the appropriate agency personnel in the use of all the research. No research was carried out without all concerned at Nicholas Products and Royds being aware of what research was being carried out and the reasons for using research.

4 Perhaps most important of all, the Bio-Tex research was never carried out as a substitute for decision-making. In this launch, research fulfilled its proper role as an objective aid for decision-makers.

The research techniques used in connexion with the Bio-Tex launch have not been described in detail in this chapter, because the techniques employed have already been fully explained and discussed in previous chapters. The techniques used were not in themselves of particular interest since they were merely drawn, in effect, from the everyday practice of professional market researchers. Our intention in this chapter has been to show the practical value of market research in a fairly typical new product launch situation.

Index